English Victorian Literature : Critical Assessments

English Victorian Literature : Critical Assessments

J. Symonds

CYBER TECH PUBLICATIONS
4264/3, Ansari Road, Daryaganj, New Delhi-110002 (India)
Ph.: 011-23244078. Fax: 011-23280028
E-Mail: cyberpublicationsdelhi@yahoo.com

English Victorian Literature : Critical Assessments
J. Symonds

First Edition 2009

Published by :

G.S. Rawat for Cyber Tech Publications
4264/3, Ansari Road, Daryaganj, New Delhi-110002 (India)
Ph.: 011-23244078. Fax: 011-23280028
E-Mail: cyberpublicationsdelhi@yahoo.com

Printed at : **Amit Enterprises**, Maujpur, Delhi, (9810878184)

Preface

In Victorian literature we engage with the astounding variety of poetic forms, themes, missions, and performances appearing in Britain during the years 1830-1901. Victorian poetry reflects, records, and wrestles with all the problems and successes of the era: a rapidly growing and increasingly problematic empire; restless, dissatisfied, and potentially revolutionary groups of citizens at home; immense capitalist wealth alongside shocking poverty; revolutionary travel and communication technologies thrilling to advocates and distressing to those yearning for the good old days; competing political and social philosophers butting heads in both the halls of Parliament and the taverns of Manchester; simultaneous excitement about and fear over feminism; religious upheaval rivaling the Reformation; and fierce debates over the control, use, and purpose of language, education, and art. We will, therefore, not only engage with the poetry itself, but also with its historical, cultural, and intellectual contexts in the present book..

I am confident enough that this work of mine would be informative to the readers of Vitorian literature. Your valuable suggestions are always welcome.

—Author

CONTENTS

Preface

1. Introduction 1
2. An Apologie for Poetry 77
3. Preface to the Fables 130
4. The Metaphysical Poets 157
5. Poetic Genius and Poetic Diction 178
6. Poetry in General 195
7. The Artificial Comedy of the Last Century 220
8. A Defence of Poetry 233
9. The Goethe 271
10. Sandro Botticelli 281

Bibliography 291

Index 294

1

INTRODUCTION

In England, as elsewhere, criticism was a late birth of the literary spirit. English poets had sung and literary prose been written for centuries before it struck men to ask themselves, What is the secret of the power that these things have on our mind, and by what principles are they to be judged? And it could hardly have been otherwise. Criticism is a self-conscious art, and could not have arisen in an age of intellectual childhood. It is a derivative art, and could scarcely have come into being without a large body of literature to suggest canons of judgment, and to furnish instances of their application.

The age of Chaucer might have been expected to bring with it a new departure. It was an age of self-scrutiny and of bold experiment. A new world of thought and imagination had dawned upon it; and a new literature, that of Italy, was spread before it. Yet who shall say that the facts answer to these expectations? In the writings of Chaucer himself a keen eye, it is true, may discern the faint beginnings of the critical spirit. No poet has written with more nicely calculated art; none has passed a cooler judgment upon the popular taste of his generation.

We know that Chaucer despised the "false gallop" of chivalrous verse; we know that he had small respect for the marvels of Arthurian romance. And his admiration is at least as frank as his contempt. What poet has felt and avowed a deeper reverence for the great Latins? What poet has been so alert to recognize the master-spirits of his own time and his father's? De Meung and Granson among the French--Dante, Petrarch and Boccaccio of the Italians--each comes in for his share of praise from Chaucer, or of the princely borrowings which are still more eloquent than praise.

Yet, for all this, Chaucer is far indeed from founding the art of criticism. His business was to create, and not to criticise. And, had he set himself to do so, there is no warrant that his success would have been great. In many ways he was still in bondage to the mediaval, and wholly uncritical, tradition. One classic, we may almost say, was as good to him as another. He seems to have placed Ovid on a line with Virgil; and the company in his House of Fame is undeniably mixed. His judgments have the healthy instinct of the consummate artist. They do not show, as those of his master, Petrarch, unquestionably do, the discrimination and the tact of the born critic.

For this, or for any approach to it, English literature had to wait for yet two centuries more. In the strict sense, criticism did not begin till the age of Elizabeth; and, like much else in our literature, it was largely due to the passion for classical study, so strongly marked in the poets and dramatists of Shakespeare's youth, and inaugurated by Surrey and others in the previous generation. These conditions are in themselves significant. They serve to explain much both of the strength and the weakness of criticism, as it has grown up on English soil. From the Elizabethans to Milton, from Milton to Johnson, English criticism was dominated by constant reference to classical models. In the latter half of this period the influence of these models, on the whole, was harmful. It acted as a curb rather than as a spur to the imagination of poets; it tended to cripple rather than give energy to the judgment of critics.

But in earlier days it was not so. For nearly a century the influence of classical masterpieces was altogether for good. It was not the regularity but the richness, not the self-restraint but the freedom, of the ancients that came home to poets such as Marlowe, or even to critics such as Meres. And if adventurous spirits, like Spenser and Sidney, were for a time misled into the vain attempt to graft exotic forms upon the homely growths of native poetry, they soon saw their mistake and revolted in silence against the ridiculous pedant who preferred the limping hexameters of the Arcadia to Sidney's sonnets, and the spavined iambics of Spenser to the Faerie Queene.

In the main, the worship of the classics seems to have counted at this time rather for freedom than restraint. And it is well that it was so. Yet restraint too was necessary; and, like freedom, it was found-- though in less ample measure--through devotion to the classics. There can be little doubt that, consciously or no, the Elizabethans, with their quick eye for beauty of every kind, were swayed, as men in all ages have been swayed, by the finely chiselled forms of classical art. The besetting sin of their imagination was the tendency to run riot; and it may well be that, save for the restraining influence of ancient poetry, they would have sinned in this matter still more boldly than they did. Yet the chastening power of classical models may be easily overrated. And we cannot but notice that it was precisely where the classical influence was strongest that the force of imagination was the least under control. Jonson apart, there were no more ardent disciples of the ancients than Marlowe and Chapman. And no poets of that age are so open to the charge of extravagance as they.

It is with Milton that the chastening influence of the ancients first makes itself definitely felt. But Milton was no less alive to the fervour than to the self-mastery of his classical models. And it was not till the Restoration that "correctness" was recognized as the highest, if not the only, quality of the ancients, or accepted as the one worthy object of poetic effort. For more than a century correctness remained the idol both of poetry and of criticism in England; and nothing less than the furious onslaught of the Lyrical Ballads was needed to overthrow it. Then the floodgates were opened. A new era both of-poetic and critical energy had dawned.

Thus the history of English criticism, like that of English literature, divides itself roughly into three periods. The first is the period of the Elizabethans and of Milton; the second is from the Restoration to the French Revolution; the third from the Revolution to the present day. The typical critic of the first period is Sidney; Dryden opens and Johnson closes the second; the third, a period of far more varied tendencies than either of the others, is perhaps most fitly represented by Lamb, Hazlitt, and Carlyle. It will be the aim of the following pages to sketch the broader outlines of the course that critical inquiry has taken in each.

I. The first thing that strikes us in the early attempts of criticism is that its problems are to a large extent remote from those which have engrossed critics of more recent times. There is little attempt to appraise accurately the worth of individual authors; still less, to find out the secret of their power, or to lay bare the hidden lines of thought on which their imagination had set itself to work. The first aim both of Puttenham and of Webbe, the pioneers of Elizabethan criticism, was either to classify writers according to the subjects they treated and the literary form that each had made his own, or to analyse the metre and other more technical elements of their poetry.

But this, after all, was the natural course in the infancy of the study. All science begins with classification; and all classification with the external and the obvious. The Greek critics could take no step forward until they had classified all poems as either lyric, epic, or dramatic. And how necessary that division was may be seen from the length at which Plato discusses the nature of the distinction in the second book of the Republic. Even Aristotle, in this as in other things the 'master of those who know', devotes no inconsiderable space of the Poetics to technical matters such as the analysis of vocal sounds, and the aptness of different metres to different forms of poetic thought.

There is another matter in which the methods of Elizabethan critics run side by side with those of the early Greeks. In Plato and Aristotle we are not seldom startled by the sudden transition from questions of form to the deepest problems suggested by imaginative art. The same is true of the Elizabethan critics. It is doubtless true that the latter give a proportionally larger space to the more technical sides of the subject than their Greek forerunners. They could not reasonably be expected to write with the width of view that all the world has admired in Aristotle and Plato. Moreover, they were from the first confronted with a practical difficulty from which the Greek critics were so fortunate as to be free. Was rhyme a "brutish" form of verse? and, if so, was its place to be taken by the alliterative rhythm, so dear to the older poets, or by an importation of classical metres, such as was attempted by Sidney and Spenser, and enforced by the unwearied lectures of Harvey and of Webbe? This, however technical, was a fundamental question; and, until it was settled, there was but little use in debating the weightier matters of the law.

The discussion, which might have raged for ever among the critics, was happily cut short by the healthy instinct of the poets. Against alliteration the question had already been given by default. Revived, after long disuse, by Langland and other poets of the West Midlands in the fourteenth century, it had soon again been swept out of fashion by the irresistible charm of the genius of Chaucer. The Tale of Gamelyn dating apparently from the first quarter of the fifteenth century, is probably the last poem of note in which the once universal metre is even partially employed. And what could prove more clearly that the old metrical form was dead? The rough rhythm of early English poetry, it is true, is kept; but alliteration is dropped, and its place is taken by rhyme.

Nor were the efforts to impose classical measures on English poetry more blest in their results. The very men on whom the literary Romanizers had fixed their hopes were the first to abandon the enterprise in despair. If any genius was equal to the task of naturalizing hexameters in a language where strict quantity is unknown, it was the genius of Spenser. But Spenser soon ranged himself heart and soul with the champions of rhyme; his very name has passed down to us as a synonym for the most elaborate of all rhyming stanzas that have taken root in our verse. For the moment, rhyme had fairly driven all rivals from the field. Over the lyric its sway was undisputed. In narrative poetry, where its fitness was far more disputable, it maintained its hold till the closing years of Milton. In the drama itself, where its triumph would have been fatal, it disputed the ground inch by inch against the magnificent instrument devised by Surrey and perfected by Marlowe.

It was during the ten years preceding the publication of Webbe's Discourse (1586) that this controversy seems to have been hottest. From the first, perhaps, it bulked more largely with the critics than with the poets themselves. Certainly it allowed both poets and critics sufficient leisure for the far more important controversy which has left an enduring monument in Sidney's Apologie for Poetrie. The most important pieces of Elizabethan criticism are:--

Gosson's School of Abuse 1579.

Lodge's Defence of Poetry, Musick, and Stage Plays 1579(?).

Sidney's Apologie for Poetrie 1580(?).

Webbe's Discourse of English Poetrie 1586.

Puttenham's Arte of English Poesie 1589.

Harington's Apologie of Poetrie 1591.

Meres' Palladis Tamia 1598.

Campion's Observations in the Arte of English Poesie 1602.

Daniel's Defence of Ryme 1603.

The historical bearing of Sidney's treatise has been too commonly overlooked. It forms, in truth, one move in the long struggle which ended only with the restoration of Charles II.; or, to speak more accurately, which has lasted, in a milder form, to the present day. In its immediate object it was a reply to the Puritan assaults upon the theatre; in its ultimate scope, a defence of imaginative art against the suspicions with which men of high but narrow purpose have always, consciously or unconsciously, tended to regard it. It is a noble plea for liberty, directed no less against the unwilling scruples of idealists, such as Plato or Rousseau, than against the ruthless bigotry of practical moralists and religious partisans.

From the first dawn of the Elizabethan drama, the stricter Protestants had declared war upon the stage. Intrenched within the city they were at once able to drive the theatres beyond the walls (1575); just as seventy years later, when it had seized the reins of central government, the same party, embittered by a thousand insults and brutalities, hastened to close the theatres altogether. It would be an evident mistake to suppose that this was merely a municipal prejudice, or to forget that the city council was backed by a large body of serious opinion throughout the country. A proof of this, if proof were needed, is to be found in the circumstances that gave rise to the Apologie of Sidney.

The attack on the stage had been opened by the corporation and the clergy. It was soon joined by the men of letters. And the essay of Sidney was an answer neither to a town councillor, nor to a preacher, but to a former dramatist and actor. This was Stephen Gosson, author of the School of Abuse. The style of Gosson's pamphlet is nothing if not literary. It is full of the glittering conceits and the fluent rhetoric which the ready talent of Lyly had just brought into currency. It is euphuism of the purest water, with all the merits and all the drawbacks of the euphuistic manner. For that very reason the blow was felt the more keenly. It was violently resented as treason by the playwrights and journalists who still professed to reckon Gosson among their ranks. Lodge writes, "I should blush from a Player to become an enviouse Preacher".-- Ancient Critical Essays ed. Haslewood, ii. 7.

A war of pamphlets followed, conducted with the usual fury of literary men. Gosson on the one side, Lodge, the dramatist, upon the other, exchanged compliments with an energy which showed that one at least of them had not in vain graduated in "the school of abuse". "Raw devises", "hudder mudder", "guts and garbage", such are the phrases hurled by Gosson at the arguments and style of his opponents; "bawdy charms", "the very butchery of Christian souls", are samples of the names fastened by him upon the cause which they defended. Lodge, in his Defence of Poetry, Musick, and Stage Plays (1579 or 1580), is hardly less scurrilous. "There came into my hand lately a little (would God a wittye) pamphelet.... Being by me advisedly wayed, I find it the oftscome of imperfections, the writer fuller of words than judgement, the matter certainely as ridiculus as serius."-- In Ancient Critical Essays ii. 5.

From this war of words Sidney turned loftily aside. Pointedly challenged at the outset--for the first and second pamphlets of Gosson had, without permission, been dedicated to "the right noble gentleman, Maister Philip Sidney"--he seldom alludes to the arguments, and never once mentions the name of Gosson. He wrote to satisfy his own mind, and not to win glory in the world of letters. And thus his Apologie though it seems to have been composed while the controversy was still fresh in men's memory, was not published until nearly ten years after his death (1595). It was not written for controversy, but for truth. From the first page it rises into the atmosphere of calm, in which alone great questions can be profitably discussed.

The Apologie of Sidney is, in truth, what would now be called a Philosophy of Poetry. It is philosophy taken from the side of the moralist; for that was the side to which the disputants had confined themselves, and in which--altogether apart from the example of others--the interest of Sidney, as man of action, inevitably lay. It is philosophy as conceived by the mind of a poet. But, none the less, it pierces to the eternal problems which underlie the workings of all creative art, and presents them with a force, for the like of which we must go back to Plato and Aristotle, or look forward to the philosophers and inspired critics of a time nearer our own. It recalls the Phadrus and the Ion ; it anticipates the utterance of a still more kindred spirit, the Defence of Poetry by Shelley.

Philosopher as he was, Sidney arranges his thoughts in the loose order of the poet or the orator. It may be well, therefore, to give a brief sketch of his argument; and to do so without much regard to the arrangement of the Apologie itself.

The main argument of the Apologie may indeed be called a commentary on the saying of Aristotle, cited by Sidney himself, that "Poetry is more philosophical and more studiously serious than History"--that is, as Sidney interprets it, than the scientific fact of any kind; or again, on that yet more pregnant saying of Shelley, that "poets are the unacknowledged legislators of the world". Gosson had denounced poetry as "the vizard of vanity, wantonness, and folly"; or, in Sidney's paraphrase, as "the mother of lies and the nurse of abuse". Sidney replies by urging that of all arts poetry is the most true and the most necessary to men.

All learning, he pleads, and all culture begin with poetry. Philosophy, religion, and history herself, speak through the lips of poetry. There is indeed a sense in which poetry stands on higher ground than any science. There is no science, not even metaphysics, the queen of all sciences, that does not "build upon nature", and that is not, so far, limited by the facts of nature. The poet alone is "not tied to any such subjection"; he alone "freely ranges within the zodiac of his own wit".

This, no doubt, is dangerous ground, and it is enforced by still more dangerous illustrations. But Sidney at once guards himself by insisting, as Plato had done before him, that the poet too is bound by laws which he finds but does not make; they are, however, laws not of fact but of thought, the laws of the idea--that is, of the inmost truth of things, and of God. Hence it is that the works of the poet seem to come from God, rather than from man. They stand rather on a level with nature, the material of all sciences, than with the sciences themselves, which are nothing more than man's interpretation of nature. In some sense, indeed, they are above nature; they stand midway between nature and him who created nature. They are a first nature, "beyond and over the works of that second nature". For they are the self-revelation of that which is the noblest work of God, and which in them finds utterance at its best and brightest.

Thus, so far from being the "mother of lies", poetry is the highest form of truth. Avowedly so, in what men have always recognized to be the noblest poetry, the psalms and parables and other writings that "do imitate the inconceivable excellences of God". To a less degree, but still avowedly, in that poetry whose theme is philosophy or history. And so essentially, however men may overlook it, in that poetry which, professedly dealing with human life as we know it, does not content itself with reproducing the character of this man or that, but "reined only with learned discretion, ranges into the divine consideration of what may be and should be"--of the universal and complete rather than the individual and imperfect.

But, if truth be the essence of the poet's work, "the right describing note to know a poet by", it would seem that the outward form of it, the metre and the ornament, are of little moment. "There have been many most excellent poets that never versified." And verse is nothing more than a means, and not the only means, of securing a "fitting raiment" for their matter and suiting their manner "according to the dignity of their subject". In this suggestion--that harmonious prose may, for certain forms of poetic thought, be hardly less suitable than verse--Sidney is at one with Shelley. And neither critic must be taken to disparage verse, or to mean more than that the matter, the conception, is the soul of poetry, and that the form is only of moment so far as it aids--as undoubtedly it does aid--to "reveal the soul within". It is rather as a witness to the whole scope of their argument than as a particular doctrine, to be left or taken, that the suggestion is most profitably regarded.

Having settled the speculative base of poetry, Sidney turns to a yet more cherished theme, its influence upon character and action. The "highest end" of all knowledge, he urges, is "the knowledge of a man's self, with the end of well doing and not of well knowing only". Now by no artist is this end served so perfectly as by the poet. His only serious rivals are the moral philosopher and the historian. But neither of these flies so straight to his mark as the poet. The one gives precepts that fire no heart to action; the other gives examples without the precepts that should interpret and control them. The one lives in the world of ideas, the other in the world of hard and literal fact. Neither, therefore, has power to bridge the gulf that parts thought from action; neither can hope to take hold of beings in whose life, by its very nature, thought and action are indissolubly interwoven. "Now doth the peerless poet perform both. For whatsoever the philosopher saith should be done, he giveth a perfect picture of it in some one, by whom he presupposeth it was done. So as he coupleth the general notion with the particular example.... Therein of all sciences is our poet the monarch."

Once more we feel that Sidney is treading upon dangerous ground. But once more he saves himself by giving a wider definition both to thought and action, both to "well knowing and to well doing", than is common with moralists. By the former most moralists are apt to understand the bare "precept", thought as crystallized in its immediate bearing upon action. By the latter they commonly mean the passive rather than the active virtues, temperance and self-restraint rather than energy and resolve. From both these limitations Sidney, on the whole, is nobly free.

To him the "delight which is all the good fellow poet seemeth to promise", "the words set in delightful proportion and prepared for the well enchanting skill of music", "the tale which holdeth children from play and old men from the chimney corner"--all these, its indefinable and purely artistic elements, are an inseparable part of the "wisdom" which poetry has to offer. In other words, it is the frame of mind produced by poetry, the "thought hardly to be packed into the narrow act", no less than the prompting to this action or to that, which Sidney values in the work of the poet.

And if this be true, none but the most fanatical champion of "art for art's sake" will dispute the justice of his demands on poetry. None but such will deny that, whether by attuning the mind to beauty and nobleness, or by means yet more direct and obvious, art must have some bearing upon the life of man and on the habitual temper of his soul. No doubt, we might have wished that, in widening the scope of poetry as a moral influence, Sidney had been yet more explicit than in fact he is. We cannot but regret that, however unjustly, he should have laid himself open to the charge of desiring to turn poetry into sermons. But it is bare justice to point out that such a charge cannot fairly be brought against him; or that it can only be brought with such qualifications as rob it of its sting.

On the other matter the record of Sidney is yet clearer. By "well doing" he does not mean, as is too often meant, mere abstinence from evil, but the active pursuit of whatsoever things are manly, noble, and of good report. It is not only the "temperance of Diomedes"-- though temperance too may be conceived as an active virtue--but the wisdom of Ulysses, the patriotism of Aneas, "the soon repenting pride of Agamemnon", the valour of Achilles--it is courage, above all courage, that stirs his soul in the great works of ancient poetry. It is the same quality that moves him in the ballads and romances of the moderns. "Certainly I must confess my own barbarousness; I never heard the old song of Percy and Douglas that I found not my heart moved more than with a trumpet." And again: "Truly I have known men that, even with reading Amadis de Gaule (which, God knoweth, wanteth much of a perfect poesy), have found their hearts moved to the exercise of courtesy, liberality, and especially courage." The man who wrote these words had no starved conception of what poetry should be.

Once again. Sidney has small patience with those who would limit art by the banishment of all that recalls the baser side of life. "Now, as in geometry, the oblique must be known as well as the right. So in the actions of our life, who seeth not the filthiness of evil, wanteth a great foil to perceive the beauty of virtue. This doth the comedy handle so... as with hearing it we get, as it were, an experience.... So that the right use of comedy will, I think, by no body be blamed." No doubt, the moral aspect of comedy is here marked with what must be called immoderate stress. Here, too, as when he deals with the kindred side of tragedy, Sidney demands that the poet shall, in his villains, "show you nothing that is not to be shunned"; in other words, that, so far as it paints evil, comedy shall take the form of satire.

But, even with this restriction, it must be allowed that Sidney takes a wider view than might appear at a hasty reading; wider, it is probable, than was at all common among the men of his generation. No Shakespeare had yet arisen to touch the baser qualities of men with a gleam of heroism or to humanize the most stoical endurance with a strain of weakness. And even Shakespeare, in turning from the practice to the theory of his art, could find no words very different from those of Sidney. To him, as to Sidney, the aim of the drama is "to show virtue her own image and scorn her own feature"; though by a saving clause, which Sidney perhaps would hardly have accepted, it is further defined as being to show "the very age and body of the time his form and pressure". Yet it must be remembered that Sidney is loud in praise of so unflinching a portraiture of life, base and noble, as Chaucer's Troilus and Cressida. And on the whole it remains true that the limitations of Sidney are the limitations of his age, while his generosity is his own.

The remainder of the Apologie is necessarily of slighter texture. Apart from the examination of Plato's banishment of the poets--a theme on which Harington also discourses, though with less weight than Sidney--it is concerned mainly with two subjects: an assertion that each form of poetry has its peculiar moral import, and a lament over the decay into which English poetry had fallen in the sixteenth century.

Such a lament sounds strangely to us, accustomed as we are to regard the age of Elizabeth, already half ended when Sidney wrote, as the most fruitful period of our literature. But, when the Apologie was composed, no one of the authors by whose fame the Elizabethan age is now commonly known--Sidney himself and Spenser alone excepted--had begun to write. English poetry was about to wake from the long night that lies between the age of Chaucer and the age of Shakespeare. But it was not yet fully awakened. And the want of a full and free life in creative art goes far to account for the shortcomings of Elizabethan criticism.

Vague the Elizabethan critics undeniably are; they tend to lose themselves either in far-fetched analogies or in generalities that have but a slight bearing upon the distinctive problems of literary appreciation. When not vague, they are apt to fritter their strength on technical details which, important to them, have long lost their significance for the student of literature. But both technicalities and vagueness may be largely traced to the uncertain practice of the poets upon whom, in the first instance, their criticism was based. The work of Surrey and of Sackville was tentative; that of Webbe and Puttenham was necessarily the same. It is the more honour to Sidney that, shackled as he was by conditions from which no man could escape altogether, he should have struck a note at once so deep and so strong as is sounded in the Apologie.

II. In turning from Sidney to Dryden we pass into a different world. The philosophy, the moral fervour, the prophetic strain of the Elizabethan critic have vanished. Their place is taken by qualities less stirring in themselves, but more akin to those that modern times have been apt to associate with criticism. In fact, whatever qualities we now demand from a critic may be found at least foreshadowed, and commonly much more than foreshadowed, in Dryden. Dryden is master of comparative criticism: he has something of the historical method; he is unrivalled in the art of seizing the distinctive qualities of his author and of setting them before us with the lightest touch. His very style, so pointed yet so easy, is enough in itself to mark the gulf that lies between the age of Elizabeth and the age of the Restoration. All the Elizabethan critics, Sidney himself hardly excepted, bore some trace of the schoolmaster. Dryden was the first to meet his readers entirely as an equal, and talk to them as a friend with friends. It is Dryden, and not Sainte-Beuve, who is the true father of the literary causerie ; and he still remains its unequalled master. There may be other methods of striking the right note in literary criticism. Lamb showed that there may be; so did Mr. Pater. But few indeed are the critics who have known how to attune the mind of the reader to a subject, which beyond all others cries out for harmonious treatment, so skilfully as Dryden.

That the first great critic should come with the Restoration, was only to be expected. The age of Elizabeth was essentially a creative age. The imagination of men was too busy to leave room for self-scrutiny. Their thoughts took shape so rapidly that there was no time to think about the manner of their coming. Not indeed that there is, as has sometimes been urged, any inherent strife between the creative and the critical spirit. A great poet, we can learn from Goethe and Coleridge, may also be a great critic. More than that: without some touch of poetry in himself, no man can hope to do more than hack-work as a critic of others. Yet it may safely be said that, if no critical tradition exists in a nation, it is not an age of passionate creation, such as was that of Marlowe and Shakespeare, that will found it.

With all their alertness, with all their wide outlook, with all their zeal for classical models, the men of that time were too much of children, too much beneath the spell of their own genius, to be critics. Compare them with the great writers of other ages; and we feel instinctively that, in spite of their surroundings, they have far more of vital kindred with Homer or the creators of the mediaval epic, than with the Greek dramatists--Aschylus excepted--or with Dante or with Goethe. The "freshness of the early world" is still upon them; neither they nor their contemporaries were born to the task of weighing and pondering, which is the birthright of the critic.

It was far otherwise with the men of the Restoration. The creative impulse of a century had at length spent its force. For the first time since Wyatt and Surrey, England deserted the great themes of literature, the heroic passions of Tamburlaine and Faustus, of Lear and Othello, for the trivial round of social portraiture and didactic discourse; for Essays on Satire and on Translated Verse for the Tea-Table of the Spectator, for dreary exercises on the Pleasures of the Imagination and the Art of Preserving Health. A new era had opened. It was the day of small things.

Yet it would be wrong to regard the new movement as merely negative. Had that been all, it would be impossible to account for the passionate enthusiasm it aroused in those who came beneath its spell; an enthusiasm which lived long after the movement itself was spent, and which--except in so far as it led to absurd comparisons with the Elizabethans--was abundantly justified by the genius of Butler and Dryden, of Congreve and Swift and Pope. Negative, on one side, the ideal of Restoration and Augustan poetry undoubtedly was. It was a reaction against the "unchartered freedom", the real or fancied extravagances, of the Elizabethan poets. But, on the higher side, it was no less positive, though doubtless far less noble, than the ideal it displaced.

The great writers of the eighty years following the Restoration were consumed by a passion for observation--observation of the men and things that lay immediately around them. They may have seen but little; but what they did see, they grasped with surprising force and clearness. They may not have gone far beneath the surface; but, so far as they went, their work was a model of acuteness and precision. This was the secret of their power. To this may be traced their victory in the various tasks that they undertook.

Hence, on the one hand, their success in painting the manners of their own day--a task from which, with some notable exceptions, the greatest of the Elizabethans had been apt to shrink, as from something alien to their genius; and, on the other hand, the range and keenness of their satire. Hence, finally, the originality of their work in criticism, and their new departure in philosophy. The energies of these men were diverse: but all sprang from the same root--from their invincible resolve to see and understand their world; to probe life, as they knew it, to the bottom.

Thus the new turn given to criticism by Dryden was part of a far- reaching intellectual movement; a movement no less positive and self- contained than, in another aspect, it was negative and reactionary. And it is only when taken as part of that movement, as side by side with the philosophy of Locke and the satire of Swift or Pope, that its true meaning can be understood. Nor is it the least important or the least attractive of Dryden's qualities, as a critic, that both the positive and the negative elements of the prevailing tendency--both the determination to understand and the wish to bring all things under rule--should make themselves felt so strongly and, on the whole, so harmoniously in his Essays. No man could have felt more keenly the shortcomings of the Elizabethan writers. No man could have set greater store by that "art of writing easily" which was the chief pride of the Restoration poets. Yet no man has ever felt a juster admiration for the great writers of the opposite school; and no man has expressed his reverence for them in more glowing words. The highest eulogy that has yet been passed on Milton, the most discriminating but at the same time the most generous tribute that has ever been offered to Shakespeare--both these are to be found in Dryden. And they are to be found in company with a perception, at once reasoned and instinctive, of what criticism means, that was altogether new to English literature.

The finest and most characteristic of Dryden's critical writings--but it is unfortunately also the longest--is without doubt the Essay of Dramatic Poesy. The subject was one peculiarly well suited to Dryden's genius. It touched a burning question of the day, and it opened the door for a discussion of the deeper principles of the drama. The Essay itself forms part of a long controversy between Dryden and his brother-in-law, Sir Robert Howard. The dispute was opened by Dryden's preface to his tragi-comedy, The Rival Ladies, published probably, as it was certainly first acted, in 1664; and in the beginning Dryden, then first rising "To a play at the King's house, The Rival Ladies, a very innocent and most pretty witty play"--is Pepys' entry for August 4, 1664: Diary, ii. 155. Contrast his contemptuous description of Dryden's first comedy, The Wild Gallant, in the preceding year (Feb. 23)--"So poor a thing as I never saw in my life almost".-- Ib., i. 390. into fame as a dramatist, confines himself to pleading the cause of rhyme against blank verse in dramatic writing.

But, from the general drift of the argument, it seems probable that Dryden was speaking of the drama in general. At a later stage of the dispute, however, he distinguishes between tragedy and comedy, and allows that the arguments in favour of rhyme apply only to the former--a curious inversion of the truth, as it would appear to the modern mind.-- Ib., pp. 561, 566. Howard--who, it may reasonably be guessed, had had some brushes with Dryden over their joint tragedy, The Indian Queen --at once took up the cudgels. He had written rhymed plays himself, it is true; the four plays, to which his attack on rhyme was prefixed, were such; but he saw a chance of paying off old scores against his brother-in-law, and he could not resist it. Dryden began his reply at once; but three years passed before it was published. And the world has no reason to regret his tardiness. There are few writings of which we can say with greater certainty, as Dryden himself said of a more questionable achievement,

'T is not the hasty product of a day, But the well-ripened fruit of wise delay.

The very form of the Essay bears witness to the spirit in which it is written. It is cast as a dialogue, "related"--as Dryden truly says--"without passion or interest, and leaving the reader to decide in favour of which part he shall judge most reasonable". The balance between opposing views is held as evenly as may be. It is a search for truth, carried out in the "rude and undigested manner" of a friendly conversation. Roughly speaking, the subjects of the Essay are two. The first, and the more slightly treated, is the quarrel of rhyme against blank verse. The second is the far more important question, How far is the dramatist bound by conventional restrictions? The former--a revival under a new form of a dispute already waged by the Elizabethans--leads Dryden to sift the claims of the "heroic drama"; and his treatment of it has the special charm belonging to an author's defence of his artistic hearth and home. The latter is a theme which, under some shape or other, will be with us wherever the stage itself has a place in our life.

This is not the place to discuss at length the origin or the historical justification of the Heroic Drama. There is perhaps no form of art that so clearly marks the transition from the Elizabethan age to that of the Restoration. Transitional it must certainly be called; for, in all vital points, it stands curiously apart from the other forms of Restoration literature. It has nothing either of the negative or the positive qualities, nothing of the close observation and nothing of the measure and self-restraint, that all feel to be the distinctive marks of the Restoration temper. On the other hand the heroic drama, of which Dryden's Conquest of Granada and Tyrannic Love may be taken as fair samples, has obvious affinities with the more questionable side of the Elizabethan stage. It may be defined as wanting in all the virtues and as exaggerating all the vices of the Elizabethan dramatists.

Whatever was most wild in the wildest of the Elizabethan plays--the involved plots, the extravagant incidents, the swelling metaphors and similes--all this reappears in the heroic drama. And it reappears without any of the dramatic force or of the splendid poetry which are seldom entirely absent from the work of the Elizabethan and Jacobean dramatists. The term "heroic drama" is, in fact, a fraud. The plays of Dryden and his school are at best but moc-heroic; and they are essentially undramatic. The truth is that these plays take something of the same place in the history of the English drama that is held by the verse of Donne and Cowley in the history of the English lyric. The extravagant incidents correspond to the far-fetched conceits which, unjustly enough, made the name of Donne a by-word with the critics of the last century.

The metaphors and similes are as abundant and overcharged, though assuredly not so rich in imagination, as those of the "metaphysical" poets. And Dryden, if we may accept the admission of Bayes, "loved argument in verse"; a confession that Donne and Cowley would heartily have echoed. The exaggerations of the heroic drama are the exaggerations of the metaphysical poets transferred from the study to the stage; with the extravagance deepened, as was natural, by the glare of their new surroundings. And, just as the extravagance of the "metaphysicians" led to the reaction that for a hundred years stifled the lyric note in English song, so the extravagance of the heroic drama gave the death-blow to English tragedy.

Against this parallel the objection may be raised that it takes no reckoning of the enormous gulf that, when all is said, separates even the weakest of the Elizabethan plays from the rant and fustian of Dryden: a gulf wider, it must be admitted, than that which parts the metaphysical poets from the "singing birds" of the Elizabethan era. And, so far as we have yet gone, the objection undoubtedly has force. It is only to be met if we can find some connecting link; if we can point to some author who, on the one hand, retains something of the dramatic instinct, the grace and flexibility of the Elizabethans; and, on the other hand, anticipates the metallic ring, the declamation and the theatrical conventions of Dryden.

Such an author is to be found in Shirley; in Shirley, as he became in his later years; at the time, for instance, when he wrote The Cardinal (1641). The Cardinal is, in many respects, a powerful play. It is unmistakably written under the influence of Webster; and of Webster at his most sombre and his best--the Webster of the Duchess of Malfi. But it is no less unmistakably wanting in the subtle strength, the dramatic grip and profound poetry, of its model. The villainy of the Cardinal is mere mechanism beside the satanic, yet horribly human, iniquity of Ferdinand and Bosolo. And, at least in one scene, Shirley sinks--it is true, in the person of a subordinate character--to a foul-mouthed vulgarity which recalls the shameless bombast of the heroes and heroines of Dryden.

I would this soldier had the Cardinal

Upon a promontory; with what a spring

The churchman would leap down! It were a spectacle

Most rare to see him topple from the precipice,

And souse in the salt water with a noise

To stun the fishes. And if he fell into

A net, what wonder would the simple sea-gulls

Have to draw up the o'ergrown lobster,

So ready boiled! He shall have my good wishes.

-- The Cardinal, act v. sc, 2.

Yet, with all his shortcomings, Shirley preserves in the main the great tradition of the Elizabethans. A further step downwards, a more deadly stage in the history of decadence, is marked by Sir William Davenant.

That arch-impostor, as is well known, had the effrontery to call himself the "son of Shakespeare": a phrase which the unwary have taken in the physical sense, but which was undoubtedly intended to mark his literary kinship with the Elizabethans in general and with the greatest of Elizabethan dramatists in particular.

So far as dates go, indeed, the work of Davenant may be admitted to fall within what we loosely call the Elizabethan period; or, more strictly, within the last stage of the period that began with Elizabeth and continued throughout the reigns of her two successors. His first tragedy, Albovine, King of the Lombards, was brought out in 1629; and his earlier work was therefore contemporary with that of Massinger and Ford.

But much beyond this his relation to the Elizabethans can hardly claim to go. Charity may allow him some faint and occasional traces of the dramatic power which is their peculiar glory; and this is perhaps more strongly marked in his earliest play than in any of its successors. What strikes us most forcibly, however--and that, even in his more youthful work--is the obvious anticipation of much that we associate only with the Restoration period. The historical plot, the metallic ring of the verse,

I take two instances from Albovine.--

(1) Let all glad hymns in one mix'd concord sound, And make the echoing heavens your mirth rebound.--Act i.

(2) I am the broom of heaven; when the world grows foul, I'll sweep the nations into the sea, like dust.--Act ii.

It is noticeable that both passages are spoken by Albovine himself, a very creditable elder brother of Dryden's Maximin and Almanzor. One more passage may be quoted, from the Just Italian (1630):--

The sacred noise attend that, whilst we hear,

Our souls may dance into each others' ear.--Act v.

It will be observed that two out of the above passages, coming at the end of scenes, are actually in rhyme, and rhyme which is hardly distinguishable from that of Dryden. the fustian and the bombast-- we have here every mark, save one, of what afterwards came to be known as the heroic drama.

The rhymed couplet alone is wanting. And that was added by Davenant himself at a later stage of his career. It was in The Siege of Rhodes, of which the first part was published in 1656, that the heroic couplet, after an interval of about sixty years, made its first reappearance on the English stage. It was garnished, no doubt, with much of what then passed for Pindaric lyric; it was eked out with music. But the fashion was set; and within ten years the heroic couplet and the heroic drama had swept everything before them. A few lines may be quoted to make good the above description of The Siege of Rhodes :--

What various voices do mine ears invade

And have a concert of confusion made?

The shriller trumpet and tempestuous drum,

The deafening clamour from the cannon's womb.

--Part i. First Entry.

The following lines from part ii. (published in 1662) might have been signed by Dryden:--

No arguments by forms of senate made

Can magisterial jealousy persuade;

It takes no counsel, nor will be in awe

Of reason's force, necessity, or law.

Or, again,

Honour's the soul which nought but guilt can wound,

Fame is the trumpet which the people sound.

The above dates are enough to disprove the common belief that the heroic drama, rhymed couplet and all, was imported from France. Albovine, as we have seen, has every mark of the heroic drama, except the couplet; and Albovine was written seven years before the first masterpiece of Corneille, one year before his first attempt at tragedy. A superficial likeness to the drama of Corneille and, subsequently, of Racine may doubtless have given wings to the popularity of the new style both with Davenant and his admirers.

But the heroic drama is, in truth, a native growth: for good or for evil, to England alone must be given the credit of its birth. Dryden, no doubt, more than once claims French descent for the literary form with which his fame was then bound up. He is, however, as explicit as could be wished in tracing the descent through Davenant. "For Heroick Plays... the first light we had of them on the English theatre was from the late Sir W. Davenant. He heightened his characters, as I may probably imagine, from the example of Corneille and some French Poets."-- Of Heroic Plays, printed as preface to The Conquest of Granada, Dramatic Works (fol.), i. 381. It was for this reason that Davenant was taken as the original hero of that burlesque masterpiece, The Rehearsal (1671); and even when the part of Bayes was transferred to Dryden, the make-up still remained largely that of Davenant.

In a well-known prologue he describes his tragic-comedy, The Maiden Queen, as:

a mingled chime

Of Jonson's humour and

Corneille's rhyme.

The greater part of The Maiden Queen, however, is written either in prose or in blank verse.

But the fact is that of Corneille there is no more trace in Dryden's tragedy than there is of Jonson in his comedy; that is, just none at all. The heroic temper, which was at once the essence of Corneille's plays and true to the very soul of the man, was mere affectation and mise-en-scene with Dryden. The heroes of Corneille reflect that nobility of spirit which never entirely forsook France till the days of the Regency; those of Dryden give utterance to nothing better than the insolent swagger of the Restoration.

To the peculiar spirit of the heroic drama--to its strength as well as to its weakness--no metrical form could have been more closely adapted than the heroic couplet. It was neither flexible nor delicate; but in the hands of Dryden, even more than in those of Davenant, it became an incomparably vigorous and effective weapon of declamation.

As the most unmistakable and the most glaring mark of the new method it was naturally placed in the forefront of the battle waged by Dryden in defence of the heroic drama. It seems, indeed, to have struck him as the strongest advantage possessed by the Restoration drama over the Elizabethan, and as that which alone was wanting to place the Elizabethan drama far ahead both of the Greek and of the French.

The claims of rhyme to Dryden's regard would seem to have been twofold. On the one hand, he thought that it served to "bound and circumscribe" the luxuriance of the poet's fancy. Dedication to The Rival Ladies : English Garner,

iii. 492. On the other hand, it went to "heighten" the purely dramatic element and to "move that admiration which is the delight of serious plays" and to which "a bare imitation" will not suffice. Essay of Dramatic Poesy : ib. 582 Both grounds of defence will seem to the modern reader questionable enough. Howard at once laid his finger upon the weak spot of the first. "It is", he said, "no argument for the matter in hand. For the dispute is not what way a man may write best in; but which is most proper for the subject he writes upon. And, if this were let pass, the argument is yet unsolved in itself; for he that wants judgment in the liberty of his fancy may as well shew the want of it in its confinement." Preface to Four New Plays : ib. 498. Besides, he adds in effect on the next page, so far from "confining the fancy" rhyme is apt to lead to turgid and stilted writing.

The second argument stands on higher ground. It amounts to a plea for the need of idealization; and, so far, may serve to remind us that the extravagances of the heroic drama had their stronger, as well as their weaker, side. No one, however, will now be willing to admit that the cause of dramatic idealization is indeed bound up with the heroic couplet; and a moment's thought will show the fallacy of Dryden's assumption that it is. In the first place, he takes for granted that, the further the language of the drama is removed from that of actual life, the nearer the spirit of it will approach to the ideal. An unwarrantable assumption, if there ever was one; and an assumption, as will be seen, that contains the seeds of the whole eighteenth-century theory of poetic diction. In the second place--but this is, in truth, only the deeper aspect of the former plea--Dryden comes perilously near to an acceptance of the doctrine that idealization in a work of art depends purely on the outward form and has little or nothing to do with the conception or the spirit.

The bond between form and matter would, according to this view, be purely arbitrary. By a mere turn of the hand, by the substitution of rhyme for prose--or for blank verse, which is on more than "measured" or harmonious prose--the baldest presentment of life could be converted into a dramatic poem. From the grosser forms of this fallacy Dryden's fine sense was enough to save him. Indeed, in the remarks on Jonson's comedies that immediately follow, he expressly rejects them; and seldom does he show a more nicely balanced judgment than in what he there says on the limits of imitation in the field of art.

But in the passage before us--in his assertion that "the converse must be heightened with all the arts and ornaments of poetry"--it is hard to resist a vision of the dramatist first writing his dialogue in bald and skimble-skamble prose, and then wringing his brains to adorn it "with all the arts" of the dramatic gradus. Here again we have the seeds of the fatal theory which dominated the criticism and perverted the art of the eighteenth century; the theory which, finding in outward form the only distinction between prose and poetry, was logically led to look for the special themes of poetic art in the dissecting-room or the pulpit, and was driven to mark the difference by an outrageous diction that could only be called poetry on the principle that it certainly was not prose; the theory which at length received its death-blow from the joint attack of Wordsworth and Coleridge.

It remains only to note the practical issue of the battle of the metres. In the drama the triumph of the heroic couplet was for the moment complete; but it was short-lived. By 1675, the date of Aurungzebe, Dryden proclaimed himself already about to "weary of his long-loved mistress, Rhyme"; and his subsequent plays were all written in blank verse or prose. But the desertion of "his mistress" brought him little luck; and the rest of his tragedies show a marked falling off in that splendid vigour which went far to redeem even the grossest absurdities of his heroic plays. A more sensitive, though a weaker, genius joined him in the rejection of rhyme; and the example of Otway--whose two crucial plays belong to 1680 and 1682--did perhaps more than that of Dryden himself, more even than the assaults of The Rehearsal, to discredit the heroic drama. With the appearance of Venice Preserved, rhyme ceased to play any part in English tragedy. But at the same time, it must be noted, tragedy itself began to drop from the place which for the last century it had held in English life. From that day to this no acting tragedy, worth serious attention, has been written for the English stage.

The reaction against rhyme was not confined to the drama. The epic, indeed--or what in those days passed for such--can hardly be said to have come within its scope. In the Essay of Dramatic Poesy Dryden--and this is one of the few judgments in which Howard heartily agrees with him--had denounced rhyme as "too low for a poem"; English Garner, iii. p. 567. by which, as the context shows, is meant an epic. This was written the very year in which Paradise Lost, with its laconic sneer at rhyme as a device "to set off wretched matter and lame metre", was given to the world. That, however, did not prevent Dryden from asking, and obtaining, leave to "tag its verses" into an opera; The following will serve as a sample of Dryden's improvements on his model:--

Seraph and Cherub, careless of their charge

And wanton in full ease, now live at large,

Unguarded leave the passes of the sky,

And all dissolved in Hallelujahs lie.

-- Dramatic Works, i. p. 596.

nor did it deter Blackmore--and, at a much later time, Wilkie Blackmore's King Arthur was published in 1695; Wilkie's Epigoniad --the subject of a patriotic puff from Hume--in 1757.--from reverting to the metre that Milton had scorned to touch. It is not till the present century that blank verse can be said to have fairly taken seisin of the epic; one of the many services that English poetry owes to the genius of Keats.

In the more nondescript kinds of poetry, however, the revolt against rhyme spread faster than in the epic. In descriptive and didactic poetry, if anywhere, rhyme might reasonably claim to hold its place. There is much to be said for the opinion that, in such subjects, rhyme is necessary to fix the wandering attention of the reader. Yet, for all that, the great efforts of the reflective muse during the next century were, with hardly an exception, in blank verse. It is enough to recall the Seasons of Thomson, the discourses of Akenside and Armstrong, and the Night Thoughts of the arch-moralist Young. It may be noted that Young's blank verse has constantly the run of the heroic couplet. In the case of Young--as later in that of Cowper--this is the more remarkable, because his Satires show him to have had complete command of the mechanism of the heroic couplet. That he should have deliberately chosen the rival metre is proof--a proof which even the exquisite work of Goldsmith is not sufficient to gainsay--that, by the middle of the eighteenth century the heroic couplet had been virtually driven from every field of poetry, save that of satire.

We may now turn to the second of the two themes with which Dryden is mainly occupied in the Essay of Dramatic Poesy. What are the conventional restrictions that surround the dramatist, and how far are they of binding force?

That the drama is by nature a convention--more than this, a convention accepted largely with a view to the need of idealization--the men of Dryden's day were in no danger of forgetting. The peril with them was all the other way. The fashion of that age was to treat the arbitrary usages of the classical theatre as though they were binding for all time. Thus, of the four men who take part in the dialogue of the Essay, three are emphatically agreed in bowing down before the three unities as laws of nature. Dryden himself (Neander) is alone in questioning their divinity: a memorable proof of his critical independence; but one in which, as he maliciously points out, he was supported by the greatest of living dramatists.

Corneille could not be suspected of any personal motive for undertaking the defence of dramatic license. Yet he closed his Discourse of the Three Unities with the admission that he had "learnt by experience how much the French stage was constrained and bound up by the observance of these rules, and how many beauties it had sacrificed". Il est facile aux speculatifs d'etre severes; mais, s'ils voulaient donner dix ou douze poemes de cette nature au public, ils elargiraient peut-etre les regles encore plus que je ne sais, si tot qu'ils auraient reconnu par l'experience quelle contrainte apporte leur exactitude et combien de belles choses elle bannit de notre theatre-- Troisieme Discours Euvres, xii. 326. See Dryden's Essay English Garner, iii 546.

On the next page is a happy hit at the shifts to which dramatists were driven in their efforts to keep up the appearance of obedience to the Unity of Place: "The street, the window, the two houses and the closet are made to walk about, and the persons to stand still." When the two leading masters of the 'Classical Drama', the French and the English, joined hands to cast doubt upon the sacred unities, its opponents might well feel easy as to the ultimate issue of the dispute.

Dryden was not the man to bound his argument by any technical question, even when it touched a point so fundamental as the unities. Nothing is more remarkable in the Essay, as indeed in all his critical work, than the wide range which he gives to the discussion. And never has the case against--we can hardly add, for--the French drama been stated more pointedly than by him. His main charge, as was to be expected, is against its monotony, and, in close connection with that, against its neglect of action and its preference for declamation.

Having defined the drama as "a just and lively image of human nature, in its actions, passions and traverses of fortune", English Garner, iii 513, ib. 567 he proceeds to test the claims of the French stage by that standard. Its characters, he finds, are wanting in variety and nature. Its range of passion and humour is lamentably narrow. Ib. 542-4. Its declamations "tire us with their length; so that, instead of grieving for their imaginary heroes, we are concerned for our own trouble, as we are in the tedious visits of bad company; we are in pain till they are gone". English Garner, iil 542. The best tragedies of the French-- Cinna and Pompey --"are not so properly to be called Plays as long discourses of Reason of State". Ib. 543. Upon their avoidance of action he is hardly less severe. "If we are to be blamed for showing too much of the action"--one is involuntarily reminded of the closing scene of Tyrannic Love and of the gibes in The Rehearsal --"the French are as faulty for discovering too little of it ". Ib. 545. Finally, on a comparison between the French dramatists and the Elizabethans, Dryden concludes that "in most of the irregular Plays of Shakespeare or Fletcher... there is a more masculine fancy, and greater spirit in all the writing, than there is in any of the French". Ib. 548.

Given the definition with which he starts--but it is a definition that no Frenchman of the seventeenth or eighteenth century would have admitted--it is hard to see how Dryden could have reached a substantially different result. Nor, if comparisons of this sort are to be made at all, is there much--so far, at least, as Shakespeare is concerned--to find fault with in the verdict with which he closes. Yet it is impossible not to regret that Dryden should have failed to recognize the finer spirit and essence of French tragedy, as conceived by Corneille: the strong-tempered heroism of soul, the keen sense of honour, the consuming fire of religion, to which it gives utterance.

The truth is that Dryden stood at once too near, and too far from, the ideals of Corneille to appreciate them altogether at their just value. Too near because he instinctively associated them with the heroic drama, which at the bottom of his heart he knew to be no better than an organized trick, done daily with a view to "elevate and surprise". Too far, because, in spite of his own candid and generous temper, it was well-nigh impossible for the Laureate of the Restoration to comprehend the highly strung nature of a man like Corneille, and his intense realization of the ideal.

But, if Dryden is blind to the essential qualities of Corneille, he is at least keenly alive to those of Shakespeare. It is a memorable thing that the most splendid tribute ever offered to the prince of Elizabethans should have come from the leading spirit of the Restoration. It has often been quoted, but it will bear quoting once again.

"Shakespeare was the man who, of all modern and perhaps ancient poets, had the largest and most comprehensive soul. All the images of nature were still present to him; and he drew them not laboriously, but luckily. When he describes anything, you more than see it, you feel it too. Those who accuse him to have wanted learning give him the great commendation. He was naturally learned. He needed not the spectacles of books to read nature; he looked inwards and found her there. I cannot say he is everywhere alike. Were he so, I should do him injury to compare him with the greatest of mankind. He is many times flat, insipid; his comic wit degenerating into clenches, his serious swelling into bombast. But he is always great when some great occasion is presented to him. No man can say, he ever had a fit subject for his wit, and did not then raise himself as high above the rest of poets,

Quantum lenta solent inter viburna cupressi." Essay of Dramatic Poesy. English Garner, iii. 549.

The same keenness of appreciation is found in Dryden's estimate of other writers who might have seemed to lie beyond the field of his immediate vision. Of Milton he is recorded to have said: "He cuts us all out, and the ancients too". The anecdote is recorded by Richardson, who says the above words were written on the copy of Paradise Lost sent by Dorset to Milton. Dryden, Poetic Works, p. 161. Comp.

Dramatic Works, i. 590; Discourse on Satire, p. 386. On Chaucer he is yet more explicit. "As he is the father of English poetry, so I hold him in the same degree of veneration as the Grecians held Homer, or the Romans Virgil. He is a perpetual fountain of good sense; learned in all sciences, and therefore speaks properly on all subjects. As he knew what to say, so he knows also when to leave off, a continence which is practised by few writers, and scarcely by any of the ancients, excepting Virgil and Horace... Chaucer followed nature everywhere, but was never so bold to go beyond her." See Preface to Fables, below.

This points to what was undoubtedly the most shining quality of Dryden, as a critic: his absolute freedom from preconceived notions, his readiness to "follow nature" and to welcome nature in whatever form she might appear. That was the more remarkable because it ran directly counter both to the general spirit of the period to which he belonged and to the prevailing practice of the critics who surrounded him. The spirit of the Restoration age was critical in the invidious, no less than in the nobler, sense of the word. It was an age of narrow ideals and of little ability to look beyond them. In particular, it was an age of carping and of fault-finding; an age within measurable distance of the pedantic system perfected in France by Boileau, Boileau's Art Poetique was published in 1674. A translation made by Soame, with the aid of Dryden, was published in 1683. and warmly adopted by a long line of English critics from Roscoromon and Buckinghamshire to the Monthly Reviewers and to Johnson. Such writers might always have "nature" on their lips; but it was nature seen through the windows of the lecture room or down the vista of a street.

With Dryden it was not so. With him we never fail to get an unbiassed judgment; the judgment of one who did not crave for nature "to advantage dressed", but trusted to the instinctive freshness of a mind, one of the most alert and open that ever gave themselves to literature. It is this that puts an impassable barrier between Dryden and the men of his own day, or for a century to come. It is this that gives him a place among the great critics of modern literature, and makes the passage from him to the schoolmen of the next century so dreary a descent.

Dryden's openness of mind was his own secret. The comparative method was, in some measure, the common property of his generation. This, in fact, was the chief conquest of the Restoration and Augustan critics. It is the mark that serves to distinguish them most clearly from those of the Elizabethan age. Not that the Elizabethans are without comparisons; but that the parallels they saw were commonly of the simplest, not to say of the most childish, cast. Every sentence of Meres' critical effort--or, to be rigorously exact, every sentence but one--is built on "as" and "so"; but it reads like a parody--a schoolmaster's parody--of Touchstone's improvement on Orlando's verses in praise of Rosalind. Shakespeare is brought into line with Ovid, Elizabeth with Achilles, and Homer with William Warner. This, no doubt, is an extreme instance; but it is typical of the artless methods dear to the infancy of criticism. In Jonson's Discoveries, such comparisons as there are have indisputable point; but they are few, and, for the most part, they are limited to the minuter matters of style.

It is with the Restoration that the comparative method first made its way into English criticism; and that both in its lawful and less lawful use. The distinction must be jealously made; for there are few matters that lend themselves so readily to confusion and misapprehension as this. Between two men, or two forms of art, a comparison may be run either for the sake of placing the one above the head of the other, or for the sake of drawing out the essential differences between the one and the other.

The latter method is indispensable to the work of the critic. Without reference, express or implied, to other types of genius or to other ways of treatment it is impossible for criticism to take a single step in definition either of an author, or a movement, or a form of art. In a vague and haphazard fashion, even the Elizabethans were comparative. Meres was so in his endless stream of classical parallels; Sidney, after a loftier strain, in his defence of harmonious prose as a form of poetry. And it is the highest achievement of modern criticism to have brought science and order into the comparative method, and largely to have widened its scope. In this sense, comparison is criticism; and to compare with increased intelligence, with a clearer consciousness of the end in view, is to reform criticism itself, to make it a keener weapon and more effective for its purpose.

A comparison of qualities, however, is one thing, and a comparison between different degrees of merit is quite another. The former is the essence of criticism; the latter, one of the most futile pastimes that can readily be imagined. That each man should have his own preferences is right enough. It would be a nerveless and unprofitable mind to which such preferences were unknown. More than that, some rough classification, some understanding with oneself as to what authors are to be reckoned supreme masters of their craft, is hardly to be avoided. The mere fact that the critic lays stress on certain writers and dismisses others with scant notice or none at all, implies that in some sense he has formed an estimate of their relative merits.

But to drag this process from the background--if we ought not rather to say, from behind the scenes--to the very foot-lights, to publish it, to insist upon it, is as irrelevant as it would be for the historian-- and he, too, must make his own perspective--to explain why he has recorded some events and left others altogether unnoticed. All this is work for the dark room; it should leave no trace, or as little as may be, upon the finished picture. Criticism has suffered from few things so much as from its incurable habit of granting degrees in poetry with honours. "The highest art", it has been well said, "is the region of equals."

It must be admitted that the Restoration critics had an immoderate passion for classing authors according to their supposed rank in the scale of literary desert. A glance at The Battle of the Books --a faint reflection of the quarrel between the ancients and the moderns--is enough to place this beyond dispute. Dryden himself is probably as guilty as any in this matter. His parallel between Juvenal and Horace, his comparison of Homer with Virgil, are largely of the nature of an attempt to show each poet to his proper place, to determine their due order of precedence in the House of Fame. In the early days of criticism this was perhaps to be expected. Men were feeling their way to the principles; and the shortest road might naturally seem to lie through a comparative table of the men. They were right in thinking that the first step was to ascertain what qualities, and what modes of treatment, give lasting pleasure in poetry; and, to do this, they could not but turn to compare the works of individual poets. But they were wrong in supposing that they could learn anything by striking the balance between the merits of one poet, as a sum total, and the merits of another.

The fault was, no doubt, largely in the Restoration critics themselves; and it is a fault which, so long as the competitive instinct holds sway with men, will never be entirely unknown. But its hold on the men of Dryden's day was in great measure due to the influence of the French critics, and to the narrow lines which criticism had taken in France. No one can read Boileau's Art Poetique, no one can compare it with the corresponding Essay of Pope, without feeling that the purely personal element had eaten into the heart of French criticism to a degree which could never have been natural in England, and which, even in the darkest days of English literature, has seldom been approached. But at the same time it will be felt that never has England come nearer to a merely personal treatment of artistic questions than in the century between Dryden and Johnson; and that it was here, rather than in the adoption of any specific form of literature--

rather, for instance, than in the growth of the heroic drama--that the influence of France is to be traced.

Side by side, however, with the baser sort of comparisons, we find in the Restoration critics no small use of the kind that profits and delights. Rymer's Remarks on the Tragedies of the Former Age are an instance of the comparative method, in its just sense, as employed by a man of talent. The essays of Dryden abound in passages of this nature, that could only have been written by a man of genius. They may have a touch of the desire to set one form of art, or one particular poet, in array against another. But, when all abatements have been made, they remain unrivalled samples of the manner in which the comparative vein can be worked by a master spirit. To the student of English literature they have a further interest--notably, perhaps, the comparison between Juvenal and Horace and the eulogy of Shakespeare--as being among the most striking examples of that change from the Latinized style of the early Stuart writers to the short, pointed sentence commonly associated with French; the change that was inaugurated by Hobbes, but only brought to completion by Dryden.

Once again. As Dryden was among the earliest to give the comparative method its due place in English criticism, so he was the first to make systematic use of the historical method. Daniel, indeed, in a remarkable essay belonging to the early years of the century, had employed that method in a vague and partial manner. A Defence of Ryme (1603). It was written in answer to a pamphlet by Campion (1602), of which the second chapter "declares the unaptness of Rime in Poesie".--Ancient Critical Essays, ii. t64, &c.

He had defended rhyme on the score of its popularity with all ages and all nations. Celts, Slavs, and Huns--Parthians and Medes and Elamites--are all pressed into the service. "The Turks, Slavonians, Arabians, Muscovites, Polacks, Hungarians... use no other harmony of words. The Irish, Britons, Scots, Danes, Saxons, English, and all the inhabiters of this island either have hither brought, or here found the same in use."--Ib. p. 198. That is, perhaps, the first instance in which English criticism can be said to have attempted tracing a literary form through the various stages of its growth. But Daniel wrote without system and without accuracy. It was reserved for Dryden--avowedly following in the steps of the French critic Dacier--to introduce the order and the fulness of knowledge--in Dryden's case, it must be admitted, a knowledge at second hand--which are indispensable to a fruitful use of the historical method. In this sense, too--as in his use of the comparative method, as in the singular grace and aptness of his style--Dryden was a pioneer in the field of English criticism.

III. Over the century that parts Dryden from Johnson it is not well to linger. During that time criticism must be said, on the whole, to have gone back rather than to have advanced. With some reservations to be noticed later, the critics of the eighteenth century are a depressing study. Their conception of the art they professed was barren; their judgments of men and things were lamentably narrow. The more valuable elements traceable in the work of Dryden--the comparative and the historical treatment--disappear or fall into the background. We are left with little but the futile exaltation of one poet at the expense of his rivals, or the still more futile insistence upon faults, shortcomings, and absurdities.

The Dunciad, the most marked critical work of the period, may be defended on the ground that it is the Dunciad; a war waged by genius upon the fool, the pedant, and the fribble. But, none the less, it had a disastrous influence upon English criticism and English taste. It gave sanction to the habit of indiscriminate abuse; it encouraged the purely personal treatment of critical discussions. Its effects may be traced on writers even of such force as Smollett; of such genius and natural kindliness as Goldsmith. But it was on Johnson that Pope's influence made itself most keenly felt. And The Lives of the Poets, though not written till the movement that gave it birth had spent its force, is the most complete and the most typical record of the tendencies that shaped English literature and gave the law to English taste from the Restoration to the French Revolution: a notable instance of the fact so often observed, and by some raised to the dignity of a general law, that both in philosophy and in art, the work of the critic does not commonly begin till the creative impulse of a given period is exhausted.

What, then, was Johnson's method? and what its practical application? The method is nothing if not magisterial. It takes for granted certain fixed laws--whether the laws formulated by Aristotle, or by Horace, or the French critics, is for the moment beside the question--and passes sentence on every work of art according as it conforms to the critical decalogue or transgresses it. The fault of this method is not, as is sometimes supposed, that it assumes principles in a subject where none are to be sought; but that its principles are built on a miserably narrow and perverted basis.

That there are principles of criticism, that the artist's search for beauty must be guided by some idea, is obvious enough. It can be questioned only by those who are prepared to deny the very possibility of criticism; who would reduce the task both of critic and of artist to a mere record of individual impressions. It need hardly be said that the very men who are most ready to profess such a doctrine with their lips, persistently, and rightly, give the lie to it in their deeds. No creative work, no critical judgment, either is or can be put forward as a mere impression; it is the impression of a trained mind--that is, of a mind which, instinctively or as a conscious process, is guided by principles or ideas.

So far, then, as he may be held to have borne witness to the need of ideas, Johnson was clearly in the right. It was when he came to ask, What is the nature of those ideas, and how does the artist or the critic arrive at them? that he began to go astray. Throughout he assumes that the principles of art--and that, not only in their general bearing (proportion, harmony, and the like), but in their minuter details-are fixed and invariable. To him they form a kind of case-law, which is to be extracted by the learned from the works of a certain number of "correct writers", ancient and modern; and which, once established, is binding for all time both on the critic and on those he summons to his bar. In effect, this was to declare that beauty can be conceived in no other way than as it presented itself, say, to Virgil or to Pope. It was to lay the dead hand of the past upon the present and the future.

More than this. The models that lent themselves to be models, after the kind desired by Johnson, were inevitably just those it was most cramping and least inspiring to follow. They were the men who themselves wrote, to some degree, by rule; in whom "correctness" was stronger than inspiration; who, however admirable in their own achievement, were lacking in the nobler and subtler qualities of the poet. They were not the Greeks; not even, at first hand, the Latins; though the names both of Greek and Latin were often on Johnson's lips. They were rather the Latins as filtered through the English poets of the preceding century; the Latins in so far as they had appealed to the writers of the "Augustan age", but no further; the Latins, as masters of satire, of declamation, and of the lighter kinds of verse. It was Latin poetry without Lucretius and Catullus, without the odes of Horace, without the higher strain of the genius of Virgil. In other words, it was poetry as conceived by Boileau or Addison-or Mr. Smith. See Johnson's extravagant eulogy of this obscure writer in the Lives of the Poets. Works, x. i.

Yet again. In the hands of Johnson--and it was a necessary consequence of his critical method--poetry becomes more and more a mere matter of mechanism. Once admit that the greatness of a poet depends upon his success in following certain models, and it is but a short step--if indeed it be a step--further to say that he must attempt no task that has not been set him by the example of his forerunners. It is doubtless true that Johnson did not, in so many words, commit himself to this absurdity. But it is equally true that any poet, who overstepped the bounds laid down by previous writers, was likely to meet with but little mercy at his hands. Milton, Cowley, Gray--for all had the audacity to take an untrodden path in poetry-one after another are dragged up for execution.

It is clear that by example, if not by precept, Johnson was prepared to "make poetry a mere mechanic art"; and Cowper was right in saying that it had become so with Pope's successors. Indeed John--son himself, in closing his estimate of Pope, seems half regretfully to anticipate Cowper's verdict. "By perusing the works of Dryden, he discovered the most perfect fabrick of English verse, and habituated himself to that only which he found the best.... New sentiments and new images others may produce; but to attempt any further improvement of versification will be dangerous. Art and diligence have now done their best, and what shall be added will be the effort of tedious toil and needless curiosity". Life of Pope. Johnson's Works, xi. pp 194, 195. But Johnson failed to see that his own view of poetry led inevitably to this lame and impotent conclusion.

To adopt Johnson's method is, in truth, to misconceive the whole nature of poetry and of poetic imagination. The ideas that have shaped the work of one poet may act as guide and spur, but can never be a rule--far less a law--to the imagination of another. The idea, as it comes to an artist, is not a law imposing itself from without; it is a seed of life and energy springing from within. This, however, was a truth entirely hidden from the eyes of Johnson and the Augustan critics. To assert it both by word and deed, both as critics and as poets, was the task of Coleridge, and of those who joined hands with Coleridge, in the succeeding generation. Apart from the undying beauty of their work as artists, this was the memorable service they rendered to poetry in England.

It remains to illustrate the method of Johnson by its practical application. As has already been said, Johnson is nothing if not a hanging judge; and it is just where originality is most striking that his sentences are the most severe. If there was one writer who might have been expected to win his favour, it was Pope; and if there is any work that bears witness to the originality of Pope's genius, it is the imitations of Horace. These are dismissed in a disparaging sentence. There is no adequate recognition of Congreve's brilliance as a dramatist; none of Swift's amazing powers as a satirist. Yet all these were men who lived more or less within the range of ideas and tendencies by which Johnson's own mind was moulded and inspired.

The case is still worse when we turn to writers of a different school. Take the poets from the Restoration to the closing years of the American war; and it is not too much to say that, with the exception of Thomson--saved perhaps by his "glossy, unfeeling diction"--there is not one of them who overstepped the bounds marked out for literary effort by the prevailing taste of the Augustan age, in its narrowest sense, without paying the price for his temerity in the sneers or reprobation of Johnson. Collins, it is true, escapes more lightly than the rest; but that is probably due to the affection and pity of his critic.

Yet even Collins, perhaps the most truly poetic spirit of the century between Milton and Burns, is blamed for a "diction often harsh, unskillfully laboured, and injudiciously selected"; for "lines commonly of slow motion"; for "poetry that may sometimes extort praise, when it gives little pleasure". Johnson's Works, xi. 270.The poems of Gray--an exception must be made, to Johnson's honour, in favour of the Elegy In the bosom of "the Club" the exception dwindled to two stanzas (Boswell's Life, ii. 300). are slaughtered in detail; Johnson's Works, xi. 372-378. Johnson is peculiarly sarcastic on the Bard and the Progress of Poetry. the man himself is given dog's burial with the compendious epitaph:

"A dull fellow, sir; dull in company, dull in his closet, dull everywhere". Boswell's Life, ii. 300. Comp. in. 435.

But most astonishing of all, as is well known, is the treatment bestowed on Milton. Of all Milton's works, Paradise Lost seems to have been the only one that Johnson genuinely admired. That he praises with as little of reservation as was in the nature of so stern a critic. On Paradise Regained he is more guarded; on Samson, more guarded yet. The two papers devoted to Samson in the Rambler are "not entitled even to this slender commendation". "This is the tragedy that ignorance has admired and bigotry applauded" (Johnson's Works, v. 436). But it is in speaking of the earlier poems that Johnson shows his hand most plainly. Comus "is a drama in the epic style, inelegantly splendid and tediously instructive". Johnson's Works, ix. 153. Of Lycidas "the diction is harsh, the rhymes uncertain, and the numbers un-pleasing" Ib. 159. As for the sonnets, "they deserve not any particular criticism. For of the best it can only be said that they are not bad; and perhaps only the eighth and twenty-first are truly entitled to this slender commendation.... These little pieces may be dismissed without much anxiety". Ib. 160. The two sonnets are those written When the assault was intended to the City, and On his Blindness.

It would be hardly worth while to record these ill-tempered judgments if they were not the natural outcome of a method which held unquestioned sway over English taste for a full century--in France for nearly two--and which, during that time, if we except Gray and his friends, was not seriously disputed by a single man of mark. The one author in whose favour the rules of "correct writing" were commonly set aside was Shakespeare; and perhaps there is no testimony to his greatness so convincing as the unwilling homage it extorted from the contemporaries of Pope, of Johnson, and of Hume. Johnson's own notes and introductions to the separate plays are at times trifling enough; Compare the assault on the "mean expressions" of Shakespeare (Rambler, No. 168). but his general preface is a solid and manly piece of work. It contrasts strangely not only with the verdicts given above, but with his jeers at Chevy Chase Ib. x. 139.--a "dull and lifeless imbecility"--at the Nonne Prestes Tale, and at the Knightes Tale Ib. ix. 432.

One more instance, and we may leave this depressing study in critical perversity. Among the great writers of Johnson's day there was none who showed a truer originality than Fielding; no man who broke more markedly with the literary superstitions of the time; none who took his own road with more sturdiness and self-reliance. This was enough fo Johnson, who persistently depreciated both the man and his work. Something of this should doubtless be set down to disapproval of the free speech and readiness to allow for human frailty, which could not but give offence to a moralist so unbending as Johnson.

But that will hardly account for the assertion that "Harry Fielding knew nothing but the outer shell of life"; still less for the petulant ruling that he "was a barren rascal". Boswell's Life, ii. 169. Diary and Letters of Madame D'Arblay, i. 91 The truth is--and Johnson felt it instinctively--that the novel, as conceived by Fielding--the novel that gloried in painting all sides of life, and above all in drawing out the humour of its "lower spheres"--dealt a fatal blow not only at the pompous canons which the Rambler was pleased to call "the indispensable laws of Aristotelian criticism", Johnson's Works, v. 431. but also at the view which found "human life to be a state where much is to be endured and little to be enjoyed". It would be hard to say whether Johnson found more in Fielding to affront him, as pessimist or as critic.

And it would be equally hard to say in which of the two characters lay the greater barrier to literary insight. Even Richardson--no less revolutionary, though in a different way, than Fielding--was only saved so as by fire; by the undying hatred which he shared with Johnson for his terrible rival. It was rather as moralist than as artist, rather for "the sentiment" than for the tragic force of his work, that Richardson seems to have won his way to Johnson's heart. See the passage referred to in the preceding note.

Is not the evidence conclusive? Is it a harsh judgment to say that no critic so narrow, so mechanical, so hostile to originality as Johnson has ever achieved the dictatorship of English letters?

The supremacy of Johnson would have been impossible, had not the way been smoothed for it by a long succession of critics like-minded with himself. Such a succession may be traced from Swift to Addison, from Addison to Pope, and--with marked reservations--from Pope to Goldsmith. It would be unjust to charge all, or indeed any, of these with the narrowness of view betrayed in Johnson's verdicts on individual writers. To arrive at this perfection of sourness was a work of time; and the nature of Addison and Goldsmith at least was too genial to allow of any approach to it.

But, with all their difference of temperament, the method of the earlier critics is hardly to be distinguished from that of Johnson. There is the same orderliness of treatment--first the fable, then the characters, lastly the sentiment and the diction; the same persistency in applying general rules to a matter which, above all others, is a law to itself; the same invincible faith in "the indispensable laws of Aristotelian criticism". It is this that, in spite of its readiness to admire, makes Addison's criticism of Paradise Lost so dreary a study; and this that, in an evil hour, prompted Goldsmith to treat the soliloquy of Hamlet as though it were a schoolboy's exercise in rhetoric and logic. Goldsmith, Essay xvi. The next essay contains a like attack on Mercutio's description of Queen Mab.

And yet it is with Goldsmith that we come to the first dawn of better things. The carping strain and the stiffness of method, that we cannot overlook in him, were the note of his generation. The openness to new ideas, the sense of nature, the fruitful use of the historical method, are entirely his own. There had been nothing like them in our literature since Dryden. In criticism, as in creative work, Goldsmith marks the transition from the old order to the new.

Perhaps the clearest indication of this is to be found in his constant appeal to nature. In itself, as we have seen, this may mean much or little. "Nature" is a vague word; it was the battle-cry of Wordsworth, but it was also the battle-cry of Boileau. And, at first sight, it might seem to be used by Goldsmith in the narrower rather than in the wider sense. "It is the business of art", he writes, "to imitate nature, but not with a servile pencil; and to choose those attitudes and dispositions only which are beautiful and engaging." Goldsmith, Essay xiii.

But a glance at the context will show that what Goldsmith had in mind was not "nature to advantage dressed", not nature with any adornments added by man; but nature stripped of all that to man has degrading associations; nature, to adopt the words used by Wordsworth on a kindred subject, "purified from all lasting or rational causes of dislike or disgust". It may well be that Goldsmith gave undue weight to this reservation. It may well be that he did not throw himself on nature with the unwavering constancy of Wordsworth. But, none the less, we have here--and we have it worked out in detail As to oratory, poetry, the drama, and acting, Ib., Essays iv., xii., xiii.; The Bee, no. ii.--the germ of the principle which, in bolder hands, gave England the Lyrical Ballads and the Essays of Lamb.

In an essay not commonly reprinted, Goldsmith, laying his finger on the one weak spot in the genius of Gray, gives the poet the memorable advice--to "study the people". And throughout his own critical work, as in his novel, his comedies, and his poems, there is an abiding sense that, without this, there is no salvation for poetry. That in itself is enough to fix an impassable barrier between Goldsmith and the official criticism of his day.

The other main service rendered by Goldsmith was his return to the historical method. It is true that his knowledge is no more at first hand, and is set out with still less system than that of Dryden a century before. But it is also true that he has a far keener sense of the strength which art may draw from history than his great forerunner. Dryden confines himself to the history of certain forms of art; Goldsmith includes the history of nations also in his view. With Dryden the past is little more than an antiquarian study; with Goldsmith it is a living fountain of inspiration for the present. The art of the past--the poetry, say, of Teutonic or Celtic antiquity--is to him an undying record of the days when man still walked hand in hand with nature.

The history of the past is at once a storehouse of stirring themes ready to the hand of the artist, and the surest safeguard against both flatness and exaggeration in his work. See Essays xiii., xiv., xx.; Present State of Polite Learning, in particular, chap. xi. It offers, moreover, the truest schooling of the heart, and insensibly "enlists the passions on the side of humanity". "Poetry", Byron said, "is the feeling of a former world, and future"; Moore's Life, p. 483 and to the first half of the statement Goldsmith would have heartily subscribed. For the historical method in his hands is but another aspect of the counsel he gave to Gray: "Study the people". It is an anticipation--vague, no doubt, but still unmistakable--of the spirit which, both in France and England, gave birth to the romantic movement a generation or two later.

That zeal for the literature of the past was in the air when Goldsmith wrote is proved by works so different as those of Gray and Percy, of Chatterton and MacPherson, of Mallet and Warton. Percy's Reliques were published in 1765; Chatterton's Rowley Poems written in 1769; MacPherson's Ossian (first instalment) in 1760; Mallet's Northern Antiquities in 1755; and Warton's History of English Poetry --a book to the learning and importance of which scant justice has been done--from 1772 to 1778. To these should be added a work, whose fine scholarship and profound learning is now universally admitted, Tyrwhitt's Chaucer (1775-78). It will be noticed that all these works fall within the space of twenty years, 1755-1775.

But it may be doubted whether any one of them, Gray excepted, saw the true bearing of the movement more clearly than Goldsmith, or did more to open fresh springs of thought and beauty for the poetry of the next age, if not of his own. It would be unpardonable to turn from the writers of the eighteenth century with no notice of a book which, seldom now read, is nevertheless perhaps the most solid piece of work that modern Europe had as yet to show in any branch of literary criticism. This is Burke's treatise On the Sublime and the Beautiful. Few will now be prepared to accept the material basis which Burke finds for the ideas of the imagination. Burke traces our ideas of the sublime to the sense of physical pain; our ideas of the beautiful to that of physical pleasure; identifying the former with a contraction or tension, and the latter with a relaxation of the muscles.

Against this theory two main objections may be urged: (1) As, on Burke's own showing, the objects of the imagination, at least as far as poetry is concerned, are, and must be, presented first to the mind, it is (in the strictest sense of the term) preposterous to attribute their power over us to a purely muscular operation (2) The argument, taken by itself, is barely relevant to the matter in hand. Even where a physical basis can be proved--as it can in the case of music, painting, and sculpture (and of poetry, so far as rhythm and harmony are an essential element of it) it is extravagant to maintain that the physiologist or the "psycho physicist" can explain the whole, or even the greater part, of what has to be explained Beyond the fraction of information that purely physical facts can give us, a vast field must be left to intellectual and imaginative association. And that is the province not of physiology but of psychology, and of what the Germans call Aesthetik This province, however, is but seldom entered by Burke.

What, then, was it that drove Burke to a position so markedly at variance with the idealism of his later years? In all probability it was his rooted suspicion of reasoning as a deliberate and conscious process. Other writers of the century--Addison, for instance--had spoken as if men reasoned from certain abstract ideas (proportion, fitness, and the like) to individual instances of beauty, deciding a thing to have beauty or no, according as it squared or failed to square with the general notion.

This, as Burke points out, is more than questionable in itself, and it was certain to affront a man who, even thus early, had shown an almost morbid hatred of abstractions. In his later years, as is well known, he sought refuge from them in instinct, in "prejudice", in the unconscious working of the "permanent reason of man". In earlier days--he was still well under thirty--he found escape by the grosser aid of a materialist explanation (Burke's treatise was published in 1756 The Laocoon of Lessing, a work which may be compared with that of Burke and which was very probably suggested by it, appeared in 1766.) But none can deny the skill with which he works out his theory, nor the easy mastery with which each part is fitted into its place. The speculative power of the book and the light it throws on the deeper springs of the imagination are alike memorable. The first is not unworthy of the Reflections or the Appeal from the New to the Old Whigs ; the second shows that fruitful study of the Bible and the poets, English and classical, to which his later writings and speeches bear witness on every page.

If the originality and depth of Burke's treatise is to be justly measured, it should be set side by side with those papers of Addison which Akenside expanded in his dismal Pleasures of the Imagination. The performance of Addison, grateful though one must be to him for attempting it, is thin and lifeless. That of Burke is massive and full of suggestion. At every turn it betrays the hand of the craftsman who works with his eye upon his tools.

The speculative side of criticism has never been a popular study with Englishmen, and it is no accident that one of the few attempts to deal seriously with it should have been made at the only time when philosophy was a living power among us, and when the desire to get behind the outward shows of things was keener than it has ever been before or since. But for Burke's treatise, a wide gap would have been left both in the philosophy and the criticism of the eighteenth century; and it is to be wished that later times had done more to work the vein which he so skilfully explored. As it is, the writers both of France and Germany--above all, Hegel in his Aesthetik --have laboured with incomparably more effect than his own countrymen, Mr. Ruskin excepted, upon the foundations that he laid.

IV. Johnson's Lives of the Poets was the last word of the school which the Restoration had enthroned; the final verdict of the supreme court which gave the law to English letters from the accession of Anne to the French Revolution. Save in the splenetic outbursts of Byron--and they are not to be taken too seriously--the indispensable laws of Aristotelian criticism fell silent at Johnson's death. A time of anarchy followed; anarchy plus the policeman's truncheon of the Edinburgh and the Quarterly. The first number of the Edinburgh appeared in 1802; the Quarterly was started in a counterblast in 1809.

The ill-fame of these Reviews, as they were in their pride of youth, is now so great that doubts may sometimes suggest themselves whether it can possibly be deserved. No one who feels such doubts can do better than turn to the earlier numbers; he will be forced to the conclusion that, whatever their services as the journeymen of letters and of party politics, few critics could have been so incompetent to judge of genius as the men who enlisted under the standard of Jeffrey or of Gifford. There is not, doubtless, in either Review the same iron wall of reasoned prejudice that has been noted in Johnson, but there is a plentiful lack of the clear vision and the openness to new impressions which are the first necessity of the critic. What Carlyle says of Jeffrey and the Edinburgh may be taken as the substantial truth also about Gifford and the Quarterly, and it is the most pregnant judgment that has yet been passed upon them.

> *"Jeffrey may be said to have begun the rash, reckless style of criticising everything in heaven and earth by appeal to Moliere's maid: 'Do you like it?' ' Don't you like it?' a style which, in hands more and more inferior to that sound-hearted old lady and him, has since grown gradually to such immeasurable length among us; and he himself is one of the first that suffers by it. If praise and blame are to be perfected, not in the mouth of Moliere's maid only but in that of mischievous, precocious babes and sucklings, you will arrive at singular judgments by degrees." Carlyle, Reminiscences n 63, 64*

Carlyle has much here to say of Jeffrey's "recklessness", his defiance of all rules, his appeal to the chance taste of the man in the crowd. He has much also to say of his acuteness, and the unrivalled authority of his decrees. "Jeffrey was by no means the supreme in criticism or in anything else, but it is certain there has no critic appeared among us since who was worth naming beside him and his influence for good and for evil in literature and otherwise has been very great. Nothing in my time has so forwarded all this--the 'gradual uprise and rule in all things of roaring, million headed &c Demos'-- "as Jeffrey and his once famous Edinburgh Review '--Ib But he is discreetly silent on their severity and short-sightedness. "You know", Byron wrote in 1808 "the system of the Edinburgh gentlemen is universal attack. They praise none, and neither the public nor the author expects praise from them."--Moore's Life, p 67.

Yet this is the unpardonable sin of both Reviews: that mediocrity was applauded, but that, whenever a man of genius came before them, the chances were ten to one that he would be held up to ridicule and contempt. The very first number of the Edinburgh lays this down as an article of faith. Taking post on the recent appearance of Thalaba, the reviewer opens fire by a laboured parallel between poetry and religion. Edinburgh Review, No. 1, pp 63, &c With an alteration of names it might have been written by a member of the English Church Union, or of the Holy Inquisition.

> *"The standards of poetry have been fixed long ago by certain inspired writers, whose authority it is no longer lawful to call in question. Many profess to be entirely devoted to poetry, who have no good works to produce in support of their pretensions. The Catholic poetical Church too... has given birth to an infinite variety of heresies and errors, the followers of which have hated and persecuted each other as heartily as other bigots."*

Then, turning to business, the writer proceeds to apply his creed to Southey and all his works, not forgetting the works also of his friends. "The author belongs to a sect of poets that has established itself in this country within these ten or twelve years"--it would be hard to say for whose benefit in particular this date was taken--"and is looked upon as one of its chief champions and apostles". "The doctrines of this sect"--the Reviewer continues, with an eye upon the Alien Act--"are of German origin, or borrowed from the great apostle of Geneva". Rousseau is then "named" for expulsion, together with a miscellaneous selection of his following: Schiller and Kotzebue (the next number includes Kant under the anathema), Quarles and Donne, Ambrose Phillips and Cowper--perhaps the most motley crew that was ever brought together for excommunication. It is not, however, till the end of the essay that the true root of bitterness between the critic and his victims is suffered fully to appear. "A splenetic and idle discontent with the existing institutions of society seems to be at the bottom of all their serious and peculiar sentiments." In other words, the Edinburgh takes up the work of the Anti-Jacobin ; with no very good grace Jeffrey affects to sit in the seat of Canning and of Frere.

So much for the "principles" of the new venture; principles, it will be seen, which appear to rest rather upon a hatred of innovation in general than upon any reasoned code, such as that of Johnson or the "Aristotelian laws", in particular. On that point, it must be clearly realized, Carlyle was in the right. It is that which marks the essential difference of the Reviewers--we can hardly say their advance--as against Johnson.

We may now turn to watch the Reviewers, knife in hand, at the dissecting-table. For the twenty-five years that followed the foundation of the Edinburgh, England was more full of literary genius than it had been at any time since the age of Elizabeth. And it is not too much to say that during that period there was not one of the men, now accepted as among the chief glories of English literature, who did not fall under the lash of one, or both, of the Reviews. The leading cases will suffice.

And first, the famous attack--not altogether undeserved, it must be allowed--of the Edinburgh upon Byron. "The poetry of this young lord belongs to the class which neither gods nor men are said to permit", and so on for two or three pages of rather vulgar and heartless merriment at the young lord's expense. Edinburgh Review, xi. 285. It is uncommonly hard to find any trace of poetic power, even of the imitative kind, in the Hours of Idleness. It is significant that the best pieces are those in the heroic couplet; an indication--to be confirmed by English Bards --of Byron's leaning towards the past.

The answer to the sneer, as all the world knows, was English Bards and Scotch Reviewers. The author of the article had reason to be proud of his feat. Never before did pertness succeed in striking such unexpected fire from genius. And it is only fair to say that the Review took its beating like a gentleman. A few years later, and the Edinburgh was among the warmest champions of the "English Bard". See the article on The Corsair and Bride of Abydos, Ib. xxiii. 198.

After speaking of the "beauty of his diction and versification, and the splendour of his description", the reviewer continues: "But it is to his pictures of the stronger passions that he is indebted for the fulness of his fame. He has delineated with unequalled force and fidelity the workings of those deep and powerful emotions.... We would humbly suggest to him to do away with the reproach of the age by producing a tragic drama of the old English school of poetry and pathos." The amende honorable with a vengeance. The review of The Giaour, Byron thought, was "so very mild and sentimental that it must be written by Jeffrey in love ".--Moore's Life, p. 191. It was reserved for Southey, a pillar of the Quarterly, to rank him as the "Goliath" of the "Satanic school".

Let us now turn to the Quarterly upon Keats. Endymion, in spite of the noble self-criticism of its preface, is denounced as "Cockney poetry" The phrase was also employed by Blackwood, vol. iii. 519-524.--a stupid and pointless vulgarism--and is branded as clothing "the most incongruous ideas in the most uncouth language". The author is dismissed with the following amenities: "Being bitten by Leigh Hunt's insane criticism, he more than rivals the insanity of his poetry"; and we are half-surprised not to find him told, as he was by Blackwood, to "go back to the shop, Mr. John; back to the plasters, pills, and ointment-boxes". Quarterly Review, xix. 204. See Blackwood, vol. iii. 524; where the Reviewer sneers at "the calm, settled, imperturbable, drivelling idiocy of Endymion ".

With this insolence it is satisfactory to contrast the verdict of the Edinburgh : "We have been exceedingly struck with the genius these poems-- Endymion, Lamia, Isabella, The Eve of St. Agnes, &c.--display, and the spirit of poetry which breathes through all their extravagance.... They are at least as full of genius as absurdity." Of Hyperion the Reviewer says: "An original character and distinct individuality is bestowed upon the poet's mythological persons.... We cannot advise its completion. For, though there are passages of some force and grandeur, it is sufficiently obvious that the subject is too far removed from all the sources of human interest to be successfully treated by any modern author". Edinburgh Review, xxxiv. 203. A blundering criticism, which, however, may be pardoned in virtue of the discernment, not to say the generosity, of the foregoing estimate.

It would have been well had the Edinburgh always written in this vein. But Wordsworth was a sure stumbling-block to the sagacity of his critics, and he certainly never failed to call forth the insolence and flippancy of Jeffrey. Two articles upon him remain as monuments to the incompetence of the Edinburgh ; the first prompted by the Poems of 1807, the second by the Excursion.

The former pronounces sentence roundly at the very start: "Mr. Wordsworth's diction has nowhere any pretence to elegance or dignity, and he has scarcely ever condescended to give the grace of correctness or dignity to his versification". From this sweeping condemnation four poems-- Brougham Castle, and the sonnets on Venice, Milton, and Bonaparte--are generously excepted. But, as though astonished at his own moderation, the reviewer quickly proceeds to deal slaughter among the rest. Of the closing lines of Resolution and Independence he writes: "We defy Mr. Wordsworth's bitterest enemy to produce anything at all parallel to this from any collection of English poetry, or even from the specimens of his friend, Mr. Southey". Of the stanzas to the sons of Burns, "never was anything more miserable". Alice Fell is "trash"; Yarrow Unvisited, "tedious and affected". The lines from the Ode to Duty.

> *"Thou dost preserve the stars from wrong, And the most ancient heavens through thee are fresh and strong," are "utterly without meaning". The poem on the Cuckoo is "absurd". The Ode on Immortality is "the most illegible and unintelligible part of the whole publication". "We venture to hope that there is now an end of this folly." Edinburgh Review, xi. 217, &c.*

But the hope is doomed to disappointment. The publication of the Excursion a few years later finds the reviewer still equal to his task. "This will never do", he begins in a fury; "the case of Mr. Wordsworth is now manifestly hopeless. We give him up as altogether incurable and beyond the power of criticism." The story of Margaret, indeed, though "it abounds, of course, with mawkish sentiment and details of preposterous minuteness, has considerable pathos". But the other passage which one would have thought must have gone home to every heart--that which describes the communing of the wanderer with nature Excursion, book i.--is singled out for ridicule; while the whole poem is judged to display "a puerile ambition of singularity, grafted on an unlucky predilection for truisms". Edinburgh Review, xxiv. I, &c.

It is but just to add that in the remainder of the essay the Reviewer takes back--so far as such things can ever be taken back--a considerable part of his abuse. It would be idle to maintain that in some of these slashing verdicts-- criticisms they cannot be called--the reviewer does not fairly hit the mark. But these are chance strokes; and they are dealt, as the whole attack is conceived, in the worst style of the professional swash- buckler. Yet, low as is the deep they sound, a lower deep is opened by the Quarterly in its article on Shelley; an article which bears unmistakable marks of having been written under the inspiration, if not by the hand, of Southey.

It is impossible to know anything about Southey without feeling that, both in character and in intellect, he had many of the qualities that go to make an enlightened critic. But his fine nature was warped by a strain of bigotry; and he had what, even in a man who otherwise gave conclusive proof of sincerity and whole-heartedness, must be set down as a strong touch of the Pharisee. After every allowance has been made, no feeling other than indignation is possible at the tone which he thought fit to adopt towards Shelley.

He opens the assault, and it is well that he does so, by an acknowledgment that the versification of the Revolt of Islam, the corpus delicti at that moment under the scalpel, is "smooth and harmonious", and that the poem is "not without beautiful passages, free from errors of taste". But the "voice of warning", as he himself would too generously have called it, is not long in making itself heard. "Mr. Shelley, with perfect deliberation and the steadiest perseverance, perverts all the gifts of his nature, and does all the injury, both public and private, which his faculties enable him to perpetrate....He draws largely on the rich stores of another mountain poet, to whose religious mind it must be matter of perpetual sorrow to see the philosophy, which comes pure and holy from his pen, degraded and perverted by this miserable crew of atheists and pantheists."

So far, perhaps, the writer may claim not to have outstepped the traditional limits of theological hatred. For what follows there is not even that poor excuse. "If we might withdraw the veil of his private life and tell what we now know about him, it would be indeed a disgusting picture that we should exhibit, but it would be an unanswerable comment on our text...Mr. Shelley is too young, too ignorant, too inexperienced, and too vicious to undertake the task of reforming any world but the little world within his own breast." Quarterly Review, xxi. 460, &c. For the credit of both Reviews it must be said that it would be difficult to find another instance of so foul a blow as this: Except in the infamous insinuations, also a crime of the Quarterly, Non ragioniam di lui, ma guarda e passa.

Against the character of Currer Bell. See also the scurrilous attack on the character of Leigh Hunt in Blackwood, vol III 453 Apart from their truculence, the early numbers of the Edinburgh and Quarterly are memorable for two reasons in the history of English literature. They mark the downfall of the absolute standard assumed by Johnson and others to hold good in criticism. And they led the way, slowly indeed but surely, to the formation of a general interest in literature, which, sooner or later, could not but be fatal to their own haphazard dogmatism. By their very nature they were an appeal to the people; and, like other appeals of the kind, they ended in a revolution.

Of the men who fixed the lines on which this revolution was to run, four stand out taller from the shoulders upwards than their fellows. These are Coleridge, Lamb, Hazlitt, and Carlyle. The critical work of all four belongs to the first thirty years or so of the present century; Some of the dates are as follows Lamb's Specimens of English Dramatic Poets was published in 1808, his Essays of Elia began to appear in the London Magazine, 1820, Coleridge's first Course of Lectures (on English poets) was delivered in 1808, his second Course, in 1811-12, his Biographia Literana in 1817

Hazlitt's Characters of Shakespeare's Plays was published in 1817, his Lectures on the English Poets in 1818, and on The English Comic Writers in 1819 Carlyle's Essays began to appear (in the Edinburgh and other Reviews) in 1827, that on Diderot--the last notable essay of a literary cast--in 1833 Hazlitt died in 1830, Coleridge and Lamb in 1834

By that time Carlyle had turned to history and kindred subjects and of the four it is probable that Carlyle, by nature certainly the least critical, had the greatest influence in changing the current of critical ideas. Space forbids any attempt to treat their work in detail. All that can be done is to indicate what were the shortcomings of English criticism as it came into their hands, and how far and in what manner they modified its methods and its aims.

Till the beginning of the present century, criticism in England had remained a very simple thing. When judgment had once been passed, for good or evil, on an individual work or an individual writer, the critic was apt to suppose that nothing further could reasonably be expected of him. The comparative method, foreshadowed but only foreshadowed by Dryden, had not been carried perceptibly further by

Dryden's successors. The historical method was still more clearly in its infancy. The connection between the two, the unity of purpose which alone gives significance to either, was hardly as yet suspected.

It may be said--an English critic of the eighteenth century would undoubtedly have said--that these, after all, are but methods; better, possibly, than other methods; but still no more than means to an end-- the eternal end of criticism, which is to appraise and to classify. The view is disputable enough. It leaves out of sight all that criticism--the criticism of literature and art--has done to throw light upon the dark places of human thought and history, upon the growth and subtle transformations of spiritual belief, upon the power of reason and imagination to mould the shape of outward institutions. All these things are included in the scope of the historical and comparative methods; and all of them stand entirely apart from the need to judge or classify the works of individual poets.

But, for the moment, such wider considerations may be put aside, and the objection weighed on its own merits. It must then be answered that, without comparison and without the appeal to history, even to judge and classify reasonably would be impossible; and hence that, however much we narrow the scope of criticism, these two methods--or rather, two aspects of the same method--must still find place within its range.

For, failing them, the critic in search of a standard--and without some standard or criterion there can be no such thing as criticism--is left with but two possible alternatives. He must either appeal to some absolute standard--the rules drawn from the "classical writers", in a sense wider or narrower, as the case may be; or he must decide everything by his own impression of the moment, eked out by the "appeal to Moliere's maid". The latter is the negation of all criticism. The former, spite of itself, is the historical method, but the historical method applied in an utterly arbitrary and irrational way. The former was the method of Johnson; the latter, of the Edinburgh and the Quarterly. Each in turn, as we have seen, had ludicrously broken down.

In the light of recent inventions, it might have been expected that some attempt would be made to limit the task of the critic to a mere record of his individual impressions. This, in fact, would only have been to avow, and to give the theory of what the Edinburgh and the Quarterly had already reduced to practice. But the truth is that the men of that day were not strong in such fine-spun speculations. It was a refinement from which even Lamb, who loved a paradox as well as any man, would have shrunk with playful indignation.

It was in another direction that Coleridge and his contemporaries sought escape from the discredit with which criticism was threatened. This was by changing the issue on which the discussion was to be fought. In its most general form, the problem of criticism amounts to this: What is the nature of the standard to be employed in literary judgments? Hitherto--at least to the Reviewers--the question may be said to have presented itself in the following shape: Is the standard to be sought within or without the mind of the critic? Is it by his own impression, or by the code handed down from previous critics, that in the last resort the critic should be guided? In the hands of Coleridge and others, this was replaced by the question: Is the touchstone of excellence to be found within the work of the poet, or outside of it? Are we to judge of a given work merely by asking: Is it clearly conceived and consistently carried out? Or are we bound to consider the further question: Is the original conception just, and capable of artistic treatment; and is the workmanship true to the vital principles of poetry? The change is significant. It makes the poet, not the critic, master of the situation. It implies that the critic is no longer to give the law to the poet; but that, in some sense more or less complete, he must begin, if not by putting himself in the place of the individual writer as he was when at work on the individual poem, at least by taking upon himself--by making his own, as far as may be--what he may conceive to be the essential temperament of the poet.

This, indeed, is one of the first things to strike us in passing from the old criticism to the new. The Edinburgh and Quarterly plunge straight into the business of the moment. From the first instant--with "This will never do"--the Reviewer poses as the critic, or rather as the accuser. Not so Coleridge and Hazlitt. Like the Edinburgh and Quarterly, they undertake to discourse on individual poets. Unlike them, each opens his enquiry with the previous question-a question that seems to have found no lodgment in the mind of the Reviewers--What is poetry? Further than this. Hazlitt, in a passage of incomparably greater force than any recorded utterance of Coleridge, makes it his task to trace poetry to the deepest and most universal springs of human nature; asserts boldly that it is poetry which, in the strictest sense, is "the life of all of us"; and calls on each one of us to assert his birthright by enjoying it. It is in virtue of the poet latent in him, that the plain man has the power to become a critic.

Starting then from the question as just stated: Is it within the mind of the individual poet, or without it, that the standard of judgment should be sought?--neither Coleridge nor Hazlitt could have any doubt as to the answer. It is not, they would tell us, in the individual work but in the nature of poetry--of poetry as written large in the common instincts of all men no less than in the particular achievement of exceptional artists--that the test of poetic beauty must be discovered. The opposite view, doubtless, finds some countenance in the precepts, if not the example, of Goethe. But, when pressed to extremes, it is neither more nor less than the impressionist conception of criticism transferred to the creative faculty; and, like its counterpart, is liable to the objection that the impression of one poet, so long as it is sincerely rendered, is as good as the impression of another. It is the abdication of art, as the other is the abdication of criticism.

Yet Hazlitt also--for, leaving Coleridge, we may now confine ourselves to him--is open to attack. His fine critical powers were marred by the strain of bitterness in his nature. And the result is that his judgment on many poets, and notably the poets of his own day, too often sounds like an intelligent version of the Edinburgh or the Quarterly. Or, to speak more accurately, he betrays some tendency to return to principles which, though assuredly applied in a more generous spirit, are at bottom hardly to be distinguished from the principles of Johnson. He too has his "indispensable laws", or something very like them. He too has his bills of exclusion and his list of proscriptions. The poetry of earth, he more than suspects, is for ever dead; after Milton, no claimant is admitted to anything more substantial than a courtesy title. This, no doubt, was in part due to his morose temper; but it was partly also the result of the imperfect method with which he started.

The fault of his conception--and it was that which determined his method--is to be too absolute. It allows too much room to poetry in the abstract; too little to the ever-varying temperament of the individual poet. And even that is perhaps too favourable a statement of the case. His idea of poetry may in part be drawn--and its strength is to have been partly drawn--direct from life and nature. But it is also taken, as from the nature of the case it must be with all of us, from the works of particular poets. And, in spite of his appeal to Dante and the Bible, it is clear that, in framing it, he was guided too exclusively by his loving study of the earlier English writers, from Chaucer to Milton. The model, so framed, is laid with heavy hand upon all other writers, who naturally fare ill in the comparison. Is it possible to account otherwise for his disparagement of Moliere, or his grudging praise of Wordsworth and of Coleridge?

It was here that Carlyle came in to redress the balance. From interests, in their origin perhaps less purely literary than have moved any man who has exercised a profound influence on literature, Carlyle was led to quicken the sense of poetic beauty, and by consequence to widen the scope of criticism, more than any writer of his day. He may have sought German literature more for its matter than for its artistic beauty--here, too, he brought a new, if in some ways a dangerous, element into criticism--but neither he nor his readers could study it, least of all could they study the work of Goethe, without awakening to a whole world of imagination and beauty, to which England had hitherto been dead. With all its shortcomings, the discovery of German literature was a greater revelation than any made to Europe since the classical Renaissance.

The shock--for it was nothing less--came at a singularly happy moment. The blow, given by Carlyle as critic, was closely followed up by the French Romantiques, as creative artists. Nothing could well have been more alien to English taste, as understood by the Edinburgh and Quarterly, than the early works, or indeed any works, of Hugo and those who owned him for chief--if it were not the works of Goethe and the countrymen of Goethe. Different as these were from each other, they held common ground in uniting the most opposite prejudices of Englishmen against them. The sarcasms of Thackeray on the French writers speak to this no less eloquently than the fluent flippancies of De Quincey upon the Germans.

See Thackeray's Paris Sketch Book, especially the chapters on Madame Sand and the New Apocalypse and French Dramas and Melodramas. See also De Quincey's Review of Carlyle's translation of Wilhelm Meister. Works, vol. xii. Yet, in the one case as in the other--thanks, in no small measure, to Matthew Arnold and Mr. Swinburne--genius, in the long run, carried the day. And the same history has been repeated, as the literatures of Russia and of Scandinavia have each in turn been brought within our ken.

These discoveries have all fallen within little more than half a century since Carlyle, by the irony of fate, reviewed Richter and the State of German Literature in the pages of the Edinburgh. And their result has been to modify the standards of taste and criticism in a thousand ways. They have opened our eyes to aspects of poetry that we should never otherwise have suspected, and unveiled to us fields of thought, as well as methods of artistic treatment which, save by our own fault, must both have widened and deepened our conception of poetry. That is the true meaning of the historical method. The more we broaden our vision, the less is our danger of confounding poetry, which is the divine genius of the whole world, with the imperfect, if not misshapen idols of the tribe, the market-place and the cave.

Of this conquest Carlyle must in justice be reckoned as the pioneer. For many years he stood almost single-handed as the champion of German thought and German art against the scorn or neglect of his countrymen. But he knew that he was right, and was fully conscious whither the path he had chosen was to lead. Aware that much in the work of Goethe would seem "faulty" to many, he forestalls the objection at the outset.

> *"To see rightly into this matter, to determine with any infallibility whether what we call a fault is in very deed a fault, we must previously have settled two points, neither of which may be so readily settled. First, we must have made plain to ourselves what the poet's aim really and truly was, how the task he had to do stood before his own eye, and how far, with such means as it afforded him, he has fulfilled it. Secondly, we must have decided whether and how far this aim, this task of his accorded--not with us and our individual crotchets, and the crotchets of our little senate where we give or take the law--but with human nature and the nature of things at large; with the universal principles of poetic*

beauty, not as they stand written in our text-books, but in the hearts and imaginations of all men. Does the answer in either case come out unfavourable; was there an inconsistency between the means and the end, a discordance between the end and the truth, there is a fault; was there not, there is no fault." Carlyle on Goethe: Miscellanies, i. 295

Nothing could ring clearer than this. No man could draw the line more accurately between the tendency to dispense with principles and the tendency to stereotype them, which are the twin dangers of the critic. But it is specially important to note Carlyle's relation, in this matter, to Hazlitt He insists with as much force as Hazlitt upon the need of basing all poetry on "human nature and the nature of things at large"; upon the fact that its principles are written "in the hearts and imaginations of all men". But, unlike Hazlitt, he bids us also consider what the aim of the individual poet was, and how far he has taken the most fitting means to reach it. In other words, he allows, as Hazlitt did not allow, for the many-sidedness of poetry, and the infinite variety of poetic genius.

And, just because he does so, he is able to give a deeper meaning to "nature" and the universal principles of imagination than Hazlitt, with all his critical and reflective brilliance, was in a position to do. Hazlitt is too apt to confine "nature" to the nature of Englishmen in general and, in his weaker moments, of Hazlitt in particular. Carlyle makes an honest attempt to bound it only by the universal instincts of man, and the "everlasting reason" of the world. Thus, in Carlyle's conception, "it is the essence of the poet to be new"; it is his mission "to wrench us from our old fixtures"; Carlyle on Goethe: Miscellanies, i. 291. for it is only by so doing that he can show us some aspect of nature or of man's heart that was hidden from us before. The originality of the poet, the impossibility of binding him by the example of his forerunners, is the necessary consequence of the infinity of truth.

That Carlyle saw this, and saw it so clearly, is no doubt partly due to a cause, of which more must be said directly; to his craving for ideas. See p. xciv.

But it was in part owing to his hearty acceptance of the historical method. Both as critic and as historian, he knew--at that time, no man so well--that each nation has its own genius; and justly pronounced the conduct of that nation which "isolates itself from foreign influence, regards its own modes as so many laws of nature, and rejects all that is different as unworthy even of examination", to be "pedantry". Miscellanies, i. 37, 38. This was the first, and perhaps the most fruitful consequence that he drew from the application of historical ideas to literature. They enlarged his field of comparison; and, by so doing, they gave both width and precision to his definition of criticism.

But there is another--and a more usual, if a narrower--sense of the historical method; and here, too, Carlyle was a pioneer. He was among the first in our country to grasp the importance of studying the literature of a nation, as a whole, and from its earliest monuments, its mythological and heroic legends, downwards to the present.

The year 1831--a turning-point in the mental history of Carlyle, for it was also the year in which Sartor Resartus took shape "among the mountain solitudes"--was largely devoted to Essays on the history of German literature, of which one, that on the Nibelungenlied, is specially memorable. And some ten years later (1840) he again took up the theme in the first of his lectures on Heroes, which still remains the most enlightening, because the most poetic, account of the primitive Norse faith, or rather successive layers of faith, in our language. See Lectures on Heroes, p. 20; compare Corpus PoeticumBorealt, i. p. ci. But what mainly concerns us here is that Carlyle, in this matter as in others, had clearly realized and as clearly defines the goal which the student, in this case the student of literary history, should set before his eyes.

> *"A History... of any national Poetry would form, taken in its complete sense, one of the most arduous enterprises any writer could engage in. Poetry, were it the rudest, so it be sincere, is the attempt which man makes to render his existence harmonious, the utmost he can do for that end; it springs, therefore, from his whole feelings, opinions, activity, and takes its character from these. It may be called the music of his whole manner of being; and, historically considered, is the test how far Music, or Freedom, existed therein; how the feeling of Love, of Beauty, and Dignity, could be elicited from that peculiar situation of his, and from the views he there had of Life and Nature, of the Universe, internal and external. Hence, in any measure to understand the Poetry, to estimate its worth and historical meaning, we ask, as a quite fundamental inquiry: What that situation was?*

Thus the History of a nation's Poetry is the essence of its History, political, economic, scientific, religious. With all these the complete Historian of a national Poetry will be familiar; the national physiognomy, in its finest traits and through its successive stages of growth, will be dear to him: he will discern the grand spiritual Tendency of each period, what was the highest Aim and Enthusiasm of mankind in each, and how one epoch naturally evolved itself from the other.

He has to record the highest Aim of a nation, in its successive directions and developments; for by this the Poetry of the nation modulates itself; this is the Poetry of the nation." Carlyle, Miscellanies, iii. 292, 293.

Never has the task of the literary historian been more accurately defined than in this passage; and never do we feel so bitterly the gulf between the ideal and the actual performance, at which more than one man of talent has since tried his hand, as when we read it. It strikes perhaps the first note of Carlyle's lifelong war against "Dryasdust". But it contains at least two other points on which it is well for us to pause.

The first is the inseparable bond which Carlyle saw to exist between the poetry of a nation and its history; the connection which inevitably follows from the fact that both one and the other are the expression of its character. This is a vein of thought that was first struck by Vico and by Montesquieu; but it was left for the German philosophers, in particular Fichte and Hegel, to see its full significance; and Carlyle was the earliest writer in this country to make it his own. It is manifest that the connection between the literature and the history of a nation may be taken from either side. We may illustrate its literature from its history, or its history from its literature. It is on the necessity of the former study that Carlyle dwells in the above.

And in the light of later exaggerations, notably those of Taine, it is well to remember, what Carlyle himself would have been the last man to forget, that no man of genius is the creature of his time or his surroundings; and, consequently, that when we have mastered all the circumstances, in Carlyle's phrase the whole "situation", of the poet, we are still only at the beginning of our task.

We have still to learn what his genius made out of its surroundings, and what the eye of the poet discovered in the world of traditional belief; in other words, what it was that made him a poet, what it was that he saw and to which all the rest were blind. We have studied the soil; we have yet to study the tree that grew from it and overshadows it. Perhaps the most striking instances of this kind of criticism, both on its strong and its weak side, are to be found in the writings of Mazzini. See Opere, ii. and iv.

In reversing the relation, in reading history by the light of literature, the danger is not so great. The man of genius may, and does, see deeper than his contemporaries; but, for that very reason, he is a surer guide to the tendencies of his time than they. He is above and beyond his time; but, just in so far as he is so, he sees over it and through it. As Shakespeare defined it, his "end, both at the first and now, was and is... to show the very age and body of the time his form and pressure". Some allowance must doubtless be made for the individuality of the poet; for the qualities in which he stands aloof from his time, and in which, therefore, he must not be taken to reflect it. But to make such allowance is a task not beyond the skill of the practised critic; and many instances suggest themselves in which it has, more or less successfully, been done. Witness not a few passages in Michelet's Histoire de France, and some to be found in the various works of Ranke.

As instances may be cited, Michelet's remarks on Rabelais (tome viii. 428-440) and on Moliere (tome xiii. 51-85): or again Ranke's Papste, i. 486-503 (on Tasso and the artistic tendencies of the middle of the sixteenth century): Franzosische Geschichte, iii. 345-368 (the age of Louis XIV.).

Witness, again, Hegel's illustration of the Greek conception of the family from the Antigone and the Oedipus of Sophocles; or, if we may pass to a somewhat different field, his "construction" of the French Revolution from the religious and metaphysical ideas of Rousseau. Hegel, Phanomenologie des Geistes, pp. 323-348, and pp. 426-436.

So far as it employs literature to give the key to the outward history of a nation or to the growth of its spiritual faith, it is clear that the historical method ceases to be, in the strict sense of the word, a literary instrument. It implies certainly that a literary judgment has been passed; but, once passed, that judgment is used for ends that lie altogether apart from the interests of literature.

But it is idle to consider that literature loses caste by lending itself to such a purpose. It would be wiser to say that it gains by anything that may add to its fruitfulness and instructiveness. In any case, and whether it pleases us or no, this is one of the things that the historical method has done for literature; and neither Carlyle, nor any other thinker of the century, would have been minded to disavow it.

This brings us to the second point that calls for remark in the foregoing quotation from Carlyle. Throughout he assumes that the matter of the poet is no less important than his manner. And here again he dwells on an aspect of literature that previous, and later, critics have tended to throw into the shade. That Carlyle should have been led to assert, and even at times to exaggerate, the claims of thought in imaginative work was inevitable; and that, not only from his temperament, but from those principles of his teaching that we have already noticed. If the poetry of a nation be indeed the expression of its spiritual aims, then it is clear that among those aims must be numbered its craving to make the world intelligible to itself, and to comprehend the working of God both within man and around him.

Not that Carlyle shows any disposition to limit "thought" to its more abstract forms; on the contrary, it is on the sense of "music, love, and beauty" that he specially insists. What he does demand is that these shall be not merely outward adornments, but the instinctive utterance of a deeper harmony within; that they shall be such as not merely to "furnish a languid mind with fantastic shows and indolent emotions, but to incorporate the everlasting reason of man in forms visible to his sense, and suitable to it". Miscellanies, i. 297. The "reason" is no less necessary to poetry than its sensible form; and whether its utterance be direct or indirect, that is a matter for the genius of the individual poet to decide. Gott und Welt, we may be sure Carlyle would have said, is poetry as legitimate as Der Erlkonig or the songs of Mignon.

In this connection he more than once appeals to the doctrine of Fichte, one of the few writers whom he was willing to recognize as his teachers. "According to Fichte, there is a 'divine idea' pervading the visible universe; which visible universe is indeed but its symbol and sensible manifestation, having in itself no meaning, or even true existence independent of it. To the mass of men this divine idea of the world lies hidden; yet to discern it, to seize it, and live wholly in it, is the condition of all genuine virtue, knowledge, freedom; and the end, therefore, of all spiritual effort in every age.

Literary men are the appointed interpreters of this divine idea; a perpetual priesthood, we might say, standing forth, generation after generation, as the dispensers and living types of God's everlasting wisdom, to show it in their writings and actions, in such particular form as their own particular times require it in. For each age, by the law of its nature, is different from every other age, and demands a different representation of the divine idea, the essence of which is the same in all; so that the literary man of one century is only by mediation and reinterpretation applicable to the wants of another." Ib., p. 69. There is a similar passage in the Lectures on Heroes (Lec. v.), p. 145. In each case the reference is to Fichte's Lectures Ueber das Wesen des Gelehrten (1805), especially to lectures i., ii., and x,; Fichte's Werke, vi. 350-371, 439-447.

The particular form of Fichte's teaching may still sound unfamiliar enough. But in substance it has had the deepest influence on the aims and methods of criticism; and, so far as England is concerned, this is mainly due to the genius of Carlyle. Compare the criticism of the last century with that of the present, and we at once see the change that has come over the temper and instincts of Englishmen in this matter.

When Johnson, or the reviewers of the next generation, quitted--as they seldom did quit--the ground of external form and regularity and logical coherence, it was only to ask: Is this work, this poem or this novel, in conformity with the traditional conventions of respectability, is it such as can be put into the hands of boys and girls? To them this was the one ground on which the matter of literature, as apart from the beggarly elements of its form, could come under the cognizance of the critic. And this narrowness, a narrowness which belonged at least in equal measure to the official criticism of the French, naturally begot a reaction almost as narrow as itself.

The cry of "art for art's sake", a cry raised in France at the moment when Carlyle was beginning his work in England, must be regarded as a protest against the moralizing bigotry of the classical school no less than against its antiquated formalities. The men who raised it were themselves not free from the charge of formalism; but the forms they worshipped were at least those inspired by the spontaneous genius of the artist, not the mechanical rules inherited from the traditions of the past. Nor, whatever may be the case with those who have taken it up in our own day, must the cry be pressed too rigorously against the men of 1830. The very man, on whom it was commonly fathered, was known to disavow it; and certainly in his own works, in their burning humanity and their "passion for reforming the world", was the first to set it at defiance. See Hugo's William Shakespeare, p. 288.

The moralist and the formalist still make their voice heard, and will always do so. But since Carlyle wrote, it is certain that a wider, a more fruitful, view of criticism has gained ground among us. And, if it be asked where lies the precise difference between such a view and that which satisfied the critics of an earlier day, the answer must be, that we are no longer contented to rest upon the outward form of a work of art, still less upon its conventional morality. We demand to learn what is the idea, of which the outward form is the harmonious utterance; and which, just because the form is individual, must itself too have more or less of originality and power.

We are resolved to know what is the artist's peculiar fashion of conceiving life, what is his insight, that which he has to teach us of God and man and nature. "Poetry", said Wordsworth, "is the breath and finer spirit of all knowledge; it is the impassioned expression which is in the countenance of all Science." Preface to Lyrical Ballads by Wordsworth: Works, vi. 328. And Wordsworth is echoed by Shelley. "Poetry is indeed something divine. It is at once the centre and circumference of knowledge; it is that which comprehends all science, and that to which all science must be referred."--Shelley, Defence of Poetry, p. 33. But it is again to Carlyle that we must turn for the explicit application of these ideas to criticism:--

"Criticism has assumed a new form...; it proceeds on other principles, and proposes to itself a higher aim. The grand question is not now a question concerning the qualities of diction, the coherence of metaphors, the fitness of sentiments, the general logical truth, in a work of art, as it was some half-century ago among most critics; neither is it a question mainly of a psychological sort, to be answered by discovering and delineating the peculiar nature of the poet from his poetry, as is usual with the best of our own critics at present: A striking example of this method, the blending of criticism with biography, is to be found in Carlyle's own Essay on Burns. The significance of the method, in such hands as those of Carlyle, is that it lays stress on the reality, the living force, of the poetry with which it deals.

It was the characteristic method of Sainte-Beuve; and it may be questioned whether it did not often lead him far enough from what can properly be called criticism;--into psychological studies, spiced with scandal, or what a distinguished admirer is kind enough to call "indiscretions". See M. Brunetiere, L'Evolution des Genres, i. 236. This book is a sketch of the history of criticism in France, and cannot be too warmly recommended to all who are interested in such subjects, but it is--not indeed exclusively, but inclusively of those two other questions--properly and ultimately a question on the essence and peculiar life of the poetry itself. The first of these questions, as we see it answered, for instance, in the criticisms of Johnson and Kames, relates, strictly speaking, to the garment of poetry: the second, indeed, to its body and material existence, a much higher point; but only the last to its soul and spiritual existence, by which alone can the body... be informed with significance and rational life.

The problem is not now to determine by what mechanism Addison composed sentences and struck out similitudes; but by what far finer and more mysterious mechanism Shakespeare organized his dramas, and gave life and individuality to his Ariel and his Hamlet? Wherein lies that life; how have they attained that shape and individuality? Whence comes that empyrean fire, which irradiates their whole being, and pierces, at least in starry gleams, like a diviner thing, into all hearts? Are these dramas of his not verisimilar only, but true; nay, truer than reality itself, since the essence of unmixed reality is bodied forth in them under more expressive symbols?

What is this unity of theirs; and can our deeper inspection discern it to be indivisible, and existing by necessity, because each work springs, as it were, from the general elements of all thought, and grows up therefrom into form and expansion by its own growth? Not only who was the poet, and how did he compose; but what and how was the poem, and why was it a poem and not rhymed eloquence, creation and not figured passion? These are the questions for the critic." Miscellanies, i. 60, 61 (1827). And, a few pages later: "As an instance we might refer to Goethe's criticism of Hamlet.... This truly is what may be called the poetry of criticism: for it is in some sort also a creative art; aiming, at least, to reproduce under a different shape the existing product of the poet; painting to the intellect what already lay painted to the heart and the imagination." Ib. p. 72.

Instances of criticism, conceived in this spirit, are unhappily still rare. But some of Coleridge's on Shakespeare, and some of Lamb's on the Plays of the Elizabethan Dramatists--in particular The Duchess of Malfi and The Broken Heart --may fairly be ranked among them. So, and with still less of hesitation, may Mr. Ruskin's rendering of the Last Judgment of Tintoret, and Mr. Pater's studies on Lionardo, Michaelangelo, and Giorgione. Of these, Mr. Pater's achievement is probably the most memorable; for it is an attempt, and an attempt of surprising power and subtlety, to reproduce not merely the effect of a single poem or picture, but the imaginative atmosphere, the spiritual individuality, of the artist. In a sense still higher than would be true even of the work done by Lamb and Ruskin, it deserves the praise justly given by Carlyle to the masterpiece of Goethe; it is "the very poetry of criticism".

We have now reviewed the whole circle traversed by criticism during the present century, and are in a position to define its limits and extent. We have seen that a change of method was at once the cause and indication of a change in spirit and in aim. The narrow range of the eighteenth century was enlarged on the one hand by the study of new literatures, and on the other hand by that appeal to history, and that idea of development which has so profoundly modified every field of thought and knowledge. In that lay the change of method. And this, in itself, was enough to suggest a wider tolerance, a greater readiness to make allowance for differences of taste, whether as between nation and nation or as between period and period, than had been possible for men whose view was practically limited to Latin literature and to such modern literatures as were professedly moulded upon the Latin. With such diversity of material, the absolute standard, absurd enough in any case, became altogether impossible to maintain. It was replaced by the conception of a common instinct for beauty, modified in each nation by the special circumstances of its temperament and history.

But even this does not cover the whole extent of the revolution in critical ideas. Side by side with a more tolerant--and, it may be added, a keener--judgment of artistic form, came a clearer sense of the inseparable connection between form and matter, and the impossibility of comprehending the form, if it be taken apart from the matter, of a work of art. This, too, was in part the natural effect of the historical method, one result of which was to establish a closer correspondence between the thought of a nation and its art than had hitherto been suspected. But it was in part also a consequence of the intellectual and spiritual revolution of which Rousseau was the herald and which, during fifty years, found in German philosophy at once its strongest inspiration and its most articulate expression.

Men were no longer satisfied to explain to themselves what Carlyle calls the "garment" and the "body" of art; they set themselves to pierce through these to the soul and spirit within. They instinctively felt that the art which lives is the art that gives man something to live by; and that, just because its form is more significant than other of man's utterances, it must have a deeper significance also in substance and in purport. Of this purport Criticism of life --the phrase suggested by one who was at once a poet and a critic--is doubtless an unhappy, because a pedantic definition; and it is rather creation of life, than the criticism of it, that art has to offer. But it must be life in all its fulness and variety; as thought, no less than as action; as energy, no less than as beauty-- As power, as love, as influencing soul.

This is the mission of art; and to unfold its working in the art of all times and of all nations, to set it forth by intuition, by patient reason, by every means at his command, is the function of the critic. To have seen this, and to have marked out the way for its performance, is not the least among the services rendered by Carlyle to his own generation and to ours. Later critics can hardly be said to have yet filled out the design that he laid. They have certainly not gone beyond it.

2

An Apologie for Poetry

SIR PHILIP SIDNEY

The Apologie was probably written about 1580; Gosson's pamphlet, which clearly suggested it, having appeared in 1579. Nothing need here be added to what has been said in the Introduction.

When the right virtuous Edward Wotton and I were at the emperor's court together, we gave ourselves to learn horsemanship of John Pietro Pugliano: one that with great commendation had the place of an esquire in his stable. And he, according to the fertileness of the Italian wit, did not only afford us the demonstration of his practice, but sought to enrich our minds with the contemplations therein, which he thought most precious. But with none I remember mine ears were at any time more laden, than when (either angered with slow payment, or moved with our learner-like admiration) he exercised his speech in the praise of his faculty. He said, soldiers were the noblest estate of mankind, and horsemen, the noblest of soldiers.

He said, they were the masters of war, and ornaments of peace: speedy goers, and strong abiders, triumphers both in camps and courts. Nay, to so unbelieved a point he proceeded, as that no earthly thing bred such wonder to a prince, as to be a good horseman. Skill of government was but a pedanteria in comparison: then would he add certain praises, by telling what a peerless beast a horse was. The only serviceable courtier without flattery, the beast of most beauty, faithfulness, courage, and such more, that, if I had not been a piece of-a logician before I came to him, I think he would have persuaded me to have wished myself a horse. But thus much at least with his no few words he drove into me, that self-love is better than any gilding to make that seem gorgeous, wherein ourselves are parties. Wherein, if Pugliano his strong affection and weak arguments will not satisfy you, I will give you a nearer example of myself, who (I know not by what mischance) in these my not old years and idlest times, having slipped into the title of a poet, am provoked to say something unto you in the defence of that my unelected vocation; which if I handle with more good will than good reasons, bear with me, sith the scholar is to be pardoned that followeth the steps of his master.

And yet I must say that, as I have just cause to make a pitiful defence of poor poetry, which from almost the highest estimation of learning is fallen to be the laughing-stock of children, so have I need to bring some more available proofs: sith the former is by no man barred of his deserved credit, the silly latter hath had even the names of philosophers used to the defacing of it, with great danger of civil war among the muses. And first, truly to all them that professing learning inveigh against poetry may justly be objected, that they go very near to ungratefulness, to seek to deface that which, in the noblest nations and languages that are known, hath been the first light-giver to ignorance, and first nurse, whose milk by little and little enabled them to feed afterwards of tougher knowledges: and will they now play the hedgehog that, being received into the den, drove out his host? or rather the vipers, that with their birth kill their parents?

Let learned Greece in any of her manifold sciences, be able to show me one book, before Musaeus, Homer, and Hesiodus, all three nothing else but poets. Nay, let any history be brought, that can say any writers were there before them, if they were not men of the same skill, as

Orpheus, Linus, and some other are named: who having been the first of that country, that made pens deliverers of their knowledge to their posterity, may justly challenge to be called their fathers in learning: for not only in time they had this priority (although in itself antiquity be venerable) but went before them, as causes to draw with their charming sweetness the wild untamed wits to an admiration of knowledge.

So as Amphion was said to move stone with his poetry, to build Thebes. And Orpheus to be listened to by beasts indeed, stony and beastly people. So among the Romans were Livius Andronicus, and Ennius. So in the Italian language, the first that made it aspire to be a treasure-house of science were the poets Dante, Boccace, and Petrarch. So in our English were Gower and Chaucer.

After whom, encouraged and delighted with their excellent foregoing, others have followed, to beautify our mother tongue, as well in the same kind as in other arts. This did so notably show itself, that the philosophers of Greece durst not a long time appear to the world but under the masks of poets. So Thales, Empedocles, and Parmenides sang their natural philosophy in verses: so did Pythagoras and Phocylides their moral counsels: so did Tyrtaus in war matters, and Solon in matters of policy: or rather, they being poets, did exercise their delightful vein in those points of highest knowledge, which before them lay hid to the world. For that wise Solon was directly a poet, it is manifest, having written in verse the notable fable of the Atlantic Island, which was continued by Plato.

And truly, even Plato, whosoever well considereth, shall find, that in the body of his work, though the inside and strength were philosophy, the skin as it were and beauty depended most of poetry: for all standeth upon dialogues, wherein he feigneth many honest burgesses of Athens to speak of such matters, that if they had been set on the rack, they would never have confessed them. Besides, his poetical describing the circumstances of their meetings, as the well ordering of a banquet, the delicacy of a walk, with interlacing mere tales, as Gyges' ring, and others, which who knows not to be the flowers of poetry, did never walk into Apollo's garden.

And even historiographers (although their lips sound of things done, and verity be written in their foreheads) have been glad to borrow both fashion, and perchance weight, of poets. So Herodotus entitled his history by the name of the nine Muses: and both he, and all the rest that followed him, either stole or usurped of poetry their passionate describing of passions, the many particularities of battles, which no man could affirm: or if that be denied me, long orations put in the mouths of great kings and captains, which it is certain they never pronounced. So that truly, neither philosopher nor historiographer could at the first have entered into the gates of popular judgments, if they had not taken a great passport of poetry, which, in all nations at this day where learning flourisheth not, is plain to be seen: in all which they have some feeling of poetry.

In Turkey, besides their law-giving divines, they have no other writers but poets. In our neighbour country Ireland, where truly learning goeth very bare, yet are their poets held in a devout reverence. Even among the most barbarous and simple Indians where no writing is, yet have they their poets, who make and sing songs which they call areytos, both of their ancestors' deeds, and praises of their Gods. A sufficient probability, that, if ever learning come among them, it must be by having their hard dull wits softened and sharpened with the sweet delights of poetry. For until they find a pleasure in the exercises of the mind, great promises of much knowledge will little persuade them, that know not the fruits of knowledge.

In Wales, the true remnant of the ancient Britons, as there are good authorities to show the long time they had poets, which they called bards: so through all the conquests of Romans, Saxons, Danes, and Normans, some of whom did seek to ruin all memory of learning from among them, yet do their poets, even to this day, last; so as it is not more notable in soon beginning than in long continuing. But since the authors of most of our sciences were the Romans, and before them the Greeks, let us a little stand upon their authorities, but even so far as to see what names they have given unto this now scorned skill.

Among the Romans a poet was called vates, which is as much as a diviner, fore-seer, or prophet, as by his conjoined words vaticinium and vaticinari is manifest: so heavenly a title did that excellent people bestow upon this heart-ravishing knowledge. And so far were they carried into the admiration thereof, that they thought in the chanceable hitting upon any such verses great foretokens of their following fortunes were placed. Whereupon grew the word of Sortes Virgilianae, when, by sudden opening Virgil's book, they lighted upon any verse of his making, whereof the histories of the emperors' lives are full: as of Albinus the governor of our island, who in his childhood met with this verse

Arma amens capio nee sat rationis in armis: and in his age performed it; which although it were a very vain and godless superstition, as also it was to think that spirits were commanded by such verses (whereupon this word charms, derived of Carmina, cometh), so yet serveth it to show the great reverence those wits were held in. And altogether not without ground, since both the oracles of Delphos and Sibylla's prophecies were wholly delivered in verses. For that same exquisite observing of number and measure in words, and that high-flying liberty of conceit proper to the Poet, did seem to have some divine force in it.

And may not I presume a little further, to show the reasonableness of this word vates ? And say that the holy David's Psalms are a divine poem? If I do, I shall not do it without the testimony of great learned men, both ancient and modern: but even the name Psalms will speak for me;

which being interpreted is nothing but songs. Then that it is fully written in metre, as all learned Hebricians agree, although the rules be not yet fully found. Lastly and principally, his handling his prophecy, which is merely poetical. For what else is the awaking his musical instruments? The often and free changing of persons? His notable prosopopeias, when he maketh you, as it were, see God coming in His majesty? His telling of the beasts' joyfulness, and hills leaping, but a heavenly poesy: wherein almost he showeth himself a passionate lover of that unspeakable and everlasting beauty to be seen by the eyes of the mind, only cleared by faith? But truly now having named him, I fear me I seem to profane that holy name, applying it to poetry, which is among us thrown down to so ridiculous an estimation: but they that with quiet judgments will look a little deeper into it, shall find the end and working of it such as, being rightly applied, deserveth not to be scourged out of the Church of God.

But now, let us see how the Greeks named it, and how they deemed of it. The Greeks called him a poet, which name hath, as the most excellent, gone through other languages. It cometh of this word poiein, which is, to make: wherein I know not, whether by luck or wisdom, we Englishmen have met with the Greeks, in calling him a maker: which name, how high and incomparable a title it is, I had rather were known by marking the scope of other sciences, than by my partial allegation.

There is no art delivered to mankind, that hath not the works of nature for his principal object, without which they could not consist, and on which they so depend, as they become actors and players, as it were, of what nature will have set forth. So doth the astronomer look upon the stars, and by that he seeth, setteth down what order nature hath taken therein. So do the geometrician, and arithmetician, in their diverse sorts of quantities. So doth the musician, in times, tell you which by nature agree, which not. The natural philosopher thereon hath his name, and the moral philosopher standeth upon the natural virtues, vices, and passions of man; and follow nature (saith he) therein, and thou shalt not err.

The lawyer saith what men have determined. The historian what men have done. The grammarian speaketh only of the rules of speech; and the rhetorician, and logician, considering what in nature will soonest prove and persuade, thereon give artificial rules, which still are compassed within the circle of a question, according to the proposed matter. The physician weigheth the nature of a man's body, and the nature of things helpful, or hurtful unto it. And the metaphysic, though it be in the second and abstract notions, and therefore be counted supernatural, yet doth he indeed build upon the depth of nature: only the poet, disdaining to be tied to any such subjection, lifted up with the vigour of his own invention, doth grow in effect another nature, in making things either better than nature bringeth forth, or quite anew forms such as never were in nature, as the heroes, demigods, cyclops, chimeras, furies, and such like: so as he goeth hand in hand with nature, not inclosed within the narrow warrant of her gifts, but freely ranging only within the zodiac of his own wit.

Nature never set forth the earth in so rich tapestry, as divers poets have done, neither with pleasant rivers, fruitful trees, sweet-smelling flowers: nor whatsoever else may make the too much loved earth more lovely. Her world is brazen, the poets only deliver a golden: but let those things alone and go to man, for whom as the other things are, so it seemeth in him her uttermost cunning is employed, and know whether she have brought forth so true a lover as Theagenes, so constant a friend as Pylades, so valiant a man as Orlando, so right a prince as Xenophon's Cyrus: so excellent a man every way, as Virgil's Aneas.

Neither let this be jestingly conceived, because the works of the one be essential, the other, in imitation or fiction; for any understanding knoweth the skill of the artificer standeth in that idea or fore-conceit of the work, and not in the work itself. And that the poet hath that idea, is manifest, by delivering them forth in such excellency as he hath imagined them. Which delivering forth also is not wholly imaginative, as we are wont to say by them that build castles in the air: but so far substantially it worketh, not only to make a Cyrus, which had been but a particular excellency, as Nature might have done, but to bestow a Cyrus upon the world, to make many Cyruses, if they will learn aright, why and how that maker made him.

Neither let it be deemed too saucy a comparison to balance the highest point of man's wit with the efficacy of Nature: but rather give right honour to the heavenly Maker of that maker: who, having made man to his own likeness, set him beyond and over all the works of that second nature, which in nothing he showeth so much as in poetry: when, with the force of a divine breath, he bringeth things forth far surpassing her doings, with no small argument to the incredulous of that first accursed fall of Adam; sith our erected wit maketh us know what perfection is, and yet our infected will keepeth us from reaching unto it. But these arguments will by few be understood, and by fewer granted. Thus much (I hope) will be given me, that the Greeks, with some probability of reason, gave him the name above all names of learning. Now let us go to a more ordinary opening of him, that the truth may be more palpable: and so I hope, though we get not so unmatched a praise as the etymology of his names will grant, yet his very description, which no man will deny, shall not justly be barred from a principal commendation.

Poesy, therefore, is an art of imitation, for so Aristotle termeth it in his word Mimesis, that is to say, a representing, counterfeiting, or figuring forth: to speak metaphorically, a speaking picture: with this end, to teach and delight; of this have been three several kinds. The chief both in antiquity and excellency, were they that did imitate the inconceivable excellencies of God. Such were David in his Psalms, Solomon in his Song of Songs, in his Ecclesiastes, and Proverbs: Moses and Deborah, in their hymns, and the writer of Job; which, beside other, the learned Emanuel Tremilius and Franciscus Junius do entitle the poetical part of Scripture. Against these none will speak that hath the Holy Ghost in due holy reverence.

In this kind, though in a full wrong divinity, were Orpheus, Amphion, Homer in his hymns, and many other, both Greeks and Romans: and this poesy must be used by whosoever will follow St. James his counsel, in singing psalms when they are merry: and I know is used with the fruit of comfort by some, when, in sorrowful pangs of their death-bringing sins, they find the consolation of the never-leaving goodness.

The second kind, is of them that deal with matters philosophical; either moral, as Tyrtaus, Phocylides, and Cato: or natural, as Lucretius and Virgil's Georgics ; or astronomical, as Manilius, and Pontanus; or historical, as Lucan; which who mislike, the fault is in their judgments quite out of taste, and not in the sweet food of sweetly-uttered knowledge. But because this second sort is wrapped within the fold of the proposed subject, and takes not the course of his own invention, whether they properly be poets or no, let grammarians dispute; and go to the third, indeed right poets, of whom chiefly this question ariseth; betwixt whom and these second is such a kind of difference, as betwixt the meaner sort of painters (who counterfeit only such faces as are set before them) and the more excellent; who, having no law but wit, bestow that in colours upon you which is fittest for the eye to see; as the constant, though lamenting look of Lucretia, when she punished in herself another's fault.

Wherein he painteth not Lucretia whom he never saw, but painteth the outward beauty of such a virtue: for these third be they which most properly do imitate to teach and delight; and, to imitate, borrow nothing of what is, hath been, or shall be: but range, only reined with learned discretion, into the divine consideration of what may be, and should be. These be they that, as the first and most noble sort may justly be termed Vates, so these are waited on in the excellentest languages and best understandings, with the fore-described name of poets: for these indeed do merely make to imitate: and imitate both to delight and teach: and delight to move men to take that goodness in hand, which without delight they would fly as from a stranger: and teach, to make them know that goodness whereunto they are moved, which being the noblest scope to which ever any learning was directed, yet want there not idle tongues to bark at them.

These be subdivided into sundry more special denominations. The most notable be the heroic, lyric, tragic, comic, satiric, iambic, elegiac, pastoral, and certain others. Some of these being termed according to the matter they deal with, some by the sorts of verses they liked best to write in, for indeed the greatest part of poets have apparelled their poetical inventions in that numbrous kind of writing which is called verse: indeed but apparelled, verse being but an ornament and no cause to poetry: sith there have been many most excellent poets that never versified, and now swarm many versifiers that need never answer to the name of poets. For Xenophon, who did imitate so excellently, as to give us effigiem justi imperii the portraiture of a just empire under the name of Cyrus (as Cicero says of him), made therein an absolute heroical poem.

So did Heliodorus in his sugared invention of that picture of love in Theagenes and Chariclea, and yet both these wrote in prose: which I speak to show, that it is not rhyming and versing that maketh a poet, no more than a long gown maketh an advocate: who, though he pleaded in armour, should be an advocate and no soldier. But it is that feigning notable images of virtues, vices, or what else, with that delightful teaching which must be the right describing note to know a poet by: although, indeed, the senate of poets hath chosen verse as their fittest raiment, meaning, as in matter they passed all in all, so in manner to go beyond them: not speaking (table-talk fashion, or like men in a dream) words as they chanceably fall from the mouth, but peyzing weighing. each syllable of each word by just proportion according to the dignity of the subject.

Now, therefore, it shall not be amiss first to weigh this latter sort of poetry by his works, and then by his parts; and if in neither of these anatomies he be condemnable, I hope we shall obtain a more favourable sentence. This purifying of wit, this enriching of memory, enabling of judgment, and enlarging of conceit, which commonly we call learning, under what name soever it come forth, or to what immediate end soever it be directed, the final end is, to lead and draw us to as high a perfection, as our degenerate souls made worse by their clayey lodgings, can be capable of.

This, according to the inclination of the man, bred many formed impressions; for some that thought this felicity principally to be gotten by knowledge, and no knowledge to be so high and heavenly as acquaintance with the stars, gave themselves to astronomy; others, persuading themselves to be demigods if they knew the causes of things, became natural and supernatural philosophers; some an admirable delight drew to music; and some the certainty of demonstration, to the mathematics. But all, one and other, having this scope to know, and by knowledge to lift up the mind from the dungeon of the body, to the enjoying his own divine essence.

But when by the balance of experience it was found, that the astronomer looking to the stars might fall into a ditch, that the inquiring philosopher might be blind in himself, and the mathematician might draw forth a straight line with a crooked heart: then lo, did proof the overruler of opinions make manifest that all these are but serving sciences, which, as they have each a private end in themselves, so yet are they all directed to the highest end of the mistress knowledge, by the Greeks called Arkitektonike, which stands (as I think) in the knowledge of a man's self, in the ethic and politic consideration, with the end of well-doing, and not of well-knowing only; even as the saddler's next end is to make a good saddle: but his farther end, to serve a nobler faculty, which is horsemanship: so the horseman's to soldiery, and the soldier not only to have the skill, but to perform the practice of a soldier: so that the ending end of all earthly learning, being virtuous action, those skills that most serve to bring forth that, have a most just title to be princes over all the rest.

Wherein if we can show the poet's nobleness, by setting him before his other competitors, among whom as principal challengers step forth the moral philosophers, whom methinketh I see coming towards me with a sullen gravity, as though they could not abide vice by daylight, rudely clothed for to witness outwardly their contempt of outward things, with books in their hands against glory, whereto they set their names, sophistically speaking against subtlety, and angry with any man in whom they see the foul fault of anger; these men casting largess as they go, of definitions, divisions, and distinctions, with a scornful interrogative, do soberly ask, whether it be possible to find any path, so ready to lead a man to virtue, as that which teacheth what virtue is and teacheth it not only by delivering forth his very being, his causes, and effects: but also, by making known his enemy vice, which must be destroyed, and his cumbersome servant passion, which must be mastered, by showing the generalities that contain it, and the specialities that are derived from it: lastly, by plain setting down, how it extendeth itself out of the limits of a man's own little world, to the government of families and maintaining of public societies. A principal clause-- It will be well, or some equivalent--is unhappily lacking to this long sentence.

The historian scarcely giveth leisure to the moralist, to say so much, but that he, laden with old mouse-eaten records, authorizing himself (for the most part) upon other histories, whose greatest authorities are built upon the notable foundation of hearsay, having much ado to accord differing writers, and to pick truth out of partiality, better acquainted with a thousand years ago than with the present age, and yet better knowing how this world goeth than how his own wit runneth, curious for antiquities and inquisitive of novelties, a wonder to young folks, and a tyrant in table-talk, denieth in a great chafe that any man, for teaching of virtue and virtuous actions, is comparable to him. I am Lux vitae, Temporum Magistra, Vita memoriae, Nuncia vetustatis, &c.

The philosopher (saith he) teacheth a disputative virtue, but I do an active: his virtue is excellent in the dangerless academy of Plato, but mine showeth forth her honourable face in the battles of Marathon, Pharsalia, Poitiers, and Agincourt. He teacheth virtue by certain abstract considerations, but I only bid you follow the footing of them that have gone before you. Old-aged experience goeth beyond the fine- witted philosopher, but I give the experience of many ages. Lastly, if he make the songbook, I put the learner's hand to the lute; and if he be the guide, I am the light.

Then would he allege you innumerable examples, conferring story by story, how much the wisest senators and princes have been directed by the credit of history, as Brutus, Alphonsus of Aragon, and who not, if need be? At length the long line of their disputation maketh a point in this, that the one giveth the precept, and the other the example.

Now, whom shall we find (sith the question standeth for the highest form in the school of learning) to be moderator? Truly, as me seemeth, the poet; and if not a moderator, even the man that ought to carry the title from them both, and much more from all other serving sciences. Therefore compare we the poet with the historian and with the moral philosopher, and, if he go beyond them both, no other human skill can match him. For as for the divine, with all reverence it is ever to be excepted, not only for having his scope as far beyond any of these, as eternity exceedeth a moment, but even for passing each of these in themselves.

And for the lawyer, though Jus be the daughter of Justice, and Justice the chief of virtues, yet because he seeketh to make men good, rather Formidine poenae than Virtutis amore or to say righter, doth not endeavour to make men good, but that their evil hurt not others: having no care, so he be a good citizen, how bad a man he be. Therefore, as our wickedness maketh him necessary, and necessity maketh him honourable, so is he not in the deepest truth to stand in rank with these, who all endeavour to take naughtiness away, and plant goodness even in the secretest cabinet of our souls. And these four are all that any way deal in that consideration of men's manners, which being the supreme knowledge, they that best breed it deserve the best commendation.

The philosopher therefore and the historian are they which would win the goal: the one by precept, the other by example. But both not having both, do both halt. For the philosopher, setting down with thorny argument the bare rule, is so hard of utterance, and so misty to be conceived, that one that hath no other guide but him shall wade in him till he be old before he shall find sufficient cause to be honest; for his knowledge standeth so upon the abstract and general, that happy is that man who may understand him, and more happy that can apply what he doth understand.

On the other side, the historian wanting the precept is so tied, not to what should be, but to what is, to the particular truth of things, and not to the general reason of things, that his example draweth no necessary consequence, and therefore a less fruitful doctrine.

Now doth the peerless poet perform both: for whatsoever the philosopher saith should be done, he giveth a perfect picture of it in some one, by whom he presupposeth it was done. So as he coupleth the general notion with the particular example. A perfect picture, I say; for he yieldeth to the powers of the mind an image of that whereof the philosopher bestoweth but a wordish description: which doth neither strike, pierce, nor possess the sight of the soul so much as that other doth.

For as in outward things, to a man that had never seen an elephant or a rhinoceros, who should tell him most exquisitely all their shapes, colour, bigness, and particular marks; or of a gorgeous palace, the architecture; with declaring the full beauties, might well make the hearer able to repeat, as it were by rote, all he had heard, yet should never satisfy his inward conceits, with being witness to itself of a true lively knowledge: but the same man, as soon as he might see those beasts well painted, or the house well in model, should straightway grow without need of any description, to a judicial comprehending of them: so no doubt the philosopher with his learned definition, be it of virtue, vices, matters of public policy or private government, replenisheth the memory with many infallible grounds of wisdom: which, notwithstanding, lie dark before the imaginative and judging power, if they be not illuminated or figured forth by the speaking picture of poesy.

Tully taketh much pains and many times not without poetical helps, to make us know the force love of our country hath in us. Let us but hear old Anchises speaking in the midst of Troy's flames, or see Ulysses, in the fulness of all Calypso's delights, bewail his absence from barren and beggarly Ithaca. Anger, the Stoics say, was a short madness; let but Sophocles bring you Ajax on a stage, killing and whipping sheep and oxen, thinking them the army of Greeks, with their chieftains Agamemnon and Menelaus, and tell me if you have not a more familiar insight into anger, than finding in the schoolmen his genus and difference. See whether wisdom and temperance in Ulysses and Diomedes, valour in Achilles, friendship in Nisus and Euryalus, even to an ignorant man, carry not an apparent shining: and contrarily, the remorse of conscience in Odipus, the soon repenting pride of Agamemnon, the self-devouring cruelty in his father Atreus, the violence of ambition in the two Theban brothers, the sour-sweetness of revenge in Medea, and to fall lower, the Terentian Gnatho and our Chaucer's Pandar, so expressed, that we now use their names to signify their trades.

And finally, all virtues, vices, and passions so in their own natural seats laid to the view, that we seem not to hear of them, but clearly to see through them. But even in the most excellent determination of goodness, what philosopher's counsel can so readily detect a prince, as the feigned Cyrus in Xenophon? or a virtuous man in all fortunes, as Aneas in virgil? or a whole commonwealth, as the way of Sir Thomas More's Utopia? I say the way; because where Sir Thomas More erred, it was the fault of the man and not of the poet; for that way of patterning a commonwealth was most absolute, though he perchance hath not so absolutely performed it: for the question is, whether the feigned image of poesy, or the regular instruction of philosophy, hath the more force in teaching; wherein if the philosophers have more rightly showed themselves philosophers than the poets have obtained to the high top of their profession, as in truth Mediocribus esse poetis,

Non Di, non homines, non concessere columna: it is I say again, not the fault of the art, but that by few men that art can be accomplished.

Certainly, even our Saviour Christ could as well have given the moral commonplaces of uncharitableness and humbleness, as the divine narration of Dives and Lazarus: or of disobedience and mercy, as that heavenly discourse of the lost child and the gracious Father; but that his through-searching wisdom knew the estate of Dives burning in hell, and of Lazarus being in Abraham's bosom, would more constantly (as it were) inhabit both the memory and judgment.

Truly, for myself, meseems I see before my eyes the lost child's disdainful prodigality, turned to envy a swine's dinner:

which by the learned divines are thought not historical acts, but instructing parables. For conclusion, I say the philosopher teacheth, but he teacheth obscurely, so as the learned only can understand him: that is to say, he teacheth them that are already taught, but the poet is the food for the tenderest stomachs, the poet is indeed the right popular philosopher, whereof Asop's tales give good proof: whose pretty allegories, stealing under the formal tales of beasts, make many, more beastly than beasts, begin to hear the sound of virtue from these dumb speakers.

But now may it be alleged that, if this imagining of matters be so fit for the imagination, then must the historian needs surpass, who bringeth you images of true matters, such as indeed were done, and not such as fantastically or falsely may be suggested to have been done. Truly Aristotle himself in his discourse of poesy, plainly determineth this question, saying that poetry is philosophoteron and spoudaioteron, that is to say, it is more philosophical, and more studiously serious, than history. His reason is, because poesy dealeth with katholou, that is to say, with the universal consideration; and the history with kathekaston, the particular; now saith he, the universal weighs what is fit to be said or done, either in likelihood or necessity (which the poesy considereth in his imposed names), and the particular only marks, whether Alcibiades did, or suffered, this or that.

Thus far Aristotle: which reason of his (as all his) is most full of reason. For indeed, if the question were whether it were better to have a particular act truly or falsely set down, there is no doubt which is to be chosen, no more than whether you had rather have Vespasian's picture right as he was, or at the painter's pleasure nothing resembling. But if the question be for your own use and learning, whether it be better to have it set down as it should be, or as it was: then certainly is more doctrinable the feigned Cyrus of Xenophon than the true Cyrus in Justin: and the feigned Aeneas in Virgil, than the right Aeneas in Dares Phrygius.

As to a lady that desired to fashion her countenance to the best grace, a painter should more benefit her to portrait a most sweet face, writing Canidia upon it, than to paint Canidia as she was, who, Horace sweareth, was foul and ill-favoured.

If the poet do his part aright, he will show you in Tantalus, Atreus, and such like, nothing that is not to be shunned. In Cyrus, Aeneas, Ulysses, each thing to be followed; where the historian, bound to tell things as things were, cannot be liberal (without he will be poetical) of a perfect pattern: but as in Alexander or Scipio himself, show doings, some to be liked, some to be misliked. And then how will you discern what to follow but by your own discretion, which you had without reading Quintus Curtius?

And whereas a man may say, though in universal consideration of doctrine the poet prevaileth, yet that the history, in his saying such a thing was done, doth warrant a man more in that he shall follow; the answer is manifest: that if he stand upon that was; as if he should argue, because it rained yesterday, therefore it should rain to-day; then indeed it hath some advantage to a gross conceit: but if he know an example only informs a conjectured likelihood, and so go by reason, the poet doth so far exceed him, as he is to frame his example to that which is most reasonable: be it in warlike, politic, or private matters; where the historian in his bare Was, hath many times that which we call fortune, to overrule the best wisdom. Many times he must tell events, whereof he can yield no cause: or if he do, it must be poetical; for that a feigned example hath as much force to teach, as a true example (for as for to move, it is clear, sith the feigned may be tuned to the highest key of passion), let us take one example, wherein a poet and a historian do concur.

Herodotus and Justin do both testify that Zopyrus, King Darius' faithful servant, seeing his master long resisted by the rebellious Babylonians, feigned himself in extreme disgrace of his king: for verifying of which, he caused his own nose and ears to be cut off: and so flying to the Babylonians, was received: and for his known valour so far credited, that he did find means to deliver them over to Darius. Much like matter doth Livy record of Tarquinius and his son. Xenophon excellently feigneth such another stratagem, performed by Abradates in Cyrus' behalf. Now would I fain know, if occasion be presented unto you, to serve your prince by such an honest dissimulation, why you do not as well learn it of Xenophon's fiction, as of the others' verity: and truly so much the better, as you shall save your nose by the bargain: for Abradates did not counterfeit so far. So then the best of the historian is subject to the poet; for whatsoever action or faction, whatsoever counsel, policy or war stratagem, the historian is bound to recite, that may the poet (if he list) with his imitation make his own; beautifying it both for further teaching, and more delighting, as it pleaseth him: having all, from Dante his heaven, to his hell, under the authority of his pen. Which if I be asked what poets have done so, as I might well name some, yet say I, and say again, I speak of the art, and not of the artificer.

Now to that which commonly is attributed to the praise of histories, in respect of the notable learning is gotten by marking the success, as though therein a man should see virtue exalted, and vice punished; truly that commendation is peculiar to poetry, and far off from history. For indeed poetry ever setteth virtue so out in her best colours, making fortune her well-waiting handmaid, that one must needs be enamoured of her. Well may you see Ulysses in a storm and in other hard plights; but they are but exercises of patience and magnanimity, to make them shine the more in the near-following prosperity. And of the contrary part, if evil men come to the stage, they ever go out (as the tragedy writer answered, to one that misliked the show of such persons) so manacled, as they little animate folks to follow them. But the historian, being captived to the truth of a foolish world, is many times a terror from well-doing, and an encouragement to unbridled wickedness.

For see we not valiant Miltiades rot in his fetters? The just Phocion, and the accomplished Socrates, put to death like traitors? The cruel Severus live prosperously? The excellent Severus miserably murdered? Of the two Severi, the earlier, who persecuted the Christians, was emperor 194-210; the later (Alexander), who favoured them, 222-235. Sulla and Marius dying in their beds? Pompey and Cicero slain then, when they would have thought exile a happiness?

See we not virtuous Cato driven to kill himself? and rebel Caesar so advanced, that his name yet after 1600 years, lasteth in the highest honour? And mark but even Caesar's own words of the fore-named Sulla, (who in that only did honestly, to put down his dishonest tyranny,) literas nescivit, as if want of learning caused him to do well. He meant it not by poetry, which not content with earthly plagues deviseth new punishments in hell for tyrants: nor yet by philosophy, which teacheth occidendos esse : but no doubt by skill in history: for that indeed can afford your Cypselus, Periander, Phalaris, Dionysius, and I know not how many more of the same kennel, that speed wel' enough in their abominable unjustice or usurpation. I conclude therefore that he excelleth history, not only in furnishing the mind with knowledge, but in setting it forward, to that which deserveth to be called and accounted good: which setting forward, and moving to well-doing, indeed setteth the laurel crown upon the poet as victorious, not only of the historian, but over the philosopher: howsoever in teaching it may be questionable.

For suppose it be granted (that which I suppose with great reason may be denied) that the philosopher, in respect of his methodical proceeding, doth teach more perfectly than the poet; yet do I think that no man is so much philophilosophos, in love with philosophy. as to compare the philosopher, in moving, with the poet.

And that moving is of a higher degree than teaching, it may by this appear: that it is well-nigh the cause and the effect of teaching. For who will be taught, if he be not moved with desire to be taught? and what so much good doth that teaching bring forth (I speak still of moral doctrine) as that it moveth one to do that which it doth teach? for as Aristotle saith, it is not Gnosis but Praxis not knowledge but action. must be the fruit. And how Praxis cannot be, without being moved to practice, it is no hard matter to consider.

The philosopher showeth you the way, he informeth you of the particularities; as well of the tediousness of the way, as of the pleasant lodging you shall have when your journey is ended, as of the many by-turnings that may divert you from your way. But this is to no man but to him that will read him, and read him with attentive studious painfulness. Which constant desire, whosoever hath in him, hath already passed half the hardness of the way, and therefore is beholding to the philosopher but for the other half. Nay truly, learned men have learnedly thought, that where once reason hath so much overmastered passion, as that the mind hath a free desire to do well, the inward light each mind hath in itself is as good as a philosopher's book; seeing in nature we know it is well to do well, and what is well, and what is evil, although not in the words of art, which philosophers bestow upon us. For out of natural conceit, the philosophers drew it; but to be moved to do that which we know, or to be moved with desire to know, Hoc opus, hic labor est.

Now therein of all sciences (I speak still of human, and according to the human conceits), is our poet the Monarch. For he doth not only show the way, but giveth so sweet a prospect into the way, as will entice any man to enter into it. Nay, he doth as if your journey should lie through a fair vineyard, at the first give you a cluster of grapes: that, full of that taste, you may long to pass further. He beginneth not with obscure definitions, which must blur the margent with interpretations, and load the memory with doubtfulness: but he cometh to you with words sent in delightful proportion, either accompanied with, or prepared for the well enchanting skill of music; and with a tale forsooth he cometh unto you:

with a tale which holdeth children from play, and old men from the chimney corner.

And pretending no more, doth intend the winning of the mind from wickedness to virtue: even as the child is often brought to take most wholesome things, by hiding them in such other as have a pleasant taste: which, if one should begin to tell them the nature of Aloes or Rhubarb they should receive, would sooner take their physic at their ears than at their mouth. So it is in men (most of which are childish in the best things, till they be cradled in their graves), glad they will be to hear the tales of Hercules, Achilles, Cyrus, and Aneas; and hearing them, must needs hear the right description of wisdom, valour, and justice; which, if they had been barely, that is to say philosophically, set out, they would swear they be brought to school again.

That imitation, whereof poetry is, hath the most conveniency to Nature of all other, insomuch, that as Aristotle saith, those things which in themselves are horrible, as cruel battles, unnatural monsters, are made in poetical imitation delightful. Truly I have known men that, even with reading Amadis de Gaule (which God knoweth wanteth much of a perfect poesy), have found their hearts moved to the exercise of courtesy, liberality, and especially courage.

Who readeth Aneas carrying old Anchises on his back, that wisheth not it were his fortune to perform so excellent an act? Whom do not the words of Turnus move? (the tale of Turnus having planted his image in the imagination)--

Fugientem hoec terra videbit;

Usque adeone mori miserum est?

Where the philosophers, as they scorn to delight, so must they be content little to move: saving wrangling, whether virtue be the chief, or the only good: whether the contemplative, or the active life do excel: which Plato and Boethius well knew, and therefore made Mistress Philosophy very often borrow the masking raiment of poesy. For even those hard-hearted evil men, who think virtue a school name, and know no other good but indulgere genio, and therefore despise the austere admonitions of the philosopher, and feel not the inward reason they stand upon, yet will be content to be delighted: which is all the good fellow poet seemeth to promise: and so steal to see the form of goodness (which seen they cannot but love) ere themselves be aware, as if they took a medicine of cherries. Infinite proofs of the strange effects of this poetical invention might be alleged; only two shall serve, which are so often remembered, as I think all men know them.

The one of Menenius Agrippa, who when the whole people of Rome had resolutely divided themselves from the Senate, with apparent show of utter ruin: though he were (for that time) an excellent orator, came not among them upon trust of figurative speeches, or cunning insinuations: and much less, with far-fetched maxims of philosophy, which (especially if they were Platonic Alluding to the inscription over the door of Plato's Academy: No entrance here without Geometry.), they must have learned geometry before they could well have conceived: but forsooth he behaves himself, like a homely, and familiar poet. He telleth them a tale, that there was a time, when all the parts of the body made a mutinous conspiracy against the belly, which they thought devoured the fruits of each other's labour; they concluded they would let so unprofitable a spender starve. In the end, to be short (for the tale is notorious, and as notorious that it was a tale), with punishing the belly, they plagued themselves. This, applied by him, wrought such effect in the people, as I never read that ever words brought forth but then, so sudden and so good an alteration; for upon reasonable conditions, a perfect reconcilement ensued. The other is of Nathan the prophet, who when the holy David had so far forsaken God, as to confirm adultery with murder: when he was to do the tenderest office of a friend, in laying his own shame before his eyes, sent by God to call again so chosen a servant: how doth he it but by telling of a man, whose beloved lamb was ungratefully taken from his bosom? the application most divinely true, but the discourse itself feigned: which made David (I speak of the second and instrumental cause), as in a glass, to see his own filthiness, as that heavenly psalm of mercy well testifieth.

By these therefore examples and reasons, I think it may be manifest, that the poet, with that same hand of delight, doth draw the mind more effectually than any other art doth; and so a conclusion not unfitly ensueth: that, as virtue is the most excellent resting-place for all worldly learning to make his end of, so poetry, being the most familiar to teach it, and most princely to move towards it, in the most excellent work is the most excellent workman.

But I am content not only to decipher him by his works (although works in commendation or dispraise must ever hold an high authority), but more narrowly will examine his parts: so that (as in a man) though altogether he may carry a presence full of majesty and beauty, perchance in some one defectious piece we may find a blemish: now in his parts, kinds, or species (as you list to term them), it is to be noted, that some poesies have coupled together two or three kinds, as tragical and comical, whereupon is risen the tragi-comical. Some in the like manner have mingled prose and verse, as Sanazzar and Boethius. Some have mingled matters heroical and pastoral. But that cometh all to one in this question; for if severed they be good, the conjunction cannot be hurtful. Therefore perchance forgetting some, and leaving some as needless to be remembered, it shall not be amiss in a word to cite the special kinds, to see what faults may be found in the right use of them.

Is it then the pastoral poem which is misliked? for perchance, where the hedge is lowest, they will soonest leap over. Is the poor pipe disdained, which sometime out of Melibeus's mouth, can show the misery of people under hard lords, or ravening soldiers? And again, by Tityrus, what blessedness is derived to them that lie lowest from the goodness of them that sit highest? Sometimes, under the pretty tales of wolves and sheep, it can include the whole considerations of wrong-doing and patience. Sometimes show, that contention for trifles can get but a trifling victory. Where perchance a man may see that even Alexander and Darius, when they strave who should be cock of this world's dunghill, the benefit they got, was that the after-livers may say,

Hac memini et victum frustra contendere Thyrsin;

Ex illo Corydon, Corydon est tempore nobis. All these instances are taken from Virgil's Eclogues.

Or is it the lamenting Elegiac, which in a kind heart would move rather pity than blame, who bewails with the great philosopher Heraclitus the weakness of mankind, and the wretchedness of the world: who surely is to be praised, either for compassionate accompanying just causes of lamentation, or for rightly painting out how weak be the passions of woefulness. Is it the bitter, but wholesome Iambic Originally used by the Greeks for satire, which rubs the galled mind, in making shame the trumpet of villany, with bold and open crying out against naughtiness; or the satirist, who Omne vafer vitium ridenti tangit amico?

Who sportingly never leaveth, until he make a man laugh at folly, and at length ashamed, to laugh at himself: which he cannot avoid, without avoiding the folly. Who while

Circum pracordia ludit, giveth us to feel, how many headaches a passionate life bringeth us to. How when all is done, Est Ulubris, animus si nos non deficit aquus i.e. The wise can find happiness even in a village. ?

No perchance it is the comic, whom naughty play-makers and stage- keepers have justly made odious. To the argument of abuse To the argument that, because comedy is liable to abuse, it should therefore be prohibited altogether. I will answer after. Only thus much now is to be said, that the comedy is an imitation of the common errors of our life, which he representeth in the most ridiculous and scornful sort that may be. So as it is impossible that any beholder can be content to be such a one.

Now, as in geometry, the oblique must be known as well as the right: and in arithmetic, the odd as well as the even, so in the actions of our life, who seeth not the filthiness of evil, wanteth a great foil to perceive the beauty of virtue. This doth the comedy handle so in our private and domestical matters, as with hearing it we get as it were an experience, what is to be looked for of a niggardly Demea: of a crafty Davus: of a flattering Gnatho: of a vainglorious Thraso All characters in the Plays of Terence.: and not only to know what effects are to be expected, but to know who be such, by the signifying badge given them by the comedian. And little reason hath any man to say that men learn evil by seeing it so set out: sith, as I said before, there is no man living but, by the force truth hath in nature, no sooner seeth these men play their parts, but wisheth them in Pistrinum the tread-mill.: although perchance the sack of his own faults lie so behind his back, that he seeth not himself dance the same measure: whereto yet nothing can more open his eyes, than to find his own actions contemptibly set forth.

So that the right use of comedy will (I think) by nobody be blamed, and much less of the high and excellent tragedy, that openeth the greatest wounds, and showeth forth the vicers sinners., that are covered with tissue: that maketh kings fear to be tyrants, and tyrants manifest their tyrannical humours: that, with stirring the effects of admiration and commiseration, teacheth the uncertainty of this world, and upon how weak foundations golden roofs are builded. That maketh us know,

Qui sceptra scevus duro imperio regit,

Timet timentes, metus in auctorem redit.

But how much it can move, Plutarch yieldeth a notable testimony, of the abominable tyrant, Alexander Pheraus;

from whose eyes, a tragedy well made and represented drew abundance of tears: who, without all pity, had murdered infinite numbers, and some of his own blood. So as he, that was not ashamed to make matters for tragedies, yet could not resist the sweet violence of a tragedy.

And if it wrought no further good in him, it was, that he in despite of himself withdrew himself from hearkening to that, which might mollify his hardened heart. But it is not the tragedy they do mislike: for it were too absurd to cast out so excellent a representation of whatsoever is most worthy to be learned. Is it the lyric that most displeaseth, who with his tuned lyre, and well accorded voice, giveth praise, the reward of virtue, to virtuous acts? who gives moral precepts and natural problems, who sometimes raiseth up his voice to the height of the heavens, in singing the lauds of the immortal God. Certainly I must confess my own barbarousness, I never heard the old song of Percy and Douglas, that I found not my heart moved more than with a trumpet: and yet is it sung but by some blind crouder fiddler., with no rougher voice than rude style: which being so evil apparelled in the dust and cobwebs of that uncivil age, what would it work trimmed in the gorgeous eloquence of Pindar? In Hungary I have seen it the manner at all feasts and other such meetings, to have songs of their ancestors' valour; which that right soldier-like nation think the chiefest kindlers of brave courage. The incomparable Lacedemonians did not only carry that kind of music ever with them to the field, but even at home, as such songs were made, so were they all content to be the singers of them, when the lusty men were to tell what they did, the old men what they had done, and the young men what they would do.

And where a man may say that Pindar many times praiseth highly victories of small moment, matters rather of sport than virtue: as it may be answered, it was the fault of the poet, and not of the poetry; so indeed, the chief fault was in the time and custom of the Greeks, who set those toys at so high a price, that Philip of Macedon reckoned a horse-race won at Olympus, among his three fearful felicities. But as the inimitable Pindar often did, so is that kind most capable and most fit to awake the thoughts from the sleep of idleness, to embrace honourable enterprises.

There rests the heroical, whose very name (I think) should daunt all backbiters; for by what conceit can a tongue be directed to speak evil of that which draweth with it no less champions than Achilles, Cyrus, Aneas, Turnus, Tydeus, and Rinaldo? who doth not only teach and move to a truth, but teacheth and moveth to the most high and excellent truth? who maketh magnanimity and justice shine, throughout all misty fearfulness and foggy desires? who, if the saying of Plato and Tully be true, that who could see Virtue, would be wonderfully ravished with the love of her beauty, this man sets her out to make her more lovely in her holiday apparel, to the eye of any that will deign, not to disdain, until they understand. But if anything be already said in the defence of sweet poetry, all concurreth to the maintaining the heroical, which is not only a kind, but the best, and most accomplished kind of poetry.

For as the image of each action stirreth and instructeth the mind, so the lofty image of such worthies most inflameth the mind with desire to be worthy, and informs with counsel how to be worthy. Only let Aneas be worn in the tablet of your memory, how he governeth himself in the ruin of his country, in the preserving his old father, and carrying away his religious ceremonies sacred vessels and household gods.: in obeying the god's commandment to leave Dido, though not only all passionate kindness, but even the humane consideration of virtuous gratefulness, would have craved other of him. How in storms, how in sports, how in war, how in peace, how a fugitive, how victorious, how besieged, how besieging, how to strangers, how to allies, how to his enemies, how to his own: lastly, how in his inward self, and how in his outward government. And I think, in a mind not prejudiced with a prejudicating humour, he will be found in excellency fruitful: yea, even as Horace saith:

Melius Chrysippo et Crantore

A better teacher than the philosophers..

But truly I imagine, it falleth out with these poet-whippers, as with some good women, who often are sick, but in faith they cannot tell where. So the name of poetry is odious to them; but neither his cause, nor effects, neither the sum that contains him, nor the particularities descending from him, give any fast handle to their carping dispraise.

Sith then poetry is of all human learning the most ancient, and of most fatherly antiquity, as from whence other learnings have taken their beginnings: sith it is so universal, that no learned nation doth despise it, nor no barbarous nation is without it: sith both Roman and Greek gave divine names unto it, the one of prophesying, the other of making: and that indeed that name of making is fit for him; considering, that whereas other arts retain themselves within their subject, and receive, as it were, their being from it, the poet only bringeth his own stuff, and doth not learn a conceit out of a matter, but maketh matter for a conceit: sith neither his description, nor his end, containeth any evil, the thing described cannot be evil: sith his effects be so good as to teach goodness and to delight the learners: sith therein (namely, in moral doctrine, the chief of all knowledges), he doth not only far pass the historian, but for instructing is well- nigh comparable to the philosopher: and for moving, leaves him behind him: sith the Holy Scripture (wherein there is no uncleanness) hath whole parts in it poetical: and that even our Saviour Christ vouchsafed to use the flowers of it: sith all his kinds are not only in their united forms, but in their severed dissections fully commendable, I think (and think I think rightly), the laurel crown, appointed for triumphing captains, doth worthily (of all other learnings) honour the poet's triumph. But because we have ears as well as tongues, and that the lightest reasons that may be, will seem to weigh greatly, if nothing be put in the counter-balance: let us hear, and as well as we can ponder, what objections may be made against this art, which may be worthy, either of yielding or answering.

First truly I note, not only in these mysomousoi poet-haters, but in all that kind of people, who seek a praise by dispraising others, that they do prodigally spend a great many wandering words, in quips, and scoffs; carping and taunting at each thing, which, by stirring the spleen, may stay the brain from a through beholding the worthiness of the subject.

Those kind of objections, as they are full of very idle easiness, sith there is nothing of so sacred a majesty, but that an itching tongue may rub itself upon it: so deserve they no other answer, but instead of laughing at the jest, to laugh at the jester. We know a playing wit can praise the discretion of an ass; the comfortableness of being in debt, and the jolly commodity of being sick of the plague. So of the contrary side, if we will turn Ovid's verse:

Ut lateat virtus proximitate mali, that good lie hid in nearness of the evil: Agrippa will be as merry in showingthe vanity of science, as Erasmus was in commending of folly. Neither shall any man or matter escape some touch of these smiling railers. But for Erasmus and Agrippa, they had another foundation than the superficial part would promise. Marry, these other pleasant fault-finders, who will correct the verb, before they understand the noun, and confute others' knowledge before they confirm their own: I would have them only remember, that scoffing cometh not of wisdom.

So as the best title in true English they get with their merriments is to be called good fools: for so have our grave forefathers ever termed that humorous kind of jesters: but that which giveth greatest scope to their scorning humours is rhyming and versing. It is already said (and as I think, truly said) it is not rhyming and versing that maketh poesy.

One may be a poet without versing, and a versifier without poetry. But yet, presuppose it were inseparable (as indeed it seemeth Scaliger judgeth) truly it were an inseparable commendation. For if oratio next to ratio, speech next to reason, be the greatest gift bestowed upon mortality: that cannot be praiseless, which doth most polish that blessing of speech, which considers each word, not only (as a man may say) by his forcible quality, but by his best measured quantity, carrying even in themselves, a harmony: without (perchance) number, measure, order, proportion, be in our time grown odious. But lay aside the just praise it hath, by being the only fit speech for music (music, I say, the most divine striker of the senses): thus much is undoubtedly true, that if reading be foolish, without remembering, memory being the only treasurer of knowledge, those words which are fittest for memory, are likewise most convenient for knowledge.

Now, that verse far exceedeth prose in the knitting up of the memory, the reason is manifest. The words (besides their delight, which hath a great affinity to memory), being so set, as one word cannot be lost, but the whole work fails: which accuseth itself, calleth the remembrance back to itself, and so most strongly confirmeth it. Besides, one word so as it were begetting another, as be it in rhyme or measured verse, by the former a man shall have a near guess to the follower. Lastly, even they that have taught the art of memory have showed nothing so apt for it, as a certain room divided into many places well and thoroughly known. Now, that hath the verse in effect perfectly: every word having his natural seat, which seat must needs make the words remembered. But what needeth more in a thing so known to all men? Who is it that ever was a scholar, that doth not carry away some verses of Virgil, Horace, or Cato The moralist.

His elegiacs are constantly quoted by medieval writers, e.g. in Piers Plowman., which in his youth he learned, and even to his old age serve him for hourly lessons? But the fitness it hath for memory is notably proved by all delivery of arts: wherein for the most part, from grammar to logic, mathematic, physic, and the rest, the rules chiefly necessary to be borne away are compiled in verses. So that, verse being in itself sweet and orderly, and being best for memory, the only handle of knowledge, it must be in jest that any man can speak against it. Now then go we to the most important imputations laid to the poor poets; for aught I can yet learn, they are these: first, that there being many other more fruitful knowledges, a man might better spend his time in them, than in this.

Secondly, that it is the mother of lies. Thirdly, that it is the nurse of abuse, infecting us with many pestilent desires: with a siren's sweetness, drawing the mind to the serpent's tail of sinful fancy. And herein especially, comedies give the largest field to err, as Chaucer saith: how both in other nations and in ours, before poets did soften us, we were full of courage, given to martial exercises; the pillars of man-like liberty, and not lulled asleep in shady idleness with poets' pastimes. And lastly, and chiefly, they cry out with an open mouth, as if they outshot Robin Hood, that Plato banished them out of his commonwealth. Truly, this is much, if there be much truth in it. First to the first: that a man might better spend his time, is a reason indeed: but it doth (as they say) but petere principium.

For if it be as I affirm, that no learning is so good as that which teacheth and moveth to virtue; and that none can both teach and move thereto so much as poetry: then is the conclusion manifest, that ink and paper cannot be to a more profitable purpose employed. And certainly, though a man should grant their first assumption, it should follow (methinks) very unwillingly, that good is not good, because better is better. But I still and utterly deny that there is sprung out of earth a more fruitful knowledge. To the second, therefore, that they should be the principal liars; I answer paradoxically, but truly I think, truly; that of all writers under the sun, the poet is the least liar: and though he would, as a poet can scarcely be a liar, the astronomer, with his cousin the geometrician, can hardly escape, when they take upon them to measure the height of the stars.

How often, think you, do the physicians lie, when they aver things good for sicknesses, which afterwards send Charon a great number of souls drowned in a potion before they come to his ferry? And no less of the rest, which take upon them to affirm. Now, for the poet, he nothing affirms, and therefore never lieth. For, as I take it, to lie is to affirm that to be true which is false. So as the other artists, and especially the historian, affirming many things, can in the cloudy knowledge of mankind hardly escape from many lies. But the poet (as I said before) never affirmeth. The poet never maketh any circles about your imagination, to conjure you to believe for true what he writes.

He citeth not authorities of other histories, but even for his entry calleth the sweet Muses to inspire into him a good invention: in truth, not labouring to tell you what is or is not, but what should or should not be: and therefore, though he recount things not true, yet because he telleth them not for true, he lieth not, without we will say that Nathan lied in his speech, before alleged, to David. Which as a wicked man durst scarce say, so think I, none so simple would say, that Asop lied in the tales of his beasts: for who thinks that Asop wrote it for actually true, were well worthy to have his name chronicled among the beasts he writeth of.

What child is there, that coming to a play, and seeing Thebes written in great letters upon an old door, doth believe that it is Thebes? If then a man can arrive, at that child's age, to know that the poet's persons and doings are but pictures what should be, and not stories what have been, they will never give the lie to things not affirmatively, but allegorically and figuratively, written. And therefore as in history, looking for truth, they go away full fraught with falsehood: so in poesy, looking for fiction, they shall use the narration but as an imaginative groundplot of a profitable invention.

But hereto is replied that the poets give names to men they write of, which argueth a conceit of an actual truth, and so, not being true, proves a falsehood. And doth the lawyer lie, then, when under the names of John a stile and John a noakes, he puts his case? But that is easily answered. Their naming of men is but to make their picture the more lively, and not to build any history: painting men, they cannot leave men nameless. We see we cannot play at chess, but that we must give names to our chessmen; and yet methinks he were a very partial champion of truth that would say we lied for giving a piece of wood the reverend title of a bishop. The poet nameth Cyrus or Aneas no other way than to show what men of their fames, fortunes, and estates should do.

Their third is, how much it abuseth men's wit, training it to wanton sinfulness and lustful love; for indeed that is the principal, if not the only abuse I can hear alleged. They say the comedies rather teach than reprehend amorous conceits. They say the lyric is larded with passionate sonnets. The elegiac weeps the want of his mistress. And that even to the heroical, Cupid hath ambitiously climbed. Alas, Love! I would thou couldst as well defend thyself as thou canst offend others. I would those on whom thou dost attend could either put thee away or yield good reason why they keep thee. But grant love of beauty to be a beastly fault, although it be very hard, sith only man and no beast hath that gift, to discern beauty. Grant that lovely name of love to deserve all hateful reproaches: although even some of my masters the philosophers spent a good deal of their lamp-oil in setting forth the excellency of it. Grant, I say, whatsoever they will have granted; that not only love, but lust, but vanity, but (if they list) scurrility, possesseth many leaves of the poet's books: yet think I, when this is granted, they will find their sentence may with good manners put the last words foremost;

and not say that poetry abuseth man's wit, but that man's wit abuseth poetry.

For I will not deny but that man's wit may make poesy (which should be eikastike, which some learned have defined, figuring forth good things) to be fantastic: which doth contrariwise infect the fancy with unworthy objects. As the painter, that should give to the eye either some excellent perspective or some fine picture fit for building or fortification, or containing in it some notable example, as Abraham sacrificing his son Isaac, Judith killing Holofernes, David fighting with Goliath, may leave those and please an ill-pleased eye with wanton shows of better hidden matters. But what, shall the abuse of a thing make the right use odious? Nay, truly, though I yield that poesy may not only be abused, but that, being abused by the reason of his sweet charming force, it can do more hurt than any other army of words: yet shall it be so far from concluding that the abuse should give reproach to the abused, that contrariwise it is a good reason that whatsoever being abused, doth most harm, being rightly used (and upon the right use each thing conceiveth his title) doth most good.

Do we not see the skill of physic (the best rampire to our often- assaulted bodies), being abused, teach poison the most violent destroyer? Doth not knowledge of law, whose end is to even and right all things, being abused, grow the crooked fosterer of horrible injuries? Doth not (to go to the highest) God's word, abused, breed heresy? and His name abused, become blasphemy? Truly a needle cannot do much hurt, and as truly (with leave of ladies be it spoken) it cannot do much good. With a sword thou mayest kill thy father, and with a sword thou mayest defend thy prince and country. So that, as in their calling poets the fathers of lies they say nothing: so in this their argument of abuse they prove the commendation.

They allege herewith that, before poets began to be in price, our nation hath set their hearts' delight upon action and not upon imagination: rather doing things worthy to be written than writing things fit to be done. What that before time was, I think scarcely Sphinx can tell: sith no memory is so ancient that hath the precedence of poetry. And certain it is that, in our plainest homeliness, yet never was the Albion nation without poetry. Marry, this argument, though it be levelled against poetry, yet is it indeed a chain-shot against all learning, or bookishness, as they commonly term it. Of such mind were certain Goths, of whom it is written that, having in the spoils of a famous city taken a fair library, one hangman (belike fit to execute the fruits of their wits) who had murdered a great number of bodies, would have set fire on it. "No", said another very gravely, "take heed what you do, for while they are busy about these toys, we shall with more leisure conquer their countries."

This indeed is the ordinary doctrine of ignorance, and many words sometimes I have heard spent in it; but because this reason is generally against all learning, as well as poetry; or rather, all learning but poetry: because it were too large a digression to handle, or at least too superfluous: (sith it is manifest that all government of action is to be gotten by knowledge, and knowledge best by gathering many knowledges, which is, reading), I only with Horace, to him that is of that opinion,

Jubeo stultum esse libenter: for as for poetry itself, it is the freest from this objection. For poetry is the companion of the camps.

I dare undertake, Orlando Furioso or honest King Arthur will never displease a soldier; but the quiddity of ens and prima materia will hardly agree with a corslet; and therefore, as I said in the beginning, even Turks and Tartars are delighted with poets. Homer, a Greek, flourished before Greece flourished. And if to a slight conjecture a conjecture may be opposed, truly it may seem that, as by him their learned men took almost their first light of knowledge, so their active men received their first motions of courage. Only

Alexander's example may serve, who by Plutarch is accounted of such virtue that fortune was not his guide but his footstool; whose acts speak for him, though Plutarch did not: indeed, the Phoenix of warlike princes. This Alexander left his schoolmaster, living Aristotle, behind him, but took dead Homer with him; he put the philosopher Calisthenes to death for his seeming philosophical, indeed mutinous stubbornness. But the chief thing he ever was heard to wish for was that Homer had been alive.

He well found he received more bravery of mind by the pattern of Achilles than by hearing the definition of fortitude; and therefore, if Cato misliked Fulvius for carrying Ennius with him to the field, it may be answered that, if Cato misliked it, the noble Fulvius liked it, or else he had not done it. For it was not the excellent Cato Uticensis (whose authority I would much more have reverenced), but it was the former Cato the Censor: in truth, a bitter punisher of faults, but else a man that had never well sacrificed to the Graces.

He misliked and cried out upon all Greek learning, and yet, being 80 years old, began to learn it. Belike, fearing that Pluto understood not Latin. Indeed, the Roman laws allowed no person to be carried to the wars but he that was in the soldiers' roll; and therefore, though Cato misliked his unmustered person, he misliked not his work.

And if he had, Scipio Nasica, judged by common consent the best Roman, loved him. Both the other Scipio brothers, who had by their virtues no less surnames than of Asia and Affrick, so loved him that they caused his body to be buried in their sepulchre. So as Cato, his authority being but against his person, and that answered with so far greater than himself, is herein of no validity.

But now, indeed, my burden is great; now Plato his name is laid upon me, whom I must confess, of all philosophers, I have ever esteemed most worthy of reverence, and with great reason, sith of all philosophers he is the most poetical.

Yet if he will defile the fountain, out of which his flowing streams have proceeded, let us boldly examine with what reasons he did it.

First, truly, a man might maliciously object that Plato, being a philosopher, was a natural enemy of poets; for, indeed, after the philosophers had picked out of the sweet mysteries of poetry the right discerning true points of knowledge, they forthwith putting it in method, and making a school-art of that which the poets did only teach by a divine delightfulness, beginning to spurn at their guides like ungrateful 'prentices, were not content to set up shops for themselves, but sought by all means to discredit their masters.

Which by the force of delight being barred them, the less they could overthrow them, the more they hated them. For, indeed, they found for Homer seven cities strove who should have him for their citizen: where many cities banished philosophers, as not fit members to live among them. For only repeating certain of Euripides' verses, many Athenians had their lives saved of the Syracusians: The story is told in Balaustion's Adventure. when the Athenians themselves thought many philosophers unworthy to live.

Certain poets, as Simonides and Pindarus had so prevailed with Hiero the first, that of a tyrant they made him a just king, where Plato could do so little with Dionysius, that he himself, of a philosopher, was made a slave. But who should do thus, I confess, should requite the objections made against poets, with like cavillation against philosophers; as likewise one should do, that should bid one read Phaedrus or Symposium in Plato, or the discourse of love in Plutarch, and see whether any poet do authorize abominable filthiness, as they do. Again, a man might ask out of what commonwealth Plato did banish them? in sooth, thence where he himself alloweth community of women: so as, belike, this banishment grew not for effeminate wantonness, sith little should poetical sonnets be hurtful, when a man might have what woman he listed. But I honour philosophical instructions, and bless the wits which bred them: so as they be not abused; which is likewise stretched to poetry.

St. Paul himself, who yet (for the credit of poets) allegeth twice two poets, and one of them by the name of a prophet, setteth a watch-word upon philosophy, indeed upon the abuse. So doth Plato, upon the abuse, not upon poetry. Plato found fault, that the poets of his time filled the world with wrong opinions of the gods, making light tales of that unspotted essence; and therefore, would not have the youth depraved with such opinions. Herein may much be said, let this suffice: the poets did not induce such opinions, but did imitate those opinions already induced. For all the Greek stories can well testify, that the very religion of that time stood upon many and many-fashioned gods, not taught so by the poets, but followed, according to their nature of imitation. Who list, may read in Plutarch, the discourses of Isis, and Osiris, of the cause why oracles ceased, of the divine providence: and see, whether the theology of that nation stood not upon such dreams, which the poets superstitiously observed, and truly, (sith they had not the light of Christ,) did much better in it than the philosophers, who, shaking off superstition, brought in atheism. Plato therefore, (whose authority I had much rather justly construe, than unjustly resist,) meant not in general of poets, in those words of which Julius Scaliger saith qua auctoritate barbari quidam atque hispidi abuti velint, ad poetas e republica exigendos : but only meant, to drive out those wrong opinions of the Deity (whereof now, without further law, Christianity hath taken away all the hurtful belief) perchance (as he thought) nourished by the then esteemed poets.

And a man need go no further than to Plato himself, to know his meaning: who in his dialogue called Ion, giveth high, and rightly divine commendation to poetry. So as Plato, banishing the abuse, not the thing, not banishing it but giving due honour unto it, shall be our patron, and not our adversary. For indeed I had much rather (sith truly I may do it) show their mistaking of Plato, (under whose lion's skin they would make an ass-like braying against poesy,) than go about to overthrow his authority, whom the wiser a man is, the more just cause he shall find to have in admiration: especially, sith he attributeth unto poesy more than myself do; namely to be a very inspiring of a divine force, far above man's wit; as in the aforenamed dialogue is apparent.

Of the other side, who would show the honours have been by the best sort of judgments granted them, a whole sea of examples would present themselves. Alexanders, Caesars, Scipios, all favourers of poets. Lalius, called the Roman Socrates, himself a poet: so as part of Heautontimorumenos in Terence was supposed to be made by him. And even the Greek Socrates, whom Apollo confirmed to be the only wise man, is said to have spent part of his old time in putting Asop's fables into verses. And therefore, full evil should it become his scholar Plato to put such words in his master's mouth against poets. But what need more? Aristotle writes the Art of Poesy: and why if it should not be written? Plutarch teacheth the use to be gathered of them, and how if they should not be read? And who reads Plutarch's either history or philosophy, shall find he trimmeth both their garments with guards of poesy.

But I list not to defend poesy, with the help of her underling, historiography. Let it suffice, that it is a fit soil for praise to dwell upon: and what dispraise may set upon it is either easily overcome, or transformed into just commendation. So that, sith the excellencies of it may be so easily and so justly confirmed, and the low-creeping objections, so soon trodden down; it not being an art of lies, but of true doctrine: not of effeminateness, but of notable stirring of courage: not of abusing man's wit, but of strengthening man's wit: not banished, but honoured by Plato: let us rather plant more laurels, for to engarland our poets' heads, (which honour of being laureat, as besides them, only triumphant captains wear, is a sufficient authority, to show the price they ought to be had in,) than suffer the ill-favouring breath of such wrong-speakers, once to blow upon the clear springs of poesy.

But sith I have run so long a career in this matter, methinks, before I give my pen a full stop, it shall be but a little more lost time, to inquire, why England, (the mother of excellent minds,) should be grown so hard a step-mother to poets, who certainly in wit ought to pass all other: sith all only proceedeth from their wit, being indeed makers of themselves, not takers of others. How can I but exclaim,

Musa mihi causas memora, quo numine laso, sweet poesy, that hath anciently had kings, emperors, senators, great captains, such as, besides a thousand others, David, Adrian, Sophocles, Germanicus, not only to favour poets, but to be poets; and of our nearer times, can present for her patrons, a Robert, king of Sicily, the great king Francis of France, King James of Scotland; such cardinals as Bembus, and Bibiena; such famous preachers and teachers, as Beza and Melancthon; so learned philosophers, as Fracastorius and Scaliger; so great orators, as Pontanus and Muretus; so piercing wits as George Buchanan; so grave counsellors, as besides many, but before all, that Hospital Michel de l'Hospital, Chancellor of France 1560-1568, and the noble champion of tolerance in the evil days of Charles IX.

He narrowly escaped with his life at the massacre of S. Bartholomew, and died a few months later of France: than whom (I think) that realme never brought forth a more accomplished judgment: more firmly builded upon virtue; I say these, with numbers of others, not only to read others' poesies, but to poetise for others' reading: that poesy thus embraced in all other places, should only find, in our time, a hard welcome in England, I think the very earth lamenteth it, and therefore decketh our soil with fewer laurels than it was accustomed; for heretofore, poets have in England also flourished; and which is to be noted, even in those times, when the trumpet of Mars did sound loudest. And now, that an over-faint quietness should seem to strew the house pave the way. for poets, they are almost in as good reputation as the mountebanks at Venice.

Truly even that, as of the one side it giveth great praise to poesy, which like Venus (but to better purpose) hath rather be troubled in the net with Mars, than enjoy the homely quiet of Vulcan: so serves it for a piece of a reason, why they are less grateful to idle England, which now can scarce endure the pain of a pen. Upon this necessarily followeth, that base men with servile wits undertake it: who think it enough, if they can be rewarded of the printer. And so as Epaminondas is said, with the honour of his virtue, to have made an office, by his exercising it, which before was contemptible, to become highly respected: so these, no more but setting their names to it, by their own disgracefulness, disgrace the most graceful poesy. For now, as if all the Muses were got with child, to bring forth bastard poets, without any commission, they do post over the banks of Helicon, till they make the readers more weary than post-horses: while in the mean time, they Queis meliore luto finxit procordia Titan, are better content, to suppress the outflowing of their wit, than by publishing them to be accounted knights of the same order. But I, that before ever I durst aspire unto the dignity am admitted into the company of the paper-blurrers, do find the very true cause of our wanting estimation, is want of desert: taking upon us to be poets, in despite of Pallas. Now, wherein we want desert were a thank-worthy labour to express: but if I knew, I should have mended myself. But I, as I never desired the title, so have neglected the means to come by it. Only overmastered by some thoughts, I yielded an inky tribute unto them.

Marry, they that delight in poesy itself should seek to know what they do, and how they do; and especially, look themselves in an unflattering glass of reason, if they be inclinable unto it. For poesy must not be drawn by the ears, it must be gently led, or rather, it must lead. Which was partly the cause, that made the ancient-learned affirm, it was a divine gift, and no human skill: sith all other knowledges lie ready for any that hath strength of wit: a poet no industry can make, if his own genius be not carried unto it: and therefore is it an old proverb, orator fit; poeta nascitur. Yet confess I always, that as the fertilest ground must be manured, so must the highest-flying wit have a Dadalus to guide him.

That Dadalus, they say, both in this and in other, hath three wings, to bear itself up into the air of due commendation: that is, art, imitation, and exercise. But these, neither artificial rules, nor imitative patterns, we much cumber ourselves withal.

Exercise indeed we do, but that, very fore-backwardly: for where we should exercise to know, we exercise as having known: and so is our brain delivered of much matter, which never was begotten by knowledge. For, there being two principal parts, matter to be expressed by words, and words to express the matter, in neither, we use art, or imitation, rightly. Our matter is quodlibet indeed, though wrongly performing Ovid's verse,Quicquid conabar dicere versus erat: never marshalling it into an assured rank, that almost the readers cannot tell where to find themselves.

Chaucer undoubtedly did excellently in his Troilus and Cresseid ; of whom, truly I know not whether to marvel more, either that he in that misty time, could see so clearly, or that we in this clear age walk so stumblingly after him. Yet had he great wants, fit to be forgiven, in so reverent antiquity. I account the Mirror of Magistrates A long series of Poems, published in the early part of Elizabeth's reign. The two first, and best, pieces in it--The Induction and Complaint of the Duke of Buckingham --were by Sackville, joint-author of the earliest English Tragedy, Gorboduc. meetly furnished of beautiful parts; and in the Earl of Surrey's Lyrics, many things tasting of a noble birth, and worthy of a noble mind.

The Shepherd's Calendar hath much poetry in his eclogues: indeed worthy the reading, if I be not deceived. That same framing of his style to an old rustic language I dare not allow, sith neither Theocritus in Greek, Virgil in Latin, nor Sannazar in Italian, did affect it. Besides these, do I not remember to have seen but few (to speak boldly) printed, that have poetical sinews in them: for proof whereof, let but most of the verses be put in prose, and then ask the meaning; and it will be found that one verse did but beget another, without ordering at the first, what should be at the last: which becomes a confused mass of words, with a tingling sound of rhyme, barely accompanied with reason.

Our tragedies and comedies, (not without cause cried out against,) observing rules neither of honest civility nor of skilful poetry, excepting Gorboduc, (again, I say, of those that I have seen,) which notwithstanding as it is full of stately speeches, and well-sounding phrases, climbing to the height of Seneca his style, and as full of notable morality, which it doth most delightfully teach, and so obtain the very end of poesy: yet in truth it is very defectious in the circumstances; which grieveth me, because it might not remain as an exact model of all tragedies. For it is faulty both in place and time, the two necessary companions of all corporal actions.

For where the stage should always represent but one place, and the uttermost time presupposed in it should be, both by Aristotle's precept and common reason, but one day: there is both many days, and many places, inartificially imagined. But if it be so in Gorboduc, how much more in all the rest? where you shall have Asia of the one side, and Africa of the other, and so many other under-kingdoms, that the player, when he cometh in, must ever begin with telling where he is: or else, the tale will not be conceived. Now ye shall have three ladies walk to gather flowers, and then we must believe the stage to be a garden. By and by, we hear news of shipwreck in the same place, and then we are to blame, if we accept it not for a rock. Upon the back of that, comes out a hideous monster, with fire and smoke, and then the miserable beholders are bound to take it for a cave.

While in the meantime, two armies fly in, represented with four swords and bucklers, and then what hard heart will not receive it for a pitched field? Now, of time they are much more liberal, for ordinary it is that two young princes fall in love. After many traverses, she is got with child, delivered of a fair boy, he is lost, groweth a man, falls in love, and is ready to get another child, and all this in two hours' space: which how absurd it is in sense, even sense may imagine, and art hath taught, and all ancient examples justified: and at this day the ordinary players in Italy will not err in.

Yet will some bring in an example of Eunuchus in Terence, that containeth matter of two days, yet far short of twenty years. True it is, and so was it to be played in two days, and so fitted to the time it set forth. And though Plautus hath in one place done amiss, let us hit with him, and not miss with him. But they will say, how then shall we set forth a story, which containeth both many places, and many times? And do they not know that a tragedy is tied to the laws of poesy, and not of history? not bound to follow the story, but having liberty, either to feign a quite new matter, or to frame the history to the most tragical convenience. Again, many things may be told, which cannot be showed, if they know the difference betwixt reporting and representing. As for example, I may speak (though I am here) of Peru, and in speech digress from that, to the description of Calicut: but in action, I cannot represent it without Pacolet's horse: and so was the manner the ancients took, by some nuncius to recount things done in former time, or other place. Lastly, if they will represent a history, they must not (as Horace saith) begin ab ovo : but they must come to the principal point of that one action, which they will represent. By example this will be best expressed.

I have a story of young Polydorus, delivered for safety's sake, with great riches, by his father Priamus to Polymnestor, king of Thrace, in the Trojan war time: he after some years, hearing the overthrow of Priamus, for to make the treasure his own, murdereth the child: the body is taken up by Hecuba: she the same day findeth a slight to be revenged most cruelly of the tyrant: where now would one of our tragedy writers begin, but with the delivery of the child? Then should he sail over into Thrace, and so spend I know not how many years, and travel numbers of places. But where doth Euripides?

In his Hecuba. Even with the finding of the body, leaving the rest to be told by the spirit of Polydorus. This need no further to be enlarged, the dullest wit may conceive it. But besides these gross absurdities, how all their plays be neither right tragedies, nor right comedies: mingling kings and clowns, not because the matter so carrieth it, but thrust in clowns by head and shoulders, to play a part in majestical matters, with neither decency nor discretion. So as neither the admiration and commiseration, nor the right sportfulness, is by their mongrel tragi-comedy obtained. I know Apuleius In his Latin Romance, the Metamorphoses, or the Golden Ass. did somewhat so, but that is a thing recounted with space of time, not represented in one moment: and I know, the ancients have one or two examples of tragi-comedies, as Plautus hath Amphitryo : but if we mark them well, we shall find, that they never, or very daintily, match hornpipes and funerals.

So falleth it out, that having indeed no right comedy, in that comical part of our tragedy, we have nothing but scurrility, unworthy of any chaste ears: or some extreme show of doltishness, indeed fit to lift up a loud laughter, and nothing else: where the whole tract of a comedy should be full of delight, as the tragedy should be still maintained in a well-raised admiration. But our comedians think there is no delight without laughter, which is very wrong; for though laughter may come with delight, yet cometh it not of delight, as though delight should be the cause of laughter; but well may one thing breed both together: nay, rather in themselves, they have as it were a kind of contrariety: for delight we scarcely do, but in things that have a convenience to ourselves, or to the general nature: laughter almost ever cometh of things most disproportioned to ourselves and nature. Delight hath a joy in it, either permanent, or present. Laughter hath only a scornful tickling.

For example, we are ravished with delight to see a fair woman, and yet are far from being moved to laughter. We laugh at deformed creatures, wherein certainly we cannot delight. We delight in good chances, we laugh at mischances; we delight to hear the happiness of our friends, or country; at which he were worthy to be laughed at, that would laugh; we shall contrarily laugh sometimes, to find a matter quite mistaken, and go down the hill against the bias, in the mouth of some such men, as for the respect of them one shall be heartily sorry, yet he cannot choose but laugh; and so is rather pained, than delighted, with laughter.

Yet deny I not, but that they may go well together; for as in Alexander's picture well set out we delight without laughter, and in twenty mad antics we laugh without delight: so in Hercules, painted with his great beard, and furious countenance, in woman's attire, spinning at Omphale's commandment, it breedeth both delight and laughter. For the representing of so strange a power in love, procureth delight: and the scornfulness of the action stirreth laughter. But I speak to this purpose, that all the end of the comical part be not upon such scornful matters as stir laughter only: but mixed with it, that delightful teaching which is the end of poesy. And the great fault even in that point of laughter, and forbidden plainly by Aristotle, is that they stir laughter in sinful things; which are rather execrable than ridiculous: or in miserable, which are rather to be pitied than scorned. For what is it to make folks gape at a wretched beggar, or a beggarly clown? or, against law of hospitality, to jest at strangers, because they speak not English so well as we do? what do we learn, sith it is certain

Nil habet infēlix paupertas durius in se, Quam quod ridiculos homines facit: but rather a busy-loving courtier; a heartless threatening Thraso; a self-wise-seeming schoolmaster; an awry-transformed traveller? These if we saw walk in stage names, which we play naturally, therein were delightful laughter, and teaching delightfulness: as in the other, the tragedies of Buchanan do justly bring forth a divine admiration. But I have lavished out too many words of this play-matter. I do it because, as they are excelling parts of poesy, so is there none so much used in England, and none can be more pitifully abused. Which like an unmannerly daughter, showing a bad education, causeth her mother poesy's honesty to be called in question.

Other sorts of poetry almost have we none, but that lyrical kind of songs and sonnets: which Lord, if he gave us so good minds, how well it might be employed, and with how heavenly fruit, both private and public, in singing the praises of the immortal beauty, the immortal goodness of that God, who giveth us hands to write, and wits to conceive, of which we might well want words, but never matter, of which we could turn our eyes to nothing, but we should ever have new budding occasions.

But truly many of such writings, as come under the banner of un-resistible love, if I were a mistress, would never persuade me they were in love: so coldly they apply fiery speeches, as men that had rather read lovers' writings, and so caught up certain swelling phrases, which hang together, like a man which once told me, the wind was at north, west, and by south, because he would be sure to name winds enough, than that in truth they feel those passions, which easily (as I think) may be betrayed by that same forcibleness, or energeia (as the Greeks call it) of the writer. But let this be a sufficient, though short note, that we miss the right use of the material point of poesy.

Now, for the outside of it, which is words, or (as I may term it) diction, it is even well worse. So is that honey-flowing matron eloquence apparelled, or rather disguised, in a courtezan-like painted affectation: one time with so far-fetched words, they may seem monsters, but must seem strangers to any poor Englishman; another time, with coursing of a letter, as if they were bound to follow the method of a dictionary: another time, with figures and flowers, extremely winter-starved. But I would this fault were only peculiar to versifiers, and had not as large possession among prose-printers; and (which is to be marvelled) among many scholars; and (which is to be pitied) among some preachers. Truly I could wish, if at least I might be so bold to wish in a thing beyond the reach of my capacity, the diligent imitators of Tully and Demosthenes (most worthy to be imitated) did not so much keep Nizolian Nizolius, the compiler of a lexicon to the works of Cicero. paper-books of their figures and phrases, as by attentive translation (as it were) devour them whole, and make them wholly theirs: for now they cast sugar and spice upon every dish that is served to the table; like those Indians, not content to wear earrings at the fit and natural place of the ears, but they will thrust jewels through their nose and lips because they will be sure to be fine.

Tully, when he was to drive out Catiline, as it were with a thunderbolt of eloquence, often used that figure of repetition, Vivit? Vivit; immo in Senatum venit, &c. Indeed, inflamed with a well-grounded rage, he would have his words (as it were) double out of his mouth: and so do that artificially, which we see men do in choler naturally. And we, having noted the grace of those words, hale them in sometime to a familiar epistle, when it were to too much choler to be choleric. Now for similitudes, in certain printed discourses, I think all herbarists, all stories of beasts, fowls, and fishes, are rifled up, that they come in multitudes, to wait upon any of our conceits: An allusion to the style of Lyly and the Euphuists. which certainly is as absurd a surfeit to the ears as is possible: for the force of a similitude, not being to prove anything to a contrary disputer, but only to explain to a willing hearer, when that is done, the rest is a most tedious prattling: rather over-swaying the memory from the purpose whereto they were applied, than any whit informing the judgment, already either satisfied, or by similitudes not to be satisfied.

For my part, I do not doubt, when Antonius and Crassus, the great forefathers of Cicero in eloquence, the one (as Cicero testifieth of them) pretended not to know art, the other, not to set by it: because with a plain sensibleness they might win credit of popular ears; which credit is the nearest step to persuasion: which persuasion is the chief mark of oratory; I do not doubt (I say) but that they used these tracks very sparingly, which who doth generally use, any man may see doth dance to his own music: and so be noted by the audience more careful to speak curiously, than to speak truly.

Undoubtedly (at least to my opinion undoubtedly), I have found in divers smally learned courtiers a more sound style, than in some professors of learning: of which I can guess no other cause, but that the courtier, following that which by practice he findeth fittest to nature, therein (though he know it not) doth according to art, though not by art: where the other, using art to show art, and not to hide art (as in these cases he should do), flyeth from nature, and indeed abuseth art. But what? methinks I deserve to be pounded, for straying from poetry to oratory: but both have such an affinity in this wordish consideration, that I think this digression will make my meaning receive the fuller understanding: which is not to take upon me to teach poets how they should do, but only finding myself sick among the rest, to show some one or two spots of the common infection, grown among the most part of writers: that, acknowledging ourselves somewhat awry, we may bend to the right use both of matter and manner; whereto our language giveth us great occasion, being indeed capable of any excellent exercising of it.

I know, some will say it is a mingled language. And why not so much the better, taking the best of both the other? Both the Teutonic and the Romance elements. Another will say it wanteth grammar. Nay, truly, it hath that praise, that it wanteth not grammar; for grammar it might have, but it needs it not; being so easy of itself, and so void of those cumbersome differences of cases, genders, moods, and tenses, which I think was a piece of the Tower of Babylon's curse, that a man should be put to school to learn his mother-tongue. But for the uttering sweetly and properly the conceits of the mind, which is the end of speech, that hath it equally with any other tongue in the world: and is particularly happy, in compositions of two or three words together, near the Greek, far beyond the Latin: which is one of the greatest beauties can be in a language.

Now, of versifying there are two sorts, the one ancient, the other modern: the ancient marked the quantity of each syllable, and according to that framed his verse: the modern, observing only number (with some regard of the accent), the chief life of it standeth in that like sounding of the words, which we call rhyme. Whether of these be the most excellent, would bear many speeches. The ancient (no doubt) more fit for music, both words and tune observing quantity, and more fit lively to express divers passions, by the low and lofty sound of the well-weighed syllable.

The latter likewise, with his rhyme, striketh a certain music to the ear: and in fine, sith it doth delight, though by another way, it obtains the same purpose: there being in either sweetness, and wanting in neither majesty. Truly the English, before any other vulgar language I know, is fit for both sorts: for, for the ancient, the Italian is so full of vowels, that it must ever be cumbered with elisions. The Dutch, Sidney probably means what we should call German. so of the other side with consonants, that they cannot yield the sweet sliding fit for a verse. The French, in his whole language, hath not one word, that hath his accent in the last syllable saving two, called Antepenultima, and little more hath the Spanish: and therefore, very gracelessly may they use Dactyls. The English is subject to none of these defects.

Now, for the rhyme, though we do not observe quantity, yet we observe the accent very precisely: which other languages either cannot do, or will not do so absolutely. That Caesura, or breathing place in the midst of the verse, neither Italian nor Spanish have; the French, and we, never almost fail of. Lastly, even the very rhyme itself, the Italian cannot put in the last syllable, by the French named the masculine rhyme, but still in the next to the last, which the French call the female, or the next before that, which the Italians termed Sdrucciola. Hence the Italian verse is always of eleven, not ten, syllables. The example of the former, is Buono, Suono ; of the Sdrucciola, Femina, Semina. The French, on the other side, hath both the male, as Bon, Son, and the female, as Plaise, Taise.

But the Sdrucciola he hath not: where English hath all three, as Due, True, Father, Rather, Motion, Potion with much more which might be said, but that I find already, the triflingness of this discourse is much too much enlarged. So that sith the ever-praiseworthy poesy is full of virtue-breeding delightfulness, and void of no gift, that ought to be in the noble name of learning: sith the blames laid against it are either false, or feeble: sith the cause why it is not esteemed in England, is the fault of poet-apes, not poets: sith lastly, our tongue is most fit to honour poesy, and to be honoured by poesy, I conjure you all, that have had the evil luck to read this ink-wasting toy of mine, even in the name of the nine Muses, no more to scorn the sacred mysteries of poesy: no more to laugh at the name of poets, as though they were next inheritors to fools: no more to jest at the reverend title of a rhymer: but to believe with Aristotle, that they were the ancient treasurers of the Grecians' Divinity.

To believe with Bembus, that they were first bringers in of all civility. To believe with Scaliger, that no philosopher's precepts can sooner make you an honest man, than the reading of Virgil. To believe with Clauserus, the translator of Cornutus, that it pleased the heavenly Deity, by Hesiod and Homer, under the veil of fables, to give us all knowledge, logic, rhetoric, philosophy, natural and moral, and Quid non? To believe with me, that there are many mysteries contained in poetry, which of purpose were written darkly, lest by profane wits it should be abused. To believe with Landin, that they are so beloved of the Gods, that whatsoever they write proceeds of a divine fury. Lastly, to believe themselves, when they tell you they will make you immortal, by their verses.

Thus doing, your name shall flourish in the printers' shops; thus doing, you shall be of kin to many a poetical preface; thus doing, you shall be most fair, most rich, most wise, most all, you shall dwell upon superlatives. Thus doing, though you be libertino patre natus, you shall suddenly grow Herculis proles : Si quid mea carmina possunt.

Thus doing, your soul shall be placed with Dante's Beatrix, or Virgil's Anchises. But if (fie of such a but) you be born so near the dull making Cataphract of Nilus, that you cannot hear the planet-like music of poetry, if you have so earth-creeping a mind, that it cannot lift itself up, to look to the sky of poetry: or rather, by a certain rustical disdain, will become such a mome scorner., as to be a momus of poetry: then, though I will not wish unto you the ass's ears of Midas, nor to be driven by a poet's verses (as Bubonax was) to hang himself, nor to be rhymed to death, as is said to be done in Ireland: yet thus much curse I must send you, in the behalf of all poets, that, while you live, you live in love, and never get favour, for lacking skill of a sonnet: and when you die, your memory die from the earth, for want of an epitaph.

3

PREFACE TO THE FABLES

JOHN DRYDEN

The following Preface belongs to the last few months of Dryden's life (1700), and introduces the collection, mainly of translations and adaptations, to which he gave the title of Fables Apart from Alexander's Feast (written in 1697), the most notable pieces in this collection were the versions of Chaucer's Knightes Tale and Nonne Prestes Tale, and of three stories to be found in Boccaccio Sigismunda and Guiscardo, Cymon and Iphigenia, Theodore and Honoria. The Preface is memorable for its critical judgments on Homer, Virgil, and Ovid, still more memorable for its glowing praise of Chaucer. It closes as it was fitting that the last work of Dryden should close, with an apology, full of manliness and dignity, for the licentiousness of his comedies. For his shortcomings in this matter he had lately been attacked by Collier, and in his reply he more than wins back any esteem that he may have lost by his transgression.

It is with a poet, as with a man who designs to build, and is very exact, as he supposes, in casting up the cost beforehand; but, generally speaking, he is mistaken in his account, and reckons short in the expense he first intended. He alters his mind as the work proceeds, and will have this or that convenience more, of which he had not thought when he began. So has it happened to me. I have built a house, where I intended but a lodge; yet with better success than a certain nobleman, who, beginning with a dog-kennel, never lived to finish the palace he had contrived.

From translating the first of Homer's Iliads (which I intended as an essay to the whole work) I proceeded to the translation of the twelfth book of Ovid's Metamorphoses, because it contains, among other things, the causes, the beginning, and ending, of the Trojan war. Here I ought in reason to have stopped; but the speeches of Ajax and Ulysses lying next in my way, I could not baulk them. When I had compassed them, I was so taken with the former part of the fifteenth book (which is the masterpiece of the whole Metamorphoses), that I enjoined myself the pleasing task of rendering it into English. And now I found, by the number of my verses, that they began to swell into a little volume; which gave me an occasion of looking backward on some beauties of my author, in his former books: there occurred to me the Hunting of the Boar, Cinyras and Myrrha, the good-natured story of Baucis and Philemon, with the rest, which I hope I have translated closely enough, and given them the same turn of verse which they had in the original; and this, I may say without vanity, is not the talent of every poet.

He who has arrived the nearest to it, is the ingenious and learned Sandys, the best versifier of the former age, if I may properly call it by that name, which was the former part of this concluding century. For Spenser and Fairfax both flourished in the reign of Queen Elizabeth; great masters in our language, and who saw much farther into the beauties of our numbers than those who immediately followed them. Milton was the poetical son of Spenser, and Mr. Waller of Fairfax, for we have our lineal descents and clans as well as other families.

Spenser more than once insinuates that the soul of Chaucer was transfused into his body, and that he was begotten by him two hundred years after his decease. Milton has acknowledged to me that Spenser was his original, and many besides myself have heard our famous Waller "He first made writing easily an art"--was Dryden's verdict on Waller.--English Garner, iii. 492. own that he derived the harmony of his numbers from the Godfrey of Bulloigne, which was turned into English by Mr. Fairfax.

But to return. Having done with Ovid for this time, it came into my mind that our old English poet, Chaucer, in many things resembled him, and that with no disadvantage on the side of the modern author, as I shall endeavour to prove when I compare them; and as I am, and always have been, studious to promote the honour of my native country, so I soon resolved to put their merits to the trial, by turning some of the Canterbury Tales into our language, as it is now refined; for by this means, both the poets being set in the same light, and dressed in the same English habit, story to be compared with story, a certain judgment may be made betwixt them by the reader, without obtruding my opinion on him. Or if I seem partial to my countryman, and predecessor in the laurel, the friends of antiquity are not few; and besides many of the learned, Ovid has almost all the beaux, and the whole fair sex, his declared patrons. Perhaps I have assumed somewhat more to myself than they allow me, because I have adventured to sum up the evidence; but the readers are the jury, and their privilege remains entire, to decide according to the merits of the cause, or, if they please, to bring it to another hearing before some other court.

In the meantime, to follow the thread of my discourse (as thoughts, according to Mr. Hobbes, have always some connection), so from Chaucer I was led to think on Boccace, who was not only his contemporary, but also pursued the same studies; wrote novels in prose, and many works in verse; particularly is said to have invented the octave rhyme, or stanza of eight lines, which ever since has been maintained by the practice of all Italian writers, who are, or at least assume the title of Heroic Poets; he and Chaucer, among other things, had this in common, that they refined their mother tongue; but with this difference, that Dante had began to file their language, at least in verse, before the time of Boccace, who likewise received no little help from his master Petrarch.

But the reformation of their prose was wholly owing to Boccace himself, who is yet the standard of purity in the Italian tongue, though many of his phrases are become obsolete, as in process of time it must needs happen. Chaucer (as you have formerly been told by our learned Mr. Rymer) first adorned and amplified our barren tongue from the Provencal, No one now believes this. An excellent discussion of the subject will be found in Professor Lounsbury's Studies in Chaucer, ii. 429-458. which was then the most polished of all the modern languages; but this subject has been copiously treated by that great critic, who deserves no little commendation from us, his countrymen.

For these reasons of time, and resemblance of genius in Chaucer and Boccace, I resolved to join them in my present work, to which I have added some original papers of my own, which, whether they are equal or inferior to my other poems, an author is the most improper judge, and therefore I leave them wholly to the mercy of the reader. I will hope the best, that they will not be condemned; but if they should, I have the excuse of an old gentleman, who, mounting on horseback before some ladies, when I was present, got up somewhat heavily, but desired of the fair spectators that they would count four-score-and-eight before they judged him. By the mercy of God, I am already come within twenty years of his number, a cripple in my limbs; but what decays are in my mind, the reader must determine.

I think myself as vigorous as ever in the faculties of my soul, excepting only my memory, which is not impaired to any great degree; and if I lose not more of it, I have no great reason to complain. What judgment I had, increases rather than diminishes; and thoughts, such as they are, come crowding in so fast upon me, that my only difficulty is to choose or to reject; to run them into verse, or to give them the other harmony of prose. I have so long studied and practised both, that they are grown into a habit, and become familiar to me. In short, though I may lawfully plead some part of the old gentleman's excuse, yet I will reserve it till I think I have greater need, and ask no grains of allowance for the faults of this my present work, but those which are given of course to human frailty.

I will not trouble my reader with the shortness of time in which I writ it, or the several intervals of sickness: they who think too well of their own performances, are apt to boast in their prefaces how little time their works have cost them, and what other business of more importance interfered; but the reader will be as apt to ask the question, why they allowed not a longer time to make their works more perfect, and why they had so despicable an opinion of their judges, as to thrust their indigested stuff upon them, as if they deserved no better.

With this account of my present undertaking, I conclude the first part of this discourse: in the second part, as at a second sitting, though I alter not the draught, I must touch the same features over again, and change the dead colouring of the whole. In general, I will only say, that I have written nothing which savours of immorality or profaneness; at least, I am not conscious to myself of any such intention. If there happen to be found an irreverent expression, or a thought too wanton, they are crept into my verses through my inadvertency; if the searchers find any in the cargo, let them be staved or forfeited, like contrabanded goods; at least, let their authors be answerable for them, as being but imported merchandise, and not of my own manufacture. On the other side, I have endeavoured to choose such fables, both ancient and modern, as contain in each of them some instructive moral, which I could prove by induction, but the way is tedious; and they leap foremost into sight, without the reader's trouble of looking after them. I wish I could affirm, with a safe conscience, that I had taken the same care in all my former writings; for it must be owned, that supposing verses are never so beautiful or pleasing, yet if they contain anything which shocks religion, or good manners, they are at best what Horace says of good numbers without good sense:

Versus inopes rerum, nugaeque canorae.

Thus far, I hope, I am right in court, without renouncing my other right of self-defence, where I have been wrongfully accused, and my sense wire-drawn into blasphemy or bawdry, as it has often been by a religious lawyer, Jeremy Collier. See conclusion of the Preface. in a late pleading against the stage; in which he mixes truth with falsehood, and has not forgotten the old rule of calumniating strongly, that something may remain.

I resume the thread of my discourse with the first of my translation, which was the first Iliad of Homer. If it shall please God to give me longer life, and moderate health, my intentions are to translate the whole Ilias ; provided still that I meet with those encouragements from the public, which may enable me to proceed in my undertaking with some cheerfulness. And this I dare assure the world beforehand, that I have found, by trial, Homer a more pleasing task than Virgil (though I say not the translation will be less laborious). For the Grecian is more according to my genius than the Latin poet. In the works of the two authors we may read their manners and inclinations, which are wholly different. Virgil was of a quiet, sedate temper; Homer was violent, impetuous, and full of fire. The chief talent of Virgil was propriety of thoughts, and ornament of words; Homer was rapid in his thoughts, and took all the liberties, both of numbers and of expressions, which his language, and the age in which he lived, allowed him: Homer's invention was more copious, Virgil's more confined; so that if Homer had not led the way, it was not in Virgil to have begun heroic poetry; for nothing can be more evident, than that the Roman poem is but the second part of the Ilias ; a continuation of the same story, and the persons already formed; the manners of Aeneas are those of Hector superadded to those which Homer gave him.

The Adventures of Ulysses in the Odysseis are imitated in the first six books of Virgil's Aeneis ; and though the accidents are not the same (which would have argued him of a servile copying, and total barrenness of invention), yet the seas were the same in which both the heroes wandered; and Dido cannot be denied to be the poetical daughter of Calypso. The six latter books of Virgil's poem are the four and twenty Iliads contracted; a quarrel occasioned by a lady, a single combat, battles fought, and a town besieged. I say not this in derogation to Virgil, neither do I contradict anything which I have formerly said in his just praise: for his Episodes are almost wholly of his own invention; and the form which he has given to the telling, makes the tale his own, even though the original story had been the same. But this proves, however, that Homer taught Virgil to design; and if invention be the first virtue of an Epic poet, then the Latin poem can only be allowed the second place.

Mr. Hobbes, in the preface to his own bald translation of the Ilias (studying poetry as he did mathematics, when it was too late), Mr. Hobbes, I say, begins the praise of Homer where he should have ended it. He tells us that the first beauty of an Epic poem consists in diction, that is, in the choice of words, and harmony of numbers; now the words are the colouring of the work, which in the order of nature is the last to be considered. The design, the disposition, the manners, and the thoughts are all before it; where any of those are wanting or imperfect, so much wants or is imperfect in the imitation of human life; which is in the very definition of a poem. Words, indeed, like glaring colours, are the first beauties that arise, and strike the sight: but if the draught be false or lame, the figures ill-disposed, the manners obscure or inconsistent, or the thoughts unnatural, then the finest colours are but daubing, and the piece is a beautiful monster at the best. Neither Virgil nor Homer were deficient in any of the former beauties; but in this last, which is expression, the Roman poet is at least equal to the Grecian, as I have said elsewhere; supplying the poverty of his language by his musical ear, and by his diligence.

But to return: our two great poets, being so different in their tempers, one choleric and sanguine, the other phlegmatic and melancholic; that which makes them excel in their several ways is, that each of them has followed his own natural inclination, as well in forming the design, as in the execution of it. The very heroes show their authors; Achilles is hot, impatient, revengeful, Impiger, iracundus, inexorabilis, acer, &c. Aeneas patient, considerate, careful of his people, and merciful to his enemies; ever submissive to the will of heaven, quo fata trahunt, retrahuntque, sequamur. I could please myself with enlarging on this subject, but am forced to defer it to a fitter time. From all I have said I will only draw this inference, that the action of Homer being more full of vigour than that of Virgil, according to the temper of the writer, is of consequence more pleasing to the reader. One warms you by degrees; the other sets you on fire all at once, and never intermits his heat.

'T is the same difference which Longinus makes betwixt the effects of eloquence in Demosthenes and Tully. One persuades, the other commands. You never cool while you read Homer, even not in the second book (a graceful flattery to his countrymen); but he hastens from the ships, and concludes not that book till he has made you an amends by the violent playing of a new machine. From thence he hurries on his action with variety of events, and ends it in less compass than two months. This vehemence of his, I confess, is more suitable to my temper; and therefore I have translated his first book with greater pleasure than any part of Virgil; but it was not a pleasure without pains: the continual agitations of the spirits must needs be a weakening of any constitution, especially in age; and many pauses are required for refreshment betwixt the heats; the Iliad of itself being a third part longer than all Virgil's works together.

This is what I thought needful in this place to say of Homer. I proceed to Ovid and Chaucer, considering the former only in relation to the latter. With Ovid ended the golden age of the Roman tongue; from Chaucer the purity of the English tongue began. The manners of the poets were not unlike: both of them were well-bred, well-natured, amorous, and libertine, at least in their writings, it may be also in their lives. Their studies were the same, philosophy and philology. Both of them were known in astronomy, of which Ovid's books of the Roman feasts, and Chaucer's treatise of the Astrolabe, are sufficient witnesses.

But Chaucer was likewise an astrologer, as were Virgil, Horace, Persius, and Manilius. Both writ with wonderful facility and clearness: neither were great inventors; for Ovid only copied the Grecian fables; and most of Chaucer's stories were taken from his Italian contemporaries, or their predecessors. Boccace's Decameron was first published, and from thence our Englishman has borrowed many of his Canterbury tales; It is doubtful whether Chaucer had any knowledge of the Decameron. yet that of Palamon and Arcite was written in all probability by some Italian wit in a former age, as I shall prove hereafter. The tale of Grizild was the invention of Petrarch; by him sent to Boccace, from whom it came to Chaucer. Troilus and Cressida was also written by a Lombard author Boccaccio himself., but much amplified by our English translator, as well as beautified; the genius of our countrymen in general being rather to improve an invention than to invent themselves, as is evident not only in our poetry, but in many of our manufactures.

I find I have anticipated already, and taken up from Boccace before I come to him; but there is so much less behind; and I am of the temper of most kings, who love to be in debt, are all for present money, no matter how they pay it afterwards; besides, the nature of a preface is rambling, never wholly out of the way, nor in it. This I have learned from the practice of honest Montaigne, and return at my pleasure to Ovid and Chaucer, of whom I have little more to say. Both of them built on the inventions of other men; yet since Chaucer had something of his own, as the Wife of Bath's Tale, The Cock and the Fox, which I have translated, and some others, I may justly give our countryman the precedence in that part, since I can remember nothing of Ovid which was wholly his. Both of them understood the manners, under which name I comprehend the passions, and, in a larger sense, the descriptions of persons, and their very habits; for an example, I see Baucis and Philemon as perfectly before me, as if some ancient painter had drawn them; and all the pilgrims in the Canterbury Tales, their humours, their features, and the very dress, as distinctly as if I had supped with them at the Tabard in Southwark; yet even there too the figures in Chaucer are much more lively, and set in a better light: which though I have not time to prove, yet I appeal to the reader, and am sure he will clear me from partiality. The thoughts and words remain to be considered in the comparison of the two poets; and I have saved myself one half of that labour, by owning that Ovid lived when the Roman tongue was in its meridian, Chaucer in the dawning of our language; therefore that part of the comparison stands not on an equal foot, any more than the diction of Ennius and Ovid, or of Chaucer and our present English.

The words are given up as a post not to be defended in our poet, because he wanted the modern art of fortifying. The thoughts remain to be considered, and they are to be measured only by their propriety, that is, as they flow more or less naturally from the persons described, on such and such occasions. The vulgar judges, which are nine parts in ten of all nations, who call conceits and jingles wit, who see Ovid full of them, and Chaucer altogether without them, will think me little less than mad, for preferring the Englishman to the Roman; yet, with their leave, I must presume to say, that the things they admire are only glittering trifles, and so far from being witty, that in a serious poem they are nauseous, because they are unnatural.

Would any man, who is ready to die for love, describe his passion like Narcissus? Would he think of inopem me copia fecit, and a dozen more of such expressions, poured on the neck of one another, and signifying all the same thing? If this were wit, was this a time to be witty, when the poor wretch was in the agony of death? This is just John Littlewit in Bartholomew Fair, Jonson's play of that name, act i. sc. i. who had a conceit (as he tells you) left him in his misery; a miserable conceit. On these occasions the poet should endeavour to raise pity; but instead of this, Ovid is tickling you to laugh. Virgil never made use of such machines, when he was moving you to commiserate the death of Dido: he would not destroy what he was building. Chaucer makes Arcite violent in his love, and unjust in the pursuit of it; yet when he came to die, he made him think more reasonably: he repents not of his love, for that had altered his character, but acknowledges the injustice of his proceedings, and resigns Emilia to Palamon. What would Ovid have done on this occasion? He would certainly have made Arcite witty on his death-bed. He had complained he was farther off from possession by being so near, and a thousand such boyisms, which Chaucer rejected as below the dignity of the subject.

They, who think otherwise, would by the same reason prefer Lucan and Ovid to Homer and Virgil, and Martial to all four of them. As for the turn of words, in which Ovid particularly excels all poets, they are sometimes a fault, and sometimes a beauty, as they are used properly or improperly; but in strong passions always to be shunned, because passions are serious, and will admit no playing. The French have a high value for them; and I confess, they are often what they call delicate, when they are introduced with judgment; but Chaucer writ with more simplicity, and followed nature more closely, than to use them. I have thus far, to the best of my knowledge, been an upright judge betwixt the parties in competition, not meddling with the design nor the disposition of it, because the design was not their own, and in the disposing of it they were equal. It remains that I say somewhat of Chaucer in particular.

In the first place, as he is the father of English poetry, so I hold him in the same degree of veneration as the Grecians held Homer or the Romans Virgil: he is a perpetual fountain of good sense, learned in all sciences, and therefore speaks properly on all subjects; as he knew what to say, so he knows also when to leave off, a continence which is practised by few writers, and scarcely by any of the ancients, excepting Virgil and Horace. One of our late great poets is sunk in his reputation, because he could never forgive any conceit which came in his way, but swept like a drag net great and small.

There was plenty enough, but the dishes were ill-sorted; whole pyramids of sweetmeats for boys and women, but little of solid meat for men: all this proceeded not from any want of knowledge, but of judgment; neither did he want that in discerning the beauties and faults of other poets, but only indulged himself in the luxury of writing, and perhaps knew it was a fault, but hoped the reader would not find it. For this reason, though he must always be thought a great poet, he is no longer esteemed a good writer; and for ten impressions, which his works have had in so many successive years, yet at present a hundred books are scarcely purchased once a twelvemonth; for as my last Lord Rochester said, though somewhat profanely, "Not being of God, he could not stand".

Chaucer followed nature everywhere, but was never so bold to go beyond her; and there is a great difference of being poeta and nimis poeta if we believe Catullus, as much as betwixt a modest behaviour and affectation. The verse of Chaucer, I confess, is not harmonious to us, but it is like the eloquence of one whom Tacitus commends, it was auribus istius temporis accommodata : they who lived with him, and some time after him, thought it musical; and it continues so even in our judgment, if compared with the numbers of Lydgate and Gower, his contemporaries; there is the rude sweetness of a Scotch tune in it, which is natural and pleasing, though not perfect.

It is true I cannot go so far as he who published the last edition of him; That of 1687, which was little more than a reprint of Speght's editions (1598, 1602). for he would make us believe the fault is in our ears, and that there were really ten syllables in a verse where we find but nine, but this opinion is not worth confuting, it is so gross and obvious an error that common sense (which is a rule in everything but matters of faith and revelation) must convince the reader that equality of numbers in every verse, which we call Heroic, was either not known, or not always practised in Chaucer's age. It were an easy matter to produce some thousands of his verses, which are lame for want of half a foot, and sometimes a whole one, and which no pronunciation can make otherwise. We can only say that he lived in the infancy of our poetry, and that nothing is brought to perfection at the first. We must be children before we grow men.

There was an Ennius, and in process of time a Lucilius and a Lucretius, before Virgil and Horace; even after Chaucer there was a Spenser, a Harrington, a Fairfax, before Waller and Denham were in being; and our numbers were in their nonage till these last appeared. I need say little of his parentage, life, and fortunes: they are to be found at large in all the editions of his works. He was employed abroad, and favoured by Edward the Third, Richard the Second, and Henry the Fourth, and was poet, as I suppose, to all three of them.

In Richard's time, I doubt, he was a little dipt in the rebellion of the commons, There is no evidence for this 'doubt', though in his Balade, Lak of Stedfastnesse, Chaucer speaks plainly both to Richard and his subjects. and being brother-in-law to John of Gaunt, it was no wonder if he followed the fortunes of that family, and was well with Henry the Fourth when he had deposed his predecessor. Neither is it to be admired that Henry, who was a wise as well as a valiant prince, who claimed by succession, and was sensible that his title was not sound, but was rightfully in Mortimer, who had married the heir of York; it was not to be admired, I say, if that great politician should be pleased to have the greatest wit of those times in his interests, and to be the trumpet of his praises.

Augustus had given him the example, by the advice of Maecenas, who recommended Virgil and Horace to him, whose praises helped to make him popular while he was alive, and after his death have made him precious to posterity. As for the religion of our poet, he seems to have some little bias towards the opinions of Wickliff, after John of Gaunt his patron; somewhat of which appears in the tale of Piers Plowman: The Plowman's Tale, which was printed as one of the Canterbury Tales in Speght's editions. It is now rejected by all authorities yet I cannot blame him for inveighing so sharply against the vices of the clergy in his age; their pride, their ambition, their pomp, their avarice, their worldly interest deserved the lashes which he gave them, both in that and in most of his Canterbury tales: neither has his contemporary Boccace spared them.

Yet both these poets lived in much esteem with good and holy men in orders; for the scandal which is given by particular priests, reflects not on the sacred function. Chaucer's Monk, his Canon, and his Friar took not from the character of his Good Parson. A satirical poet is the check of the laymen on bad priests. We are only to take care that we involve not the innocent with the guilty in the same condemnation.

The good cannot be too much honoured, nor the bad too coarsely used; for the corruption of the best becomes the worst. When a clergyman is whipped his gown is first taken off, by which the dignity of his order is secured; if he be wrongfully accused, he has his action of slander; and it is at the poet's peril if he transgress the law But they will tell us that all kinds of satire, though never so well-deserved by particular priests, yet brings the whole order into contempt. Is, then, the peerage of England anything dishonoured when a peer suffers for his treason? If he be libelled, or any way defamed, he has his Scandalum Magnatum to punish the offender.

They who use this kind of argument seem to be conscious to themselves of somewhat which has deserved the poet's lash, and are less concerned for their public capacity than for their private; at least there is pride at the bottom of their reasoning. If the faults of men in orders are only to be judged among themselves, they are all in some sort parties; for, since they say the honour of their order is concerned in every member of it, how can we be sure that they will be impartial judges? How far I may be allowed As a Catholic. to speak my opinion in this case I know not, but I am sure a dispute of this nature caused mischief in abundance betwixt a King of England and an Archbishop of Canterbury, one standing up for the laws of his land, and the other for the honour (as he called it) of God's Church, which ended in the murder of the prelate, and in the whipping of his majesty from post to pillar for his penance.

The learned and ingenious Dr. Drake has saved me the labour of inquiring into the esteem and reverence which the priests have had of old; and I would rather extend than diminish any part of it: yet I must needs say, that when a priest provokes me without any occasion given him, I have no reason, unless it be the charity of a Christian, to forgive him. Prior laesit is justification sufficient in the Civil Law. If I answer him in his own language, self-defence, I am sure, must be allowed me; and if I carry it farther, even to a sharp recrimination, somewhat may be indulged to human frailty. Yet my resentment has not wrought so far, but that I have followed Chaucer in his character of a holy man, and have enlarged on that subject with some pleasure, reserving to myself the right, if I shall think fit hereafter, to describe another sort of priests, such as are more easily to be found than the good parson; such as have given the last blow to Christianity in this age, by a practice so contrary to their doctrine. But this will keep cold till another time. In the meanwhile, I take up Chaucer where I left him.

He must have been a man of a most wonderful comprehensive nature, because, as it has been truly observed of him, he has taken into the compass of his Canterbury tales the various manners and humours (as we now call them) of the whole English nation, in his age. Not a single character has escaped him. All his pilgrims are severally distinguished from each other; and not only in their inclinations, but in their very physiognomies and persons. Baptista Porta could not have described their natures better than by the marks which the poet gives them. The matter and manner of their tales, and of their telling, are so suited to their different educations, humours, and callings that each of them would be improper in any other mouth.

Even the grave and serious characters are distinguished by their several sorts of gravity: their discourses are such as belong to their age, their calling, and their breeding; such as are becoming of them, and of them only. Some of his persons are vicious, and some virtuous; some are unlearned, or (as Chaucer calls them) lewd, and some are learned. Even the ribaldry of the low characters is different: the Reeve, the Miller, and the Cook are several men, and distinguished from each other, as much as the mincing lady prioress, and the broad-speaking gap-toothed wife of Bath. But enough of this: there is such a variety of game springing up before me, that I am distracted in my choice, and know not which to follow. 'Tis sufficient to say, according to the proverb, that here is God's plenty. We have our forefathers and great-grand-dames all before us, as they were in Chaucer's days; their general characters are still remaining in mankind, and even in England, though they are called by other names than those of Monks and Friars and Canons, and Lady Abbesses and Nuns; for mankind is ever the same, and nothing lost out of nature, though everything is altered.

May I have leave to do myself the justice (since my enemies will do me none, and are so far from granting me to be a good poet that they will not allow me so much as to be a Christian, or a moral man), may I have leave, I say, to inform my reader that I have confined my choice to such tales of Chaucer as savour nothing of immodesty? If I had desired more to please than to instruct, the Reeve, the Miller, the Shipman, the Merchant, the Summoner, and, above all, the Wife of Bath, in the prologue to her tale, would have procured me as many friends and readers as there are beaux and ladies of pleasure in the town. But I will no more offend against good manners; I am sensible, as I ought to be, of the scandal I have given by my loose writings, and make what reparation I am able by this public acknowledgment. If anything of this nature, or of profaneness, be crept into these poems, I am so far from defending it that I disown it. Totum hoc indictum volo. Chaucer makes another manner of apology for his broad speaking, and Boccace makes the like; but I will follow neither of them. Our countryman, in the end of his characters, before the Canterbury tales, thus excuses the ribaldry, which is very gross in many of his novels.

But first, I pray you of your courtesie,
That ye ne arrette it nought my villanie,
Though that I plainly speak in this matere
To tellen yon her words, and eke her chere:
Ne though I speak her wordes properly,
For this ye knowen al so well as I,
Who-so shall tell a tale after a man,
He mote rehearse as nye as ever he can
Everich a word, if it be in his charge,

All speke he never so rudely and large.
Or elles he mot telle his tale untrue.
Or feine things, or finde wordes new:
He may not spare, although he were his brother,
He mot as well say o word as another,
Christ spake himself full broad in holy writ,
And well ye wot no villany is it.
Eke Plato saith, who so that can him rede,
The wordes mote be cousin to the dede.

Yet if a man should have inquired of Boccace or of Chaucer, what need they had of introducing such characters where obscene words were proper in their mouths, but very indecent to be heard; I know not what answer they could have made; for that reason, such tale shall be left untold by me. You have here a specimen of Chaucer's language, which is so obsolete, that his sense is scarce to be understood; and you have likewise more than one example of his unequal numbers, The lines have been corrected in the text, and may easily be seen to be perfectly metrical. which were mentioned before. Yet many of his verses consist of ten syllables, and the words not much behind our present English: as, for example, these two lines, in the description of the carpenter's young wife:--

Wincing she was, as is a jolly colt,
Long as a mast, and upright as a bolt.

I have almost done with Chaucer, when I have answered some objections relating to my present work. I find some people are offended that I have turned these tales into modern English; because they think them unworthy of my pains, and look on Chaucer as a dry, old-fashioned wit, not worth reviving. I have often heard the late Earl of Leicester say, that Mr. Cowley himself was of that opinion; who, having read him over at my lord's request, declared he had no taste of him. I dare not advance my opinion against the judgment of so great an author: but I think it fair, however, to leave the decision to the public. Mr. Cowley was too modest to set up for a dictator; and being shocked perhaps with his old style, never examined into the depth of his good sense. Chaucer, I confess, is a rough diamond, and must first be polished ere he shines. I deny not, likewise, that, living in our early times he writes not always of a piece, but sometimes mingles trivial things with those of greater moment. Sometimes also, though not often, he runs riot, like Ovid, and knows not when he has said enough.

But there are more great wits besides Chaucer, whose fault is their excess of conceits, and those ill sorted. An author is not to write all he can, but only all he ought. Having observed this redundancy in Chaucer (as it is an easy matter for a man of ordinary parts to find a fault in one of greater), I have not tied myself to a literal translation; but have often omitted what I judged unnecessary, or not of dignity enough to appear in the company of better thoughts. I have presumed farther, in some places, and added somewhat of my own where I thought my author was deficient, and had not given his thoughts their true lustre, for want of words in the beginning of our language.

And to this I was the more emboldened, because (if I may be permitted to say it of myself) I found I had a soul congenial to his, and that I had been conversant in the same studies. Another poet, in another age, may take the same liberty with my writings; if at least they live long enough to deserve correction. It was also necessary sometimes to restore the sense of Chaucer, which was lost or mangled in the errors of the press: let this example suffice at present; in the story of Palamon and Arcite, where the temple of Diana is described, you find these verses, in all the editions of our author:

There saw I Dane turned into a tree,

I mean not the goddess Diane,

But Venus daughter, which that hight Dane:

Which, after a little consideration, I knew was to be reformed into this sense, that Daphne, the daughter of Peneus, was turned into a tree. I durst not make thus bold with Ovid, lest some future Milbourn should arise, and say, I varied from my author, because I understood him not.

But there are other judges who think I ought not to have translated Chaucer into English, out of a quite contrary notion: they suppose there is a certain veneration due to his old language; and that it is a little less than profanation and sacrilege to alter it. They are farther of opinion, that somewhat of his good sense will suffer in this transfusion, and much of the beauty of his thoughts will infallibly be lost, which appear with more grace in their old habit. Of this opinion was that excellent person, whom I mentioned, the late Earl of Leicester, who valued Chaucer as much as Mr. Cowley despised him. My lord dissuaded me from this attempt (for I was thinking of it some years before his death), and his authority prevailed so far with me, as to defer my undertaking while he lived, in deference to him: yet my reason was not convinced with what he urged against it. If the first end of a writer be to be understood, then as his language grows obsolete, his thoughts must grow obscure: multa renascentur quae nunc cecidere; cadentque, quae nunc sunt in honore vocabula, si volet usus, quem penes arbitrium est et jus et norma loquendi.

When an ancient word for its sound and significancy deserves to be revived, I have that reasonable veneration for antiquity, to restore it. All beyond this is superstition. Words are not like landmarks, so sacred as never to be removed; customs are changed, and even statutes are silently repealed, when the reason ceases for which they were enacted. As for the other part of the argument, that his thoughts will lose of their original beauty, by the innovation of words; in the first place, not only their beauty but their being is lost where they are no longer understood, which is the present case. I grant that something must be lost in all transfusion, that is, in all translations; but the sense will remain, which would otherwise be lost, or at least be maimed, when it is scarce intelligible; and that but to a few.

How few are there who can read Chaucer, so as to understand him perfectly! And if imperfectly, then with less profit and no pleasure. 'Tis not for the use of some old Saxon friends that I have taken these pains with him: let them neglect my version because they have no need of it. I made it for their sakes who understand sense and poetry as well as they, when that poetry and sense is put into words which they understand.

I will go farther, and dare to add, that what beauties I lose in some places, I give to others which had them not originally; but in this I may be partial to myself; let the reader judge, and I submit to his decision. Yet I think I have just occasion to complain of them, who, because they understand Chaucer, would deprive the greater part of their countrymen of the same advantage, and hoard him up, as misers do their grandam gold, only to look on it themselves, and hinder others from making use of it.

In some I seriously protest, that no man ever had, or can have, a greater veneration for Chaucer, than myself. I have translated some part of his works, only that I might perpetuate his memory, or at least refresh it, amongst my countrymen.

If I have altered him anywhere for the better, I must at the same time acknowledge that I could have done nothing without him: Facile est inventis addere, is no great commendation; and I am not so vain to think I have deserved a greater.

I will conclude what I have to say of him singly, with this one remark: a lady of my acquaintance, who keeps a kind of correspondence with some authors of the fair sex in France, has been informed by them that Mademoiselle de Scudery, who is as old as Sibyl, and inspired like her by the same god of poetry, is at this time translating Chaucer into modern French.

From which I gather that he has been formerly translated into the old Provencal (for how she should come to understand old English I know not). But the matter of fact being true, it makes me think that there is something in it like fatality; that, after certain periods of time, the fame and memory of great wits should be renewed, as Chaucer is both in France and England. If this be wholly chance, 'tis extraordinary, and I dare not call it more for fear of being taxed with superstition.

Boccace comes last to be considered, who, living in the same age with Chaucer, had the same genius, and followed the same studies; both writ novels, and each of them cultivated his mother tongue.

But the greatest resemblance of our two modern authors being in their familiar style, and pleasing way of relating comical adventures, I may pass it over, because I have translated nothing from Boccace of that nature. In the serious part of poetry, the advantage is wholly on Chaucer's side; for though the Englishman has borrowed many tales from the Italian, yet it appears that those of Boccace were not generally of his own making, but taken from authors of former ages, and by him only modelled; so that what there was of invention in either of them may be judged equal.

But Chaucer has refined on Boccace, and has mended the stories which he has borrowed in his way of telling, though prose allows more liberty of thought, and the expression is more easy when unconfined by numbers.

Our countryman carries weight, and yet wins the race at disadvantage. I desire not the reader should take my word, and therefore I will set two of their discourses on the same subject, in the same light, for every man to judge betwixt them. I translated Chaucer first, and amongst the rest pitched on the Wife of Bath's tale--not daring, as

I have said, to adventure on her prologue, because it is too licentious.

There Chaucer introduces an old woman of mean parentage, whom a youthful knight of noble blood was forced to marry, and consequently loathed her. The crone being in bed with him on the wedding-night, and finding his aversion, endeavours to win his affection by reason, and speaks a good word for herself (as who could blame her?) in hope to mollify the sullen bridegroom.

She takes her topics from the benefits of poverty, the advantages of old age and ugliness, the vanity of youth, and the silly pride of ancestry and titles without inherent virtue, which is the true nobility.

When I had closed Chaucer I returned to Ovid, and translated some more of his fables; and by this time had so far forgotten the Wife of Bath's tale that, when I took up Boccace unawares, I fell on the same argument of preferring virtue to nobility of blood, and titles, in the story of Sigismunda, which I had certainly avoided for the resemblance of the two discourses, if my memory had not failed me. Let the reader weigh them both, and if he thinks me partial to Chaucer, it is in him to right Boccace.

I prefer in our countryman, far above all his other stories, the noble poem of Palamon and Arcite, which is of the Epic kind, and perhaps not much inferior to the Ilias or the Aeneis. The story is more pleasing than either of them--the manners as perfect, the diction as poetical, the learning as deep and various, and the disposition full as artful--only it includes a greater length of time, as taking up seven years at least; but Aristotle has left undecided the duration of the action, which yet is easily reduced into the compass of a year by a narration of what preceded the return of Palamon to Athens.

I had thought for the honour of our nation, and more particularly for his whose laurel, though unworthy, I have worn after him, that this story was of English growth and Chaucer's own; but I was undeceived by Boccace, for casually looking on the end of his seventh Giornata, I found Dioneo (under which name he shadows himself) and Fiametta (who represents his mistress the natural daughter of Robert, King of Naples), of whom these words are spoken, Dioneo e la Fiametta granpezza contarono insieme d'Arcita, e di Palamone, by which it appears that this story was written before the time of Boccace; It was really written by Boccaccio himself, but, as Dryden himself says, Chaucer has greatly improved upon his original (La Teseide). but the name of its author being wholly lost, Chaucer is now become an original, and I question not but the poem has received many beauties by passing through his noble hands.

Besides this tale, there is another of his own invention, after the manner of the Provencals, called the Flower and the Leaf, with which I was so particularly pleased, both for the invention and the moral, that I cannot hinder myself from recommending it to the reader.

As a corollary to this preface, in which I have done justice to others, I owe somewhat to myself; not that I think it worth my time to enter the lists with one Milbourn and one Blackmore, but barely to take notice that such men there are who have written scurrilously against me without any provocation.

Milbourn, who is in orders, pretends amongst the rest this quarrel to me, that I have fallen foul on priesthood; if I have, I am only to ask pardon of good priests, and am afraid his part of the reparation will come to little. Let him be satisfied that he shall not be able to force himself upon me for an adversary. I contemn him too much to enter into competition with him. His own translations of Virgil have answered his criticisms on mine.

If (as they say he has declared in print) he prefers the version of Ogilby to mine, the world has made him the same compliment, for it is agreed on all hands that he writes even below Ogilby. That, you will say. is not easily to be done; but what cannot Milbourn bring about? I am satisfied, however, that while he and I live together, I shall not be thought the worst poet of the age.

It looks as if I had desired him underhand to write so ill against me; but upon my honest word, I have not bribed him to do me this service, and am wholly guiltless of his pamphlet. 'Tis true, I should be glad if I could persuade him to continue his good offices, and write such another critique on anything of mine; for I find by experience he has a great stroke with the reader, when he condemns any of my poems, to make the world have a better opinion of them.

He has taken some pains with my poetry, but nobody will be persuaded to take the same with his. If I had taken to the church (as he affirms, but which was never in my thoughts), I should have had more sense, if not more grace, than to have turned myself out of my benefice by writing libels on my parishioners. But his account of my manners and my principles are of a piece with his cavils and his poetry; and so I have done with him for ever.

As for the City Bard, or Knight Physician, I hear his quarrel to me is, that I was the author of Absalom and Achitophel, which he thinks was a little hard on his fanatic patrons in London.

But I will deal the more civilly with his two poems, because nothing ill is to be spoken of the dead, and therefore peace be to the Manes of his Arthurs. I will only say that it was not for this noble knight that I drew the plan of an Epic poem on King Arthur in my preface to the translation of Juvenal.

The guardian angels of kingdoms were machines too ponderous for him to manage; and therefore he rejected them, as Dares did the whirlbats of Eryx, when they were thrown before him by Entellus. Yet from that preface he plainly took his hint; for he began immediately upon his story, though he had the baseness not to acknowledge his benefactor; but instead of it, to traduce me in a libel.

I shall say the less of Mr. Collier, His Short View of the Immorality and Profaneness of the English Stage (1698) was largely directed against Dryden. See the account of it given in Macaulay's Comic Dramatists of the Restoration. because in many things he has taxed me justly, and I have pleaded guilty to all thoughts and expressions of mine which can be truly argued of obscenity, profaneness, or immorality, and retract them. If he be my enemy, let him triumph; if he be my friend, as I have given him no personal occasion to be otherwise, he will be glad of my repentance. It becomes me not to draw my pen in the defence of a bad cause when I have so often drawn it for a good one. Yet it were not difficult to prove that in many places he has perverted my meaning by his glosses, and interpreted my words into blasphemy and bawdry, of which they were not guilty--besides that he is too much given to horseplay in his raillery, and comes to battle like a dictator from the plough.

I will not say the zeal of God's house has eaten him up, but I am sure it has devoured some part of his good manners and civility. It might also be doubted whether it were altogether zeal which prompted him to this rough manner of proceeding; perhaps it became not one of his function to rake into the rubbish of ancient and modern plays. A divine might have employed his pains to better purpose than in the nastiness of Plautus and Aristophanes, whose examples, as they excuse not me, so it might be possibly supposed that he read them not without some pleasure. They who have written commentaries on those poets, or on Horace, Juvenal, and Martial, have explained some vices which, without their interpretation, had been unknown to modern times. Neither has he judged impartially betwixt the former age and us.

There is more bawdry in one play of Fletcher's, called the Custom of the Country, than in all ours together. Yet this has been often acted on the stage in my remembrance. Are the times so much more reformed now than they were five and twenty years ago? If they are, I congratulate the amendment of our morals. But I am not to prejudice the cause of my fellow-poets, though I abandon my own defence; they have some of them answered for themselves, and neither they nor I can think Mr. Collier so formidable an enemy that we should shun him. He has lost ground at the latter end of the day by pursuing his point too far, like the Prince of Conde at the battle of Senneffe: from immoral plays to no plays-- ab abusu ad usum, non valet consequentia. From the fact that there are immoral plays to the inference that there should be no plays the argument does not follow. But being a party, I am not to erect myself into a judge. As for the rest of those who have written against me, they are such scoundrels that they deserve not the least notice to be taken of them. Blackmore and Milbourn are only distinguished from the crowd by being remembered to their infamy.

----Demetri teque, Tigelli,

Discipulorum inter jubeo plorare cathedras.

4

The Metaphysical Poets

SAMUEL JOHNSON

The criticism of the 'metaphysical poets' occurs in the Life of Cowley, published as one of the Lives of the Poets in 1780. The name 'metaphysical poetry' was first devised by Dryden, in his Essay of Dramatic Poesy. It was revived by Johnson, and is now generally accepted by historians of English literature. It is used by Johnson, as it was used by Dryden, to express the love of remote analogies, which was a mark of the poetry of Donne and those who wrote more or less after the manner of Donne. But it has a deeper meaning than was probably intended by its inventors.

It is no unapt term to indicate the vein of weighty thought and brooding imagination which runs like a thread of gold through all the finer work of these poets. Johnson did no harm in calling attention to the extravagance of much of the imagery beloved by the lyric poets of the Stuart period. But it is unpardonable that he should have had no eye for the nobler and subtler qualities of their genius, and equally unpardonable that he should have drawn no distinction between three men so incomparable in degree and kind of power as Cleveland, Cowley, and Donne. Some remarks on the place of the metaphysical poets in English literature will be found in the Introduction.

Cowley, like other poets who have written with narrow views, and, instead of tracing intellectual pleasure to its natural sources in the mind of man, paid their court to temporary prejudices, has been at one time too much praised, and too much neglected at another.

Wit, like all other things subject by their nature to the choice of man, has its changes and fashions, and at different times takes different forms. About the beginning of the seventeenth century appeared a race of writers that may be termed the metaphysical poets; of whom, in a criticism on the works of Cowley, it is not improper to give some account.

The metaphysical poets were men of learning, and to show their learning was their whole endeavour; but, unluckily resolving to show it in rhyme, instead of writing poetry, they only wrote verses, and very often such verses as stood the trial of the finger better than of the ear; for the modulation was so imperfect, that they were only found to be verses by counting the syllables.

If the father of criticism has rightly denominated poetry, an imitative art, these writers will, without great wrong, lose their right to the name of poets; for they cannot be said to have imitated anything; they neither copied nature nor life; neither painted the forms of matter, nor represented the operations of intellect.

Those, however, who deny them to be poets, allow them to be wits. Dryden confesses of himself and his contemporaries that they fall below Donne in wit, but maintains that they surpass him in poetry.

If wit be well described by Pope, as being "that which has been often thought, but was never before so well expressed", they certainly never attained, nor ever sought it; for they endeavoured to be singular in their thoughts, and were careless of their diction. But Pope's account of wit is undoubtedly erroneous: he depresses it below its natural dignity, and reduces it from strength of thought to happiness of language.

If by a more noble and more adequate conception that be considered as wit which is at once natural and new, that which, though not obvious, is, upon its first production, acknowledged to be just; if it be that which he that never found it wonders how he missed; to wit of this kind the metaphysical poets have seldom risen. Their thoughts are often new, but seldom natural; they are not obvious, but neither are they just; and the reader, far from wondering that he missed them, wonders more frequently by what perverseness of industry they were ever found.

But wit, abstracted from its effects upon the hearer, may be more rigorously and philosophically considered as a kind of discordia concors ; a combination of dissimilar images, or discovery of occult resemblances in things apparently unlike. Of wit, thus defined, they have more than enough. The most heterogeneous ideas are yoked by violence together; nature and art are ransacked for illustrations, comparisons, and allusions; their learning instructs, and their subtlety surprises; but the reader commonly thinks his improvement dearly bought, and, though he sometimes admires, is seldom pleased.

From this account of their compositions it will be readily inferred that they were not successful in representing or moving the affections. As they were wholly employed on something unexpected and surprising, they had no regard to that uniformity of sentiment which enables us to conceive and to excite the pains and the pleasure of other minds: they never inquired what, on any occasion, they should have said or done; but wrote rather as beholders than partakers of human nature; as Beings looking upon good and evil, impassive and at leisure; as Epicurean deities making remarks on the actions of men and the vicissitudes of life without interest and without emotion.

Their courtship was void of fondness, and their lamentation of sorrow. Their wish was only to say what they hoped had never been said before.

Nor was the sublime more within their reach than the pathetic; for they never attempted that comprehension and expanse of thought which at once fills the whole mind, and of which the first effect is sudden astonishment, and the second rational admiration. Sublimity is produced by aggregation, and littleness by dispersion. Great thoughts are always general, and consist in positions not limited by exceptions, and in descriptions not descending to minuteness. It is with great propriety that subtlety, which in its original import means exility of particles, is taken in its metaphorical meaning for nicety of distinction.

Those writers who lay on the watch for novelty could have little hope of greatness; for great things cannot have escaped former observation. Their attempts were always analytic; they broke every image into fragments: and could no more represent, by their slender conceits and laboured particularities, the prospects of nature or the scenes of life, than he who dissects a sunbeam with a prism can exhibit the wide effulgence of a summer noon.

What they wanted, however, of the sublime, they endeavoured to supply by hyperbole; their amplification had no limits; they left not only reason but fancy behind them; and produced combinations of confused magnificence that not only could not be credited, but could not be imagined.

Yet great labour, directed by great abilities, is never wholly lost: if they frequently threw away their wit upon false conceits, they likewise sometimes struck out unexpected truth: if their conceits were far-fetched, they were often worth the carriage.

To write on their plan, it was at least necessary to read and think. No man could be born a metaphysical poet, nor assume the dignity of a writer, by descriptions copied from descriptions, by imitations borrowed from imitations, by traditional imagery and hereditary similes, by readiness of rhyme and volubility of syllables.

In perusing the works of this race of authors, the mind is exercised either by recollection or inquiry; either something already learned is to be retrieved, or something new is to be examined.

If their greatness seldom elevates, their acuteness often surprises; if the imagination is not always gratified, at least the powers of reflection and comparison are employed; and in the mass of materials which ingenious absurdity has thrown together, genuine wit and useful knowledge may be sometimes found, buried perhaps in grossness of expression, but useful to those who know their value; and such as, when they are expanded to perspicuity and polished to elegance, may give lustre to works which have more propriety though less copiousness of sentiment.

This kind of writing, which was, I believe, borrowed from Marino As Marino's chief poem, L'Adone, was not published till 1623, and as most of Donne's poems must have been written earlier, this is very unlikely. Besides, the resemblance is more apparent than real. Metaphysical poetry was a native product. See Introduction. and his followers, had been recommended by the example of Donne, a man of very extensive and various knowledge; and by Jonson, whose manner resembled that of Donne more in the ruggedness of his lines than in the cast of his sentiments.

When their reputation was high, they had undoubtedly more imitators than time has left behind. Their immediate successors, of whom any remembrance can be said to remain, were Suckling, Waller, Denham, Cowley, Cleveland, and Milton. Denham and Waller sought another way to fame, by improving the harmony of our numbers. Milton tried the metaphysic style only in his lines upon Hobson the Carrier. Cowley adopted it, and excelled his predecessors, having as much sentiment and more music. Suckling neither improved versification, nor abounded in conceits. The fashionable style remained chiefly with Cowley; Suckling could not reach it, and Milton disdained it.

Critical remarks are not easily understood without examples, and I have therefore collected instances of the modes of writing by which this species of poets, for poets they were called by themselves and their admirers, was eminently distinguished.

As the authors of this race were perhaps more desirous of being admired than understood, they sometimes drew their conceits from recesses of learning not very much frequented by common readers of poetry. Thus Cowley on Knowledge :

The sacred tree midst the fair orchard grew;
The phoenix Truth did on it rest.
And built his perfum'd nest,
That right Porphyrian tree which did true logick shew.
Each leaf did learned notions give,
And th' apples were demonstrative:
So clear their colour and divine,
The very shade they cast did other lights outshine.

On Anacreon continuing a lover in his old age:

Love was with thy life entwin'd,
Close as heat with fire is join'd,
A powerful brand prescrib'd the date
Of thine, like Meleager's fate.
The antiperistasis of age
More enflam'd thy amorous rage.

In the following verses we have an allusion to a Rabbinical opinion concerning Manna:

Variety I ask not: give me one
To live perpetually upon.
The person Love does to us fit,
Like manna, has the taste of all in it.

Thus Donne shows his medicinal knowledge in some encomiastic verses:

In everything there naturally grows
A Balsamum to keep it fresh and new,
If't were not injur'd by extrinsique blows;
Your youth and beauty are this balm in you.
But you, of learning and religion,
And virtue and such ingredients, have made
A mithridate, whose operation
Keeps off, or cures what can be done or said.

Though the following lines of Donne, on the last night of the year, have something in them too scholastic, they are not inelegant:

This twilight of two years, not past nor next,
Some emblem is of me, or I of this,
Who, meteor-like, of stuff and form perplext,
Whose what and where, in disputation is,
If I should call me any thing, should miss.
I sum the years and me, and find me not
Debtor to th' old, nor creditor to th' new,
That cannot say, my thanks I have forgot,
Nor trust I this with hopes: and yet scarce true
This bravery is, since these times shew'd me you.
-- *Donne.*

Yet more abstruse and profound is Donne's reflection upon Man as a Microcosm:

If men be worlds, there is in every one
Something to answer in some proportion
All the world's riches: and in good men, this
Virtue, our form's form, and our soul's soul is.

Of thoughts so far-fetched as to be not only unexpected but unnatural, all their books are full.

TO A LADY, WHO WROTE POESIES FOR RINGS

They, who above do various circles find,
Say, like a ring th' aquator heaven does bind.
When heaven shall be adorn'd by thee,
(Which then more heaven than 't is, will be)
'T is thou must write the poesy there,
For it wanteth one as yet,
Though the sun pass through 't twice a year,
The sun, which is esteem'd the god of wit.
-- Cowley.

The difficulties which have been raised about identity in philosophy are by Cowley, with still more perplexity, applied to Love:

Five years ago (says story) I lov'd you,
For which you call me most inconstant now;
Pardon me, madam, you mistake the man;
For I am not the same that I was then;
No flesh is now the same't was then in me,
And that my mind is chang'd yourself may see.
The same thoughts to retain still, and intents,
Were more inconstant far; for accidents
Must of all things most strangely inconstant prove,
If from one subject they t' another move:
My members then, the father members were
From whence these take their birth, which now are here.
If then this body love what th' other did,
'T were incest, which by nature is forbid.

The love of different women is, in geographical poetry, compared to travels, through different countries:

Hast thou not found each woman's breast
(The land where thou hast travelled)
Either by savages possest,
Or wild, and uninhabited?
What joy could'st take, or what repose,
In countries so unciviliz'd as those?
Lust, the scorching dog-star, here
Rages with immoderate heat;
Whilst Pride, the rugged Northern Bear,
In others makes the cold too great.
And when these are temperate known,
The soil's all barren sand, or rocky stone.
-- *Cowley.*

A lover, burnt up by his affections, is compared to Egypt:

The fate of Egypt I sustain,
And never feel the dew of rain.
From clouds which in the head appear;
But all my too much moisture owe
To overflowings of the heart below.
-- *Cowley.*

The lover supposes his lady acquainted with the ancient laws of augury and rites of sacrifice:

And yet this death of mine, I fear,
Will ominous to her appear:
When found in every other part,
Her sacrifice is found without an heart.
For the last tempest of my death
Shall sigh out that too, with my breath.

That the chaos was harmonized, has been recited of old; but whence the different sounds arose remained for a modern to discover:

Th' ungovern'd parts no correspondence knew,

And artless war from thwarting motions grew;

Till they to number and fixt rules were brought.

Water and air he for the Tenor chose.

Earth made the Base, the Treble flame arose.

-- *Cowley.*

The tears of lovers are always of great poetical account, but Donne has extended them into worlds. If the lines are not easily understood, they may be read again:

On a round ball

A workman, that hath copies by, can lay

An Europe, Afric, and an Asia,

And quickly make that, which was nothing, all.

So doth each tear,

Which thee doth wear,

A globe, yea world, by that impression grow,

Till thy tears mixt with mine do overflow

This world, by waters sent from thee my heaven dissolved so.

On reading the following lines, the reader may perhaps cry out, "Confusion worse confounded":

Here lies a she sun, and a he moon here,

She gives the best light to his sphere,

Or each is both, and all, and so

They unto one another nothing owe.

-- *Donne.*

Who but Donne would have thought that a good man is a telescope?

Though God be our true glass, through which we see
All, since the being of all things is He,
Yet are the trunks, which do to us derive
Things, in proportion fit, by perspective
Deeds of good men; for by their living here,
Virtues, indeed remote, seem to be near.

Who would imagine it possible that in a very few lines so many remote ideas could be brought together?

Since't is my doom, Love's undershrieve,
Why this reprieve?
Why doth my She Advowson fly
Incumbency?
To sell thyself dost thou intend
By candle's end,
And hold the contrast thus in doubt,
Life's taper out?
Think but how soon the market fails,
Your sex lives faster than the males;
As if to measure age's span,
The sober Julian were th' account of man,
Whilst you live by the fleet Gregorian.
-- Cleveland.

Of enormous and disgusting hyperboles, these may be examples:

By every wind, that comes this way,
Send me at least a sigh or two,
Such and so many I'll repay
As shall themselves make winds to get to you.
-- Cowley.

In tears I'll waste these eyes,
By Love so vainly fed;
So lust of old the Deluge punished.
-- Cowley.

All arm'd in brass the richest dress of war,
(A dismal glorious sight) he shone afar.
The sun himself started with sudden fright,
To see his beams return so dismal bright.
-- Cowley.

An universal consternation:
His bloody eyes he hurls round, his sharp paws
Tear up the ground; then runs he wild about,
Lashing his angry tail and roaring out.
Beasts creep into their dens, and tremble there;
Trees, though no wind is stirring, shake with fear;
Silence and horror fill the place around:
Echo itself dares scarce repeat the sound.
-- Cowley.

Their fictions were often violent and unnatural.

OF HIS MISTRESS BATHING

The fish around her crowded, as they do
To the false light that treacherous fishers shew,
And all with as much ease might taken be,
As she at first took me:
For ne'er did light so clear
Among the waves appear,
Though every night the sun himself set there.
-- Cowley.

The poetical effect of a lover's name upon glass:

My name engrav'd herein
Doth contribute my firmness to this glass;
Which, ever since that charm, hath been
As hard as that which grav'd it was.
-- *Donne.*

Their conceits were sometimes slight and trifling.

ON AN INCONSTANT WOMAN

He enjoys thy calmy sunshine now,
And no breath stirring hears,
In the clear heaven of thy brow,
No smallest cloud appears.
He sees thee gentle, fair and gay,
And trusts the faithless April of thy May.
-- *Cowley.*

Upon a paper written with the juice of lemon, and read by the fire:

Nothing yet in thee is seen:
But when a genial heat warms thee within,
A new-born wood of various lines there grows;
Here buds an L, and there a B,
Here sprouts a V, and there a T,
And all the flourishing letters stand in rows.
-- *Cowley*

As they sought only for novelty, they did not much inquire whether their allusions were to things high or low, elegant or gross; whether they compared the little to the great, or the great to the little.

PHYSICK AND CHIRURGERY FOR A LOVER

Gently, ah gently, madam, touch
The wound, which you yourself have made;
That pain must needs be very much,
Which makes me of your hand afraid.
Cordials of pity give me now,
For I too weak for purgings grow.
-- Cowley.

THE WORLD AND A CLOCK

Mahol, th' inferior world's fantastic face,
Through all the turns of matter's maze did trace;
Great Nature's well-set clock in pieces took;
On all the springs and smallest wheels did look
Of life and motion; and with equal art
Made up again the whole of every part.
-- Cowley.

A coal-pit has not often found its poet; but, that it may not want its due honour, Cleveland has paralleled it with the sun:

The moderate value of our guiltless ore
Makes no man atheist, and no woman whore;
Yet why should hallow'd vestals' sacred shrine
Deserve more honour than a flaming mine?
These pregnant wombs of heat would fitter be
Than a few embers, for a deity.
Had he our pits, the Persian would admire
No sun, but warm's devotion at our fire:
He'd leave the trotting whipster, and prefer
Our profound Vulcan 'bove that waggoner.

For wants he heat or light? or would have store

Of both? 'tis here: and what can suns give more?

Nay, what's the sun but, in a different name,

A coal-pit rampant, or a mine on flame!

Then let this truth reciprocally run

The sun's heaven's coalery, and coals our sun.

DEATH, A VOYAGE

No family

E'er rigg'd a soul for heaven's discovery,

With whom more venturers might boldly dare

Venture their stakes, with him in joy to share.

-- Donne.

Their thoughts and expressions were sometimes grossly absurd, and such as no figures or licence can reconcile to the understanding.

A LOVER NEITHER DEAD NOR ALIVE

Then down I laid my head,

Down on cold earth; and for a while was dead,

And my freed soul to a strange somewhere fled:

Ah, sottish soul, said I,

When back to its cage again I saw it fly:

Fool to resume her broken chain!

And row her galley here again!

Fool, to that body to return

Where it condemn'd and destin'd is to burn!

Once dead, how can it be,

Death should a thing so pleasant seem to thee,

That thou should'st come to live it o'er again in me?

-- Cowley.

A LOVER'S HEART A HAND GRENADO

Wo to her stubborn heart, if once mine come
Into the self-same room,
'T will tear and blow up all within,
Like a grenado shot into a magazin.
Then shall Love keep the ashes, and torn parts,
Of both our broken hearts:
Shall out of both one new one make;
From hers th' allay; from mine, the metal take.
-- Cowley.

THE POETICAL PROPAGATION OF LIGHT

The Prince's favour is diffus'd o'er all,
From which all fortunes, names, and natures fall;
Then from those wombs of stars, the Bride's bright eyes,
At every glance a constellation flies,
And sows the court with stars, and doth prevent
In light and power, the all-ey'd firmament:
First her eye kindles other ladies' eyes,
Then from their beams their jewels' lustres rise;
And from their jewels torches do take fire,
And all is warmth, and light, and good desire.
-- Donne.

They were in very little care to clothe their notions with elegance of dress, and therefore miss the notice and the praise which are often gained by those who think less, but are more diligent to adorn their thoughts.

That a mistress beloved is fairer in idea than in reality is by Cowley thus expressed:

Thou in my fancy dost much higher stand,

Than woman can be plac'd by Nature's hand;
And I must needs, I'm sure, a loser be,
To change thee, as thou 'rt there, for very thee.

That prayer and labour should co-operate are thus taught by Donne:

In none but us, are such mixt engines found,
As hands of double office: for the ground
We till with them; and them to heaven we raise;
Who prayerless labours, or without this, prays,
Doth but one half, that's none.

By the same author, a common topic, the danger of procrastination, is thus illustrated:

--That which I should have begun
In my youth's morning, now late must be done;
And I, as giddy travellers must do,
Which stray or sleep all day, and having lost
Light and strength, dark and tir'd must then ride post.

All that Man has to do is to live and die; the sum of humanity is comprehended by Donne in the following lines:

Think in how poor a prison thou didst lie;
After, enabled but to suck and cry.
Think, when't was grown to most, 't was a poor inn,
A province pack'd up in two yards of skin,
And that usurp'd, or threaten'd with a rage
Of sicknesses, or their true mother, age.
But think that death hath now enfranchis'd thee;
Thou hast thy expansion now, and liberty;
Think, that a rusty piece discharg'd is flown
In pieces, and the bullet is his own,
And freely flies; this to thy soul allow,

Think thy shell broke, think thy soul hatched but now.

They were sometimes indelicate and disgusting. Cowley thus apostrophizes beauty:

--Thou tyrant, which leav'st no man free!

Thou subtle thief, from whom nought safe can be!

Thou murderer, which hast kill'd, and devil, which would'st damn me.

Thus he addresses his mistress:

Thou who, in many a propriety,

So truly art the sun to me.

Add one more likeness, which I'm sure you can,

And let me and my sun beget a man.

Thus he represents the meditations of a lover:

Though in thy thoughts scarce any tracts have been

So much as of original sin,

Such charms thy beauty wears as might

Desires in dying confest saints excite.

Thou with strange adultery

Dost in each breast a brothel keep;

Awake, all men do lust for thee,

And some enjoy thee when they sleep.

The true taste of tears:

Hither with crystal vials, lovers, come,

And take my tears, which are Love's wine,

And try your mistress' tears at home;

For all are false, that taste not just like mine.

-- Donne.

This is yet more indelicate:

As the sweet sweat of roses in a still

As that which from chaf'd musk-cat's pores doth trill,

As th' almighty balm of th' early East,

Such are the sweet drops of my mistress' breast.

And on her neck her skin such lustre sets,

They seem no sweat-drops, but pearl coronets:

Rank sweaty froth thy mistress' brow defiles.

-- Donne.

Their expressions sometimes raise horror, when they intend perhaps to be pathetic:

As men in hell are from diseases free,

So from all other ills am I.

Free from their known formality:

But all pains eminently lie in thee.

-- Cowley.

They were not always strictly curious, whether the opinions from which they drew their illustrations were true; it was enough that they were popular. Bacon remarks that some falsehoods are continued by tradition, because they supply commodious allusions.

It gave a piteous groan, and so it broke;

In vain it something would have spoke:

The love within too strong for't was,

Like poison put into a Venice-glass.

-- Cowley.

In forming descriptions, they looked out, not for images, but for conceits. Night has been a common subject, which poets have contended to adorn. Dryden's Night is well known; Donne's is as follows:

Thou seest me here at midnight, now all rest:

Time's dead low-water; when all minds divest

To-morrow's business, when the labourers have

Such rest in bed, that their last church-yard grave,

Subject to change, will scarce be a type of this;
Now when the client, whose last hearing is
To-morrow, sleeps; when the condemned man,
Who when he opens his eyes, must shut them then
Again by death, although sad watch he keep,
Doth practise dying by a little sleep,
Thou at this midnight seest me.

It must be, however, confessed of these writers that if they are upon common subjects often unnecessarily and unpoetically subtle, yet where scholastic speculation can be properly admitted, their copiousness and acuteness may justly be admired. What Cowley has written upon Hope shows an unequalled fertility of invention:

Hope, whose weak being ruin'd is,
Alike if it succeed, and if it miss;
Whom good or ill does equally confound,
And both the horns of Fate's dilemma wound.
Vain shadow, which dost vanish quite,
Both at full noon and perfect night!
The stars have not a possibility
Of blessing thee;
If things then from their end we happy call,
'T is hope is the most hopeless thing of all.
Hope, thou bold taster of delight,
Who, whilst thou shouldst but taste, devour'st it quite!
Thou bring'st us an estate, yet leav'st us poor,
By clogging it with legacies before!
The joys, which we entire should wed,
Come deflower'd virgins to our bed;
Good fortune without gain imported be.

Such mighty customs paid to thee:
For joy, like wine, kept close does better taste;
If it take air before, its spirits waste.

To the following comparison of a man that travels and his wife that stays at home, with a pair of compasses, it may be doubted whether absurdity or ingenuity has the better claim:

Our two souls therefore, which are one,
Though I must go, endure not yet
A breach, but an expansion,
Like gold to airy thinness beat.
If they be two, they are two so
As stiff twin-compasses are two,
Thy soul, the fixt foot, makes no show
To move, but doth, if th' other do.
And though it in the centre sit,
Yet when the other far doth roam,
It leans, and hearkens after it,
And grows erect, as that comes home.
Such wilt thou be to me, who must
Like th' other foot, obliquely run.
Thy firmness makes my circle just,
And makes me end where I begun.
--Donne.

In all these examples it is apparent that whatever is improper or vicious is produced by a voluntary deviation from nature in pursuit of something new and strange, and that the writers fail to give delight by their desire of exciting admiration.

5

Poetic Genius and Poetic Diction

SAMUEL TAYLOR COLERIDGE

The following passage forms Chapters xiv and xv of Coleridge's Biographia Literaria, published in 1817 It has been selected as giving a less imperfect impression of his powers as a critic than any other piece that could have been chosen The truth is that, great in talk and supreme in poetry, Coleridge was lost directly he sat down to express himself in prose His style is apt to be cumbrous, and his matter involved. We feel that the critic himself was greater than any criticism recorded either in his writings or his lectures The present extract may be defined as an attempt, and an attempt less inadequate than was common with Coleridge, to state his poetic creed, and to illustrate it by reference to his own poetry and to that of Wordsworth and of Shakespeare.

In what he says of Shakespeare he is at his best. He forgets himself, and writes with a single eye to a theme which was thoroughly worthy of his powers. In the earlier part of the piece, and indeed indirectly throughout, he has in mind Wordsworth's famous Preface to the Lyrical Ballads, which is to be found in any complete edition of Wordsworth's poems, or in his poise writings, as edited by Dr. Grosart.

During the first year that Mr. Wordsworth and I were neighbours, our conversation turned frequently on the two cardinal points of poetry, the power of exciting the sympathy of the reader by a faithful adherence to the truth of nature, and the power of giving the interest of novelty by the modifying colours of imagination. The sudden charm, which accidents of light and shade, which moonlight or sunset, diffused over a known and familiar landscape, appeared to represent the practicability of combining both. These are the poetry of nature.

The thought suggested itself (to which of us I do not recollect) that a series of poems might be composed of two sorts. In the one, the incidents and agents were to be, in part at least, supernatural; and the excellence aimed at was to consist in the interesting of the affections by the dramatic truth of such emotions, as would naturally accompany such situations, supposing them real. And real in this sense they have been to every human being who, from whatever source of delusion, has at any time believed himself under supernatural agency. For the second class, subjects were to be chosen from ordinary life; the characters and incidents were to be such as will be found in every village and its vicinity where there is a meditative and feeling mind to seek after them, or to notice them when they present themselves.

In this idea originated the plan of the Lyrical Ballads; Published in 1798. It opened with the Ancient Mariner and closed with Wordsworth's lines on Tintern Abbey. Among other poems written in Wordsworth's simplest style were The Idiot Boy, The Thorn, and We are Seven. in which it was agreed that my endeavours should be directed to persons and characters supernatural, or at least romantic; yet so as to transfer from our inward nature a human interest and a semblance of truth sufficient to procure for these shadows of imagination that willing suspension of disbelief for the moment, which constitutes poetic faith. Mr. Wordsworth, on the other hand, was to propose to himself as his object, to give the charm of novelty to things of every day, and to excite a feeling analogous to the supernatural, by awakening the mind's attention from the lethargy of custom, and directing it to the loveliness and the wonders of the world before us; an inexhaustible treasure, but for which, in consequence of the film of familiarity and selfish solicitude, we have eyes, yet see not, ears that hear not, and hearts that neither feel nor understand.

With this view I wrote the Ancient Mariner, and was preparing, among other poems, the Dark Ladie, and the Christabel, in which I should have more nearly realized my ideal than I had done in my first attempt. But Mr. Wordsworth's industry had proved so much more successful, and the number of his poems so much greater, that my compositions, instead of forming a balance, appeared rather an interpolation of heterogeneous matter.

Mr. Wordsworth added two or three poems written in his own character, in the impassioned, lofty, and sustained diction which is characteristic of his genius. In this form the Lyrical Ballads were published; and were presented by him, as an experiment, whether subjects, which from their nature rejected the usual ornaments and extra-colloquial style of poems in general, might not be so managed in the language of ordinary life as to produce the pleasurable interest which it is the peculiar business of poetry to impart.

To the second edition he added a preface of considerable length; in which, notwithstanding some passages of apparently a contrary import, he was understood to contend for the extension of this style to poetry of all kinds, and to reject as vicious and indefensible all phrases and forms of style that were not included in what he (unfortunately, I think, adopting an equivocal expression) called the language of real life.

From this preface, prefixed to poems in which it was impossible to deny the presence of original genius, however mistaken its direction might be deemed, arose the whole long-continued controversy. For from the conjunction of perceived power with supposed heresy I explain the inveteracy, and in some instances, I grieve to say, the acrimonious passions, with which the controversy has been conducted by the assailants.

Had Mr. Wordsworth's poems been the silly, the childish things which they were for a long time described as being; had they been really distinguished from the compositions of other poets merely by meanness of language and inanity of thought; had they indeed contained nothing more than what is found in the parodies and pretended imitations of them; they must have sunk at once, a dead weight, into the slough of oblivion, and have dragged the preface along with them. But year after year increased the number of Mr. Wordsworth's admirers. They were found, too, not in the lower classes of the reading public, but chiefly among young men of strong sensibility and meditative minds; and their admiration (inflamed perhaps in some degree by opposition) was distinguished by its intensity, I might almost say, by its religious fervour.

These facts, and the intellectual energy of the author, which was more or less consciously felt, where it was outwardly and even boisterously denied, meeting with sentiments of aversion to his opinions, and of alarm at their consequences, produced an eddy of criticism, which would of itself have borne up the poems by the violence with which it whirled them round and round. With many parts of this preface, in the sense attributed to them, and which the words undoubtedly seem to authorize, I never concurred; but, on the contrary, objected to them as erroneous in principle, and as contradictory (in appearance at least) both to other parts of the same preface and to the author's own practice in the greater number of the poems themselves.

Mr. Wordsworth, in his recent collection, has, I find, degraded this prefatory disquisition to the end of his second volume, to be read or not at the reader's choice. But he has not, as far as I can discover, announced any change in his poetic creed. At all events, considering it as the source of a controversy, in which I have been honoured more than I deserve by the frequent conjunction of my name with his, I think it expedient to declare, once for all, in what points I coincide with his opinions, and in what points I altogether differ. But in order to render myself intelligible, I must previously, in as few words as possible, explain my ideas, first, of a poem; and secondly, of poetry itself, in kind and in essence.

The office of philosophical disquisition consists in just distinction; while it is the privilege of the philosopher to preserve himself constantly aware that distinction is not division. In order to obtain adequate notions of any truth, we must intellectually separate its distinguishable parts; and this is the technical process of philosophy. But having so done, we must then restore them in our conceptions to the unity in which they actually co-exist; and this is the result of philosophy.

A poem contains the same elements as a prose composition; the difference, therefore, must consist in a different combination of them, in consequence of a different object proposed. According to the difference of the object will be the difference of the combination. It is possible that the object may be merely to facilitate the recollection of any given facts or observations by artificial arrangement; and the composition will be a poem, merely because it is distinguished from prose by metre, or by rhyme, or by both conjointly. In this, the lowest sense, a man might attribute the name of a poem to the well-known enumeration of the days in the several months:

Thirty days hath September, April, June, and November, &c.

and others of the same class and purpose. And as a particular pleasure is found in anticipating the recurrence of sounds and quantities, all compositions that have this charm superadded, whatever be their contents, may be entitled poems.

So much for the superficial form. A difference of object and contents supplies an additional ground of distinction. The immediate purpose may be the communication of truths; either of truth absolute and demonstrable, as in works of science; or of facts experienced and recorded, as in history. Pleasure, and that of the highest and most permanent kind, may result from the attainment of the end; but it is not itself the immediate end. In other works the communication of pleasure may be the immediate purpose; and though truth, either moral or intellectual, ought to be the ultimate end, yet this will distinguish the character of the author, not the class to which the work belongs.

Blest indeed is that state of society, in which the immediate purpose would be baffled by the perversion of the proper ultimate end; in which no charm of diction or imagery could exempt the Bathyllus even of an Anacreon, or the Alexis of Virgil, from disgust and aversion!

But the communication of pleasure may be the immediate object of a work not metrically composed; and that object may have been in a high degree attained, as in novels and romances. Would then the mere superaddition of metre, with or without rhyme, entitle these to the name of poems? The answer is, that nothing can permanently please which does not contain in itself the reason why it is so, and not otherwise. If metre be superadded, all other parts must be made consonant with it.

They must be such as to justify the perpetual and distinct attention to each part, which an exact correspondent recurrence of accent and sound are calculated to excite. The final definition then, so deduced, may be thus worded. A poem is that species of composition which is opposed to works of science, by proposing for its immediate object pleasure, not truth; and from all other species (having this object in common with it) it is discriminated by proposing to itself such delight from the whole as is compatible with a distinct gratification from each component part.

Controversy is not seldom excited in consequence of the disputants attaching each a different meaning to the same word; and in few instances has this been more striking than in disputes concerning the present subject. If a man chooses to call every composition a poem which is rhyme, or measure, or both, I must leave his opinion uncontroverted.

The distinction is at least competent to characterize the writer's intention. If it were subjoined that the whole is likewise entertaining or affecting, as a tale, or as a series of interesting reflections, I of course admit this as another fit ingredient of a poem, and an additional merit. But if the definition sought for be that of a legitimate poem, I answer, it must be one the parts of which mutually support and explain each other; all in their proportion harmonizing with, and supporting the purpose and known influences of metrical arrangement.

The philosophic critics of all ages coincide with the ultimate judgment of all countries, in equally denying the praises of a just poem, on the one hand to a series of striking lines or distichs, each of which, absorbing the whole attention of the reader to itself, disjoins it from its context, and makes it a separate whole, instead of a harmonizing part; and on the other hand, to an unsustained composition, from which the reader collects rapidly the general result unattracted by the component parts.

The reader should be carried forward, not merely or chiefly by the mechanical impulse of curiosity, or by a restless desire to arrive at the final solution; but by the pleasurable activity of mind excited by the attractions of the journey itself.

Like the motion of a serpent, which the Egyptians made the emblem of intellectual power; or like the path of sound through the air, at every step he pauses and half recedes, and from the retrogressive movement collects the force which again carries him onward. Praecipitandus est liber spiritus, says Petronius Arbiter most happily. The epithet, liber, here balances the preceding verb, and it is not easy to conceive more meaning condensed in fewer words.

But if this should be admitted as a satisfactory character of a poem, we have still to seek for a definition of poetry. The writings of Plato and Bishop Taylor, and the Theoria Sacra of Burnet, furnish undeniable proofs that poetry of the highest kind may exist without metre, and even without the contradistinguishing objects of a poem. The first chapter of Isaiah (indeed a very large proportion of the whole book) is poetry in the most emphatic sense; yet it would be not less irrational than strange to assert that pleasure, and not truth, was the immediate object of the prophet. In short, whatever specific import we attach to the word poetry, there will be found involved in it, as a necessary consequence, that a poem of any length neither can be, nor ought to be, all poetry. Yet if a harmonious whole is to be produced, the remaining parts must be preserved in keeping with the poetry; and this can be no otherwise effected than by such a studied selection and artificial arrangement as will partake of one, though not a peculiar, property of poetry. And this again can be no other than the property of exciting a more continuous and equal attention than the language of prose aims at, whether colloquial or written.

My own conclusions on the nature of poetry, in the strictest use of the word, have been in part anticipated in the preceding disquisition on the fancy and imagination. What is poetry? is so nearly the same question with, what is a poet? that the answer to the one is involved in the solution of the other. For it is a distinction resulting from the poetic genius itself, which sustains and modifies the images, thoughts, and emotions of the poet's own mind.

The poet, described in ideal perfection, brings the whole soul of man into activity, with the subordination of its faculties to each other, according to their relative worth and dignity. He diffuses a tone and spirit of unity that blends, and (as it were) fuses, each into each, by that synthetic and magical power to which we have exclusively appropriated the name of imagination. This power, first put in action by the will and understanding, and retained under their irremissive, though gentle and unnoticed, control (laxis effertur habenis), reveals itself in the balance or reconciliation of opposite or discordant qualities: of sameness, with difference; of the general, with the concrete; the idea, with the image; the individual, with the representative; the sense of novelty and freshness, with old and familiar objects; a more than usual state of emotion, with more than usual order; judgment ever awake and steady self-possession, with enthusiasm and feeling profound or vehement; and while it blends and harmonizes the natural and the artificial, still subordinates art to nature, the manner to the matter, and our admiration of the poet to our sympathy with the poetry.

Doubtless, as Sir John Davies observes of the soul (and his words may with slight alteration be applied, and even more appropriately, to the poetic imagination),--

Doubtless this could not be, but that she turns
Bodies to spirit by sublimation strange,
As fire converts to fire the things it burns,
As we our food into our nature change.
From their gross matter she abstracts their forms,
And draws a kind of quintessence from things;
Which to her proper nature she transforms
To bear them light on her celestial wings.
Thus does she, when from individual states
She doth abstract the universal kinds;
Which then re-clothed in divers names and fates
Steal access through our senses to our minds.

Finally, good sense is the body of poetic genius, fancy its drapery, motion its life, and imagination the soul that is everywhere, and in each; and forms all into one graceful and intelligent whole.

In the application of these principles to purposes of practical criticism as employed in the appraisal of works more or less imperfect, I have endeavoured to discover what the qualities in a poem are, which may be deemed promises and specific symptoms of poetic power, as distinguished from general talent determined to poetic composition by accidental motives, by an act of the will, rather than by the inspiration of a genial and productive nature. In this investigation, I could not, I thought, do better than keep before me the earliest work of the greatest genius that perhaps human nature has yet produced, our myriad-minded Shakespeare. I mean the Venus and Adonis, and the Lucrece ; works which give at once strong promises of the strength, and yet obvious proofs of the immaturity, of his genius. From these I abstracted the following marks, as characteristics of original poetic genius in general.

I. In the Venus and Adonis the first and obvious excellence is the perfect sweetness of the versification, its adaptation to the subject, and the power displayed in varying the march of the words without passing into a loftier and more majestic rhythm than was demanded by the thoughts, or permitted by the propriety of preserving a sense of melody predominant. The delight in richness and sweetness of sound, even to a faulty excess, if it be evidently original, and not the result of an easily imitable mechanism, I regard as a highly favourable promise in the compositions of a young man. "The man that hath not music in his soul" can indeed never be a genuine poet. Imagery (even taken from nature, much more when transplanted from books, as travels, voyages, and works of natural history), affecting incidents, just thoughts, interesting personal or domestic feelings, and with these the art of their combination or intertexture in the form of a poem, may all by incessant effort be acquired as a trade, by a man of talents and much reading, who, as I once before observed, has mistaken an intense desire of poetic reputation for a natural poetic genius; the love of the arbitrary end for a possession of the peculiar means. But the sense of musical delight, with the power of producing it, is a gift of imagination; and this, together with the power of reducing multitude into unity of effect, and modifying a series of thoughts by some one predominant thought or feeling, may be cultivated and improved, but can never be learnt. It is in these that Poeta nascitur non fit.

A second promise of genius is the choice of subjects very remote from the private interests and circumstances of the writer himself. At least I have found that where the subject is taken immediately from the author's personal sensations and experiences, the excellence of a particular poem is but an equivocal mark, and often a fallacious pledge, of genuine poetic power. We may perhaps remember the tale of the statuary, who had acquired considerable reputation for the legs of his goddesses, though the rest of the statue accorded but indifferently with ideal beauty; till his wife, elated by her husband's praises, modestly acknowledged that she herself had been his constant model.

In the Venus and Adonis this proof of poetic power exists even to excess. It is throughout as if a superior spirit, more intuitive, more intimately conscious even than the characters themselves, not only of every outward look and act, but of the flux and reflux of the mind in all its subtlest thoughts and feelings, were placing the whole before our view; himself meanwhile unparticipating in the passions, and actuated only by that pleasurable excitement which had resulted from the energetic fervour of his own spirit, in so vividly exhibiting what it had so accurately and profoundly contemplated.

I think I should have conjectured from these poems that even then the great instinct which impelled the poet to the drama was secretly working in him, prompting him by a series and never-broken chain of imagery, always vivid, and because unbroken, often minute; by the highest effort of the picturesque in words, of which words are capable, higher perhaps than was ever realized by any other poet, even Dante not excepted; to provide a substitute for that visual language, that constant intervention and running comment by tone, look, and gesture, which, in his dramatic works, he was entitled to expect from the players. His Venus and Adonis seem at once the characters themselves, and the whole representation of those characters by the most consummate actors.

You seem to be told nothing, but to see and hear everything. Hence it is that from the perpetual activity of attention required on the part of the reader; from the rapid flow, the quick change, and the playful nature of the thoughts and images; and, above all, from the alienation, and, if I may hazard such an expression, the utter aloofness of the poet's own feelings from those of which he is at once the painter and the analyst; that, though the very subject cannot but detract from the pleasure of a delicate mind, yet never was poem less dangerous on a moral account.

Instead of doing as Ariosto, and as, still more offensively, Wieland has done; instead of degrading and deforming passion into appetite, the trials of love into the struggles of concupiscence, Shakespeare has here represented the animal impulse itself so as to preclude all sympathy with it, by dissipating the reader's notice among the thousand outward images, and now beautiful, now fanciful circumstances, which form its dresses and its scenery; or by diverting our attention from the main subject by those frequent witty or profound reflections which the poet's ever active mind has deduced from, or connected with, the imagery and the incidents. The reader is forced into too much action to sympathize with the merely passive of our nature. As little can a mind thus roused and awakened be brooded on by mean and instinct emotion, as the low, lazy mist can creep upon the surface of a lake while a strong gale is driving it onward in waves and billows.

It has been before observed that images, however beautiful, though faithfully copied from nature, and as accurately represented in words, do not of themselves characterize the poet. They become proofs of original genius only as far as they are modified by a predominant passion; or by associated thoughts or images awakened by that passion; or when they have the effect of reducing multitude to unity, or succession to an instant; or, lastly, when a human and intellectual life is transferred to them from the poet's own spirit,

Which shoots its being through earth, sea, and air.

In the two following lines, for instance, there is nothing objectionable, nothing which would preclude them from forming, in their proper place, part of a descriptive poem:

Behold yon row of pines, that shorn and bow'd
Bend from the sea-blast, seen at twilight eve.

But with the small alteration of rhythm, the same words would be equally in their place in a book of topography, or in a descriptive tour. The same image will rise into a semblance of poetry if thus conveyed:

Yon row of bleak and visionary pines,
By twilight-glimpse discerned, mark! how they flee
From the fierce sea-blast, all their tresses wild
Streaming before them.

I have given this as an illustration, by no means as an instance, of that particular excellence which I had in view, and in which Shakespeare, even in his earliest as in his latest works, surpasses all other poets. It is by this that he still gives a dignity and a passion to the objects which he presents. Unaided by any previous excitement, they burst upon us at once in life and in power.

Full many a glorious morning have I seen
Flatter the mountain-tops with sovereign eye.

-- *Sonnet 33.*

Not mine own fears, nor the prophetic soul
Of the wide world dreaming on things to come,
Can yet the lease of my true love control,
Supposed as forfeit to a confined doom.
The mortal moon hath her eclipse endured,
And the sad augurs mock their own presage:
Incertainties now crown themselves assured,
And peace proclaims olives of endless age.
Now with the drops of this most balmy time
My love looks fresh: and Death to me subscribes,
Since, spite of him, I'll live in this poor rhyme,
While he insults o'er dull and speechless tribes.
And thou in this shalt find thy monument,
When tyrants' crests and tombs of brass are spent.
-- Sonnet 107.

As of higher worth, so doubtless still more characteristic of poetic genius does the imagery become, when it moulds and colours itself to the circumstances, passion, or character, present and foremost in the mind.

For unrivalled instances of this excellence the reader's own memory will refer him to the Lear, Othello, in short, to which not of the 'great, ever living, dead man's' dramatic works? Inopem me copia fecit. How true it is to nature, he has himself finely expressed in the instance of love in Sonnet 98:

From you have I been absent in the spring,
When proud-pied April drest in all his trim
Hath put a spirit of youth in every thing,
That heavy Saturn laugh'd and leap'd with him.
Yet nor the lays of birds, nor the sweet smell
Of different flowers in odour and in hue,

Could make me any summer's story tell,
Or from their proud lap pluck them where they grew
Nor did I wonder at the lily's white,
Nor praise the deep vermilion in the rose;
They were, but sweet, but figures of delight,
Drawn after you, you pattern of all those.
Yet seem'd it winter still and, you away,
As with your shadow I with these did play!

Scarcely less sure, or if a less valuable, not less indispensable mark

Greek text, transliterated

Gonzmou men Poihtou----------

----------ostis rhma gennaion lakoi,

will the imagery supply when, with more than the power of the painter, the poet gives us the liveliest image of succession with the feeling of simultaneousness!

With this he breaketh from the sweet embrace
Of those fair arms, that bound him to her breast,
And homeward through the dark laund runs apace:
Look how a bright star shooteth from the sky!
So glides he in the night from Venus' eye.
-- Venus and Adonis, 1. 811.

The last character I shall mention, which would prove indeed but little, except as taken conjointly with the former; yet without which the former could scarce exist in a high degree, and (even if this were possible) would give promises only of transitory flashes and a meteoric power;--its depth and energy of thought.

No man was ever yet a great poet without being at the same time a profound philosopher. For poetry is the blossom and the fragrancy of all human knowledge, human thoughts, human passions, emotions, language. In Shakespeare's Poems the creative power and the intellectual energy wrestle as in a war embrace. Each in its excess of strength seems to threaten the extinction of the other. At length, in the drama they were reconciled, and fought each with its shield before the breast of the other.

Or like two rapid streams that, at their first meeting within narrow and rocky banks, mutually strive to repel each other, and intermix reluctantly and in tumult, but soon finding a wider channel and more yielding shores, blend and dilate, and flow on in one current and with one voice. The Venus and Adonis did not perhaps allow the display of the deeper passions.

But the story of Lucretia seems to favour, and even demand, their intensest workings. And yet we find in Shakespeare's management of the tale neither pathos nor any other dramatic quality. There is the same minute and faithful imagery as in the former poem, in the same vivid colours, inspirited by the same impetuous vigour of thought, and diverging and contracting with the same activity of the assimilative and of the modifying faculties; and with a yet larger display, a yet wider range of knowledge and reflection; and lastly, with the same perfect dominion, often domination, over the whole world of language.

What, then, shall we say? even this, that Shakespeare, no mere child of nature; no automaton of genius; no passive vehicle of inspiration possessed by the spirit, not possessing it; first studied patiently, meditated deeply, understood minutely, till knowledge, become habitual and intuitive, wedded itself to his habitual feelings, and at length gave birth to that stupendous power, by which he stands alone, with no equal or second in his own class; to that power which seated him on one of the two glory-smitten summits of the poetic mountain, with Milton as his compeer, not rival. While the former darts himself forth, and passes into all the forms of human character and passion, the one Proteus of the fire and the flood; the other attracts all forms and things to himself, into the unity of his own ideal. All things and modes of action shape themselves anew in the being of Milton; while Shakespeare becomes all things, yet for ever remaining himself. O what great men hast thou not produced, England, my country! Truly, indeed,

> *Must we be free or die, who speak the tongue,*
> *Which Shakespeare spake; the faith and morals hold,*
> *Which Milton held. In every thing we are sprung*
> *Of earth's first blood, have titles manifold.*

6

POETRY IN GENERAL

WILLIAM HAZLITT

This was the first of a series of lectures on English poets, delivered in 1818, and published in the same year. It has been reprinted in the collected edition of Hazlitt's works (Bohn). It is a striking sample of Hazlitt's brilliance as a writer; and it is free from the faults of temper, and consequent errors of judgment, which, especially when he is dealing with modern authors, must be held in some degree to mar his greatness as a critic. It has been chosen partly for these reasons; partly also for those assigned in the Introduction. There is perhaps no other passage in the long roll of his writings that so clearly marks his place in the development of English criticism.

The best general notion which I can give of poetry is, that it is the natural impression of any object or event, by its vividness exciting an involuntary movement of imagination and passion, and producing, by sympathy, a certain modulation of the voice, or sounds, expressing it. In treating of poetry, I shall speak first of the subject-matter of it, next of the forms of expression to which it gives birth, and afterwards of its connection with harmony of sound.

Poetry is the language of the imagination and the passions. It relates to whatever gives immediate pleasure or pain to the human mind. It comes home to the bosoms and businesses of men; for nothing but what so comes home to them in the most general and intelligible shape can be a subject for poetry. Poetry is the universal language which the heart holds with nature and itself. He who has a contempt for poetry cannot have much respect for himself, or for anything else. It is not a mere frivolous accomplishment (as some persons have been led to imagine), the trifling amusement of a few idle readers or leisure hours: it has been the study and delight of mankind in all ages. Many people suppose that poetry is something to be found only in books, contained in lines of ten syllables with like endings: but wherever there is a sense of beauty, or power, or harmony, as in the motion of a wave of the sea, in the growth of a flower that "spreads its sweet leaves to the air, and dedicates its beauty to the sun",-- there is poetry, in its birth.

If history is a grave study, poetry may be said to be a graver: its materials lie deeper, and are spread wider. History treats, for the most part, of the cumbrous and unwieldy masses of things, the empty cases in which the affairs of the world are packed, under the heads of intrigue or war, in different states, and from century to century: but there is no thought or feeling that can have entered into the mind of man, which he would be eager to communicate to others, or which they would listen to with delight, that is not a fit subject for poetry. It is not a branch of authorship: it is "the stuff of which our life is made". The rest is "mere oblivion", a dead letter: for all that is worth remembering in life is the poetry of it. Fear is poetry, hope is poetry, love is poetry, hatred is poetry; contempt, jealousy, remorse, admiration, wonder, pity, despair, or madness, are all poetry. Poetry is that fine particle within us, that expands, rarefies, refines, raises our whole being: without it "man's life is poor as beast's".

Man is a poetical animal: and those of us who do not study the principles of poetry, act upon them all our lives, like Moliere's Bourgeois Gentilhomme, who had always spoken prose without knowing it. The child is a poet, in fact, when he first plays at Hide-and-seek, or repeats the story of Jack the Giant-killer; the shepherd-boy is a poet when he first crowns his mistress with a garland of flowers; the countryman, when he stops to look at the rainbow; the city apprentice, when he gazes after the Lord Mayor's show; the miser, when he hugs his gold; the courtier, who builds his hopes upon a smile; the savage, who paints his idol with blood; the slave, who worships a tyrant; or the tyrant, who fancies himself a god; the vain, the ambitious, the proud, the choleric man, the hero and the coward, the beggar and the king, the rich and the poor, the young and the old, all live in a world of their own making; and the poet does no more than describe what all the others think and act. If his art is folly and madness, it is folly and madness at second hand. "There is warrant for it." Poets alone have not "such seething brains, such shaping fantasies, that apprehend more than cooler reason" can.

The lunatic, the lover, and the poet
Are of imagination all compact.
One sees more devils than vast hell can hold,
That is, the madman: the lover, all as frantic,
Sees Helen's beauty in a brow of Egypt.
The poet's eye, in a fine frenzy rolling,
Doth glance from heav'n to earth, from earth to heav'n;
And, as imagination bodies forth
The forms of things unknown, the poet's pen
Turns them to shape, and gives to airy nothing
A local habitation and a name.
Such tricks hath strong imagination.

If poetry is a dream, the business of life is much the same. If it is a fiction, made up of what we wish things to be, and fancy that they are, because we wish them so, there is no other nor better reality. Ariosto has described the loves of Angelica and Medoro: but was not Medoro, who carved the name of his mistress on the barks of trees, as much enamoured of her charms as he? Homer has celebrated the anger of Achilles: but was not the hero as mad as the poet? Plato banished the poets from his Commonwealth, lest their descriptions of the natural man should spoil his mathematical man, who was to be without passions and affections--who was neither to laugh nor weep, to feel sorrow nor anger, to be cast down nor elated by anything. This was a chimera, however, which never existed but in the brain of the inventor; and Homer's poetical world has outlived Plato's philosophical Republic.

Poetry then is an imitation of nature, but the imagination and the passions are a part of man's nature. We shape things according to our wishes and fancies, without poetry; but poetry is the most emphatical language that can be found for those creations of the mind "which ecstasy is very cunning in". Neither a mere description of natural objects, nor a mere delineation of natural feelings, however distinct or forcible, constitutes the ultimate end and aim of poetry, without the heightenings of the imagination. The light of poetry is not only a direct but also a reflected light, that while it shows us the object, throws a sparkling radiance on all around it: the flame of the passions, communicated to the imagination, reveals to us, as with a flash of lightning, the inmost recesses of thought, and penetrates our whole being. Poetry represents forms chiefly as they suggest other forms: feelings, as they suggest forms or other feelings. Poetry puts a spirit of life and motion into the universe. It describes the flowing, not the fixed. It does not define the limits of sense, or analyse the distinctions of the understanding, but signifies the excess of the imagination beyond the actual or ordinary impression of any object or feeling.

The poetical impression of any object is that uneasy, exquisite sense of beauty or power that cannot be contained within itself, that is impatient of all limit, that (as flame bends to flame) strives to link itself to some other image of kindred beauty or grandeur, to enshrine itself, as it were, in the highest forms of fancy, and to relieve the aching sense of pleasure by expressing it in the boldest manner, and by the most striking examples of the same quality in other instances. Poetry, according to Lord Bacon, for this reason "has something divine in it, because it raises the mind and hurries it into sublimity, by conforming the shows of things to the desires of the soul, instead of subjecting the soul to external things, as reason and history do".

It is strictly the language of the imagination; and the imagination is that faculty which represents objects, not as they are in themselves, but as they are moulded by other thoughts and feelings, into an infinite variety of shapes and combinations of power. This language is not the less true to nature, because it is false in point of fact; but so much the more true and natural, if it conveys the impression which the object under the influence of passion makes on the mind. Let an object, for instance, be presented to the senses in a state of agitation or fear, and the imagination will distort or magnify the object, and convert it into the likeness of whatever is most proper to encourage the fear. "Our eyes are made the fools" of our other faculties. This is the universal law of the imagination:

That if it would but apprehend some joy,

It comprehends some bringer of that joy:

Or in the night imagining some fear,

How easy is each bush suppos'd a bear!

When Iachimo says of Imogen:

---The flame o' th' taper

Bows toward her, and would under-peep her lids

To see the enclosed lights--

This passionate interpretation of the motion of the flame, to accord with the speaker's own feelings, is true poetry. The lover, equally with the poet, speaks of the auburn tresses of his mistress as locks of shining gold, because the least tinge of yellow in the hair has, from novelty and a sense of personal beauty, a more lustrous effect to the imagination than the purest gold. We compare a man of gigantic stature to a tower: not that he is anything like so large, but because the excess of his size beyond what we are accustomed to expect, or the usual size of things of the same class, produces by contrast a greater feeling of magnitude and ponderous strength than another object of ten times the same dimensions. The intensity of the feeling makes up for the disproportion of the objects. Things are equal to the imagination, which have the power of affecting the mind with an equal degree of terror, admiration, delight, or love. When Lear calls upon the heavens to avenge his cause, "for they are old like him", there is nothing extravagant or impious in this sublime identification of his age with theirs; for there is no other image which could do justice to the agonizing sense of his wrongs and his despair!

Poetry is the high-wrought enthusiasm of fancy and feeling. As in describing natural objects, it impregnates sensible impressions with the forms of fancy, so it describes the feelings of pleasure or pain, by blending them with the strongest movements of passion, and the most striking forms of nature. Tragic poetry, which is the most impassioned species of it, strives to carry on the feeling to the utmost point of sublimity or pathos, by all the force of comparison or contrast: loses the sense of present suffering in the imaginary exaggeration of it: exhausts the terror or pity by an unlimited indulgence of it: grapples with impossibilities in its desperate impatience of restraint: throws us back upon the past, forward into the future: brings every moment of our being or object of nature in startling review before us: and in the rapid whirl of events, lifts us from the depths of woe to the highest contemplations on human life. When Lear says of Edgar, "Nothing but his unkind daughters could have brought him to this", what a bewildered amazement, what a wrench of the imagination, that cannot be brought to conceive of any other cause of misery than that which has bowed it down, and absorbs all other sorrow in its own!

His sorrow, like a flood, supplies the sources of all other sorrow. Again, when he exclaims in the mad scene, "The little dogs and all, Tray, Blanche, and Sweetheart, see, they bark at me!" it is passion lending occasion to imagination to make every creature in league against him, conjuring up ingratitude and insult in their least looked-for and most galling shapes, searching every thread and fibre of his heart, and finding out the last remaining image of respect or attachment in the bottom of his breast, only to torture and kill it! In like manner, the "So I am" of Cordelia gushes from her heart like a torrent of tears, relieving it of a weight of love and of supposed ingratitude, which had pressed upon it for years. What a fine return of the passion upon itself is that in Othello--with what a mingled agony of regret and despair he clings to the last traces of departed happiness, when he exclaims:

---O now, for ever,

Farewell the tranquil mind: farewell content!

Farewell the plumed troop, and the big wars,

That make ambition virtue! O, farewell!

Farewell the neighing steed, and the shrill trump,

The spirit-stirring drum, the ear-piercing fife,

The royal banner; and all quality,

Pride, pomp, and circumstance of glorious war!

And O you mortal engines, whose rude throats

Th' immortal Jove's dread clamours counterfeit,

Farewell! Othello's occupation's gone!

How his passion lashes itself up and swells and rages like a tide in its sounding course, when, in answer to the doubts expressed of his returning love, he says:

Never, Iago. Like to the Pontic sea,
Whose icy current and compulsive course
Ne'er feels retiring ebb, but keeps due on
To the Propontic and the Hellespont:
Even so my bloody thoughts, with violent pace,
Shall ne'er look back, ne'er ebb to humble love,
Till that a capable and wide revenge
Swallow them up.

The climax of his expostulation afterwards with Desdemona is at that passage:

But there where I have garner'd up my heart...
To be discarded thence!

One mode in which the dramatic exhibition of passion excites our sympathy without raising our disgust is that, in proportion as it sharpens the edge of calamity and disappointment, it strengthens the desire of good. It enhances our consciousness of the blessing, by making us sensible of the magnitude of the loss. The storm of passion lays bare and shows us the rich depths of the human soul: the whole of our existence, the sum total of our passions and pursuits, of that which we desire and that which we dread, is brought before us by contrast; the action and reaction are equal; the keenness of immediate suffering only gives us a more intense aspiration after, and a more intimate participation with the antagonist world of good: makes us drink deeper of the cup of human life: tugs at the heart-strings: loosens the pressure about them, and calls the springs of thought and feeling into play with tenfold force.

Impassioned poetry is an emanation of the moral and intellectual part of our nature, as well as of the sensitive--of the desire to know, the will to act, and the power to feel; and ought to appeal to these different parts of our constitution, in order to be perfect. The domestic or prose tragedy, which is thought to be the most natural, is in this sense the least so, because it appeals almost exclusively to one of these faculties, our sensibility. The tragedies of Moore-and Lillo, For instance, The Gamester and George Barnwell They are to be found respectively in vols. xiv. and xi. of the British Theatre. for this reason, however affecting at the time, oppress and lie like a dead weight upon the mind, a load of misery which it is unable to throw off; the tragedy of Shakespeare, which is true poetry, stirs our inmost affections; abstracts evil from itself by combining it with all the forms of imagination, and with the deepest workings of the heart; and rouses the whole man within us.

The pleasure, however, derived from tragic poetry is not anything peculiar to it as poetry, as a fictitious and fanciful thing. It is not an anomaly of the imagination. It has its source and ground-work in the common love of strong excitement. As Mr. Burke observes, people flock to see a tragedy; but if there were a public execution in the next street, the theatre would very soon be empty. It is not then the difference between fiction and reality that solves the difficulty. Children are satisfied with the stories of ghosts and witches in plain prose: nor do the hawkers of full, true, and particular accounts of murders and executions about the streets find it necessary to have them turned into penny ballads, before they can dispose of these interesting and authentic documents.

The grave politician drives a thriving trade of abuse and calumnies poured out against those whom he makes his enemies for no other end than that he may live by them. The popular preacher makes less frequent mention of Heaven than of hell. Oaths and nicknames are only a more vulgar sort of poetry or rhetoric. We are as fond of indulging our violent passions as of reading a description of those of others. We are as prone to make a torment of our fears, as to luxuriate in our hopes of good. If it be asked, Why we do so, the best answer will be, Because we cannot help it. The sense of power is as strong a principle in the mind as the love of pleasure. Objects of terror and pity exercise the same despotic control over it as those of love or beauty. It is as natural to hate as to love, to despise as to admire, to express our hatred or contempt, as our love or admiration:

Masterless passion sways us to the mood

Of what it likes or loathes.

Not that we like what we loathe: but we like to indulge our hatred and scorn of it, to dwell upon it, to exasperate our idea of it by every refinement of ingenuity and extravagance of illustration, to make it a bugbear to ourselves, to point it out to others in all the splendour of deformity, to embody it to the senses, to stigmatize it by name, to grapple with it in thought--in action, to sharpen our intellect, to arm our will against it, to know the worst we have to contend with, and to contend with it to the utmost. Poetry is only the highest eloquence of passion, the most vivid form of expression that can be given to our conception of anything, whether pleasurable or painful, mean or dignified, delightful or distressing. It is the perfect coincidence of the image and the words with the feeling we have, and of which we cannot get rid in any other way, that gives an instant "satisfaction to the thought". This is equally the origin of wit and fancy, of comedy and tragedy, of the sublime and pathetic. When Pope says of the Lord Mayor's show--

Now night descending, the proud scene is o'er,

But lives in Settle's numbers one day more!

when Collins makes Danger, "with limbs of giant mould".

----Throw him on the steep

Of some loose hanging rock asleep:

when Lear calls out in extreme anguish--

Ingratitude, thou marble-hearted fiend,

More hideous, when thou shew'st thee in a child,

Than the sea-monster!

the passion of contempt in the one case, of terror in the other, and of indignation in the last, is perfectly satisfied. We see the thing ourselves, and show it to others as we feel it to exist, and as, in spite of ourselves, we are compelled to think of it. The imagination, by thus embodying and turning them to shape, gives an obvious relief to the indistinct and importunate cravings of the will. We do not wish the thing to be so; but we wish it to appear such as it is. For knowledge is conscious power; and the mind is no longer in this case the dupe, though it may be the victim, of vice or folly.

Poetry is in all its shapes the language of the imagination and the passions, of fancy and will. Nothing, therefore, can be more absurd than the outcry which has been sometimes raised by frigid and pedantic critics for reducing the language of poetry to the standard of common sense and reason; for the end and use of poetry, "both at the first and now, was and is to hold the mirror up to nature", seen through the medium of passion and imagination, not divested of that medium by means of literal truth or abstract reason. The painter of history might as well be required to represent the face of a person who has just trod upon a serpent with the still-life expression of a common portrait, as the poet to describe the most striking and vivid impressions which things can be supposed to make upon the mind, in the language of common conversation.

Let who will strip nature of the colours and the shapes of fancy, the poet is not bound to do so; the impressions of common sense and strong imagination, that is, of passion and indifference, cannot be the same, and they must have a separate language to do justice to either. Objects must strike differently upon the mind, independently of what they are in themselves, as long as we have a different interest in them, as we see them in a different point of view, nearer or at a greater distance (morally or physically speaking) from novelty, from old acquaintance, from our ignorance of them, from our fear of their consequences, from contrast, from unexpected likeness.

We can no more take away the faculty of the imagination, than we can see all objects without light or shade. Some things must dazzle us by their preternatural light; others must hold us in suspense, and tempt our curiosity to explore their obscurity. Those who would dispel these various illusions, to give us their drab-coloured creation in their stead, are not very wise. Let the naturalist, if he will, catch the glow-worm, carry it home with him in a box, and find it next morning nothing but a little gray worm: let the poet or the lover of poetry visit it at evening, when beneath the scented hawthorn and the crescent moon it has built itself a palace of emerald light. This is also one part of nature, one appearance which the glow-worm presents, and that not the least interesting; so poetry is one part of the history of the human mind, though it is neither science nor philosophy. It cannot be concealed, however, that the progress of knowledge and refinement has a tendency to circumscribe the limits of the imagination, and to clip the wings of poetry.

The province of the imagination is principally visionary, the unknown and undefined: the understanding restores things to their natural boundaries, and strips them of their fanciful pretensions. Hence the history of religious and poetical enthusiasm is much the same; and both have received a sensible shock from the progress of experimental philosophy. It is the undefined and uncommon that gives birth and scope to the imagination; we can only fancy what we do not know. As in looking into the mazes of a tangled wood we fill them with what shapes we please--with ravenous beasts, with caverns vast, and drear enchantments--so in our ignorance of the world about us, we make gods or devils of the first object we see, and set no bounds to the wilful suggestions of our hopes and fears:

And visions, as poetic eyes avow,

Hang on each leaf and cling to every bough.

There can never be another Jacob's Dream. Since that time, the heavens have gone farther off, and grown astronomical. They have become averse to the imagination; nor will they return to us on the squares of the distances, or on Doctor Chalmers's Discourses. Rembrandt's picture brings the matter nearer to us. It is not only the progress of mechanical knowledge, but the necessary advances of civilization, that are unfavourable to the spirit of poetry. We not only stand in less awe of the preternatural world, but we can calculate more surely, and look with more indifference, upon the regular routine of this.

The heroes of the fabulous ages rid the world of monsters and giants. At present we are less exposed to the vicissitudes of good or evil, to the incursions of wild beasts or "bandit fierce", or to the unmitigated fury of the elements. The time has been that "our fell of hair would at a dismal treatise rouse, and stir as life were in it". But the police spoils all; and we now hardly so much as dream of a midnight murder. Macbeth is only tolerated in this country for the sake of the music; and in the United States of America, where the philosophical principles of government are carried still further in theory and practice, we find that the Beggar's Opera is hooted from the stage. Society, by degrees, is constructed into a machine that carries us safely and insipidly from one end of life to the other, in a very comfortable prose style:

Obscurity her curtain round them drew,

And siren Sloth a dull quietus sung.

The remarks which have been here made, would, in some measure, lead to a solution of the question of the comparative merits of painting and poetry. I do not mean to give any preference, but it should seem that the argument which has been sometimes set up, that painting must affect the imagination more strongly, because it represents the image more distinctly, is not well founded. We may assume without much temerity that poetry is more poetical than painting. When artists or connoisseurs talk on stilts about the poetry of painting, they show that they know little about poetry, and have little love for the art. Painting gives the object itself; poetry what it implies. Painting embodies what a thing contains in itself; poetry suggests what exists out of it, in any manner connected with it. But this last is the proper province of the imagination. Again, as it relates to passion, painting gives the event, poetry the progress of events; but it is during the progress, in the interval of expectation and suspense, while our hopes and fears are strained to the highest pitch of breathless agony, that the pinch of the interest lies:

Between the acting of a dreadful thing
And the first motion, all the interim is
Like a phantasma, or a hideous dream
The mortal instruments are then in council;
And the state of man, like to a little kingdom,
Suffers then the nature of an insurrection.

But by the time that the picture is painted, all is over. Faces are the best part of a picture; but even faces are not what we chiefly remember in what interests us most. But it may be asked then, Is there anything better than Claude Lorraine's landscapes, than Titian's portraits, than Raphael's cartoons, or the Greek statues? Of the two first I shall say nothing, as they are evidently picturesque rather than imaginative.

Raphael's cartoons are certainly the finest comments that ever were made on the Scriptures. Would their effect be the same if we were not acquainted with the text? But the New Testament existed before the cartoons. There is one subject of which there is no cartoon: Christ washing the feet of the disciples the night before His death. But that chapter does not need a commentary. It is for want of some such resting-place for the imagination that the Greek statues are little else than specious forms. They are marble to the touch and to the heart. They have not an informing principle within them. In their faultless excellence they appear sufficient to themselves. By their beauty they are raised above the frailties of passion or suffering. By their beauty they are deified. But they are not objects of religious faith to us, and their forms are a reproach to common humanity. They seem to have no sympathy with us, and not to want our admiration.

Poetry in its matter and form is natural imagery or feeling, combined with passion and fancy. In its mode of conveyance, it combines the ordinary use of language with musical expression. There is a question of long standing in what the essence of poetry consists, or what it is that determines why one set of ideas should be expressed in prose, another in verse. Milton has told us his idea of poetry in a single line:

Thoughts that voluntary move

Harmonious numbers.

As there are certain sounds that excite certain movements, and the song and dance go together, so there are, no doubt, certain thoughts that lead to certain tones of voice, or modulations of sound, and change "the words of Mercury into the songs of Apollo". There is a striking instance of this adaptation of the movement of sound and rhythm to the subject, in Spenser's description of the Satyrs accompanying Una to the cave of Sylvanus:

So from the ground she fearless doth arise,

And walketh forth without suspect of crime.

They, all as glad as birds of joyous prime,

Thence lead her forth, about her dancing round,

Shouting and singing all a shepherd's rhyme;

And with green branches strewing all the ground,

Do worship her as queen with olive garland crown'd.

And all the way their merry pipes they sound,

That all the woods and doubled echoes ring;
And with their horned feet do wear the ground,
Leaping like wanton kids in pleasant spring;
So towards old Sylvanus they her bring,
Who with the noise awaked, cometh out.

On the contrary, there is nothing either musical or natural in the ordinary construction of language. It is a thing altogether arbitrary and conventional. Neither in the sounds themselves, which are the voluntary signs of certain ideas, nor in their grammatical arrangements in common speech, is there any principle of natural imitation, or correspondence to the individual ideas or to the tone of feeling with which they are conveyed to others. The jerks, the breaks, the inequalities and harshnesses of prose are fatal to the flow of a poetical imagination, as a jolting road or a stumbling horse disturbs the reverie of an absent man. But poetry "makes these odds all even". It is the music of language, answering to the music of the mind, untying, as it were, "the secret soul of harmony".

Wherever any object takes such a hold of the mind as to make us dwell upon it, and brood over it, melting the heart in tenderness, or kindling it to a sentiment of enthusiasm; wherever a movement of imagination or passion is impressed on the mind, by which it seeks to prolong and repeat the emotion, to bring all other objects into accord with it, and to give the same movement of harmony, sustained and continuous, or gradually varied, according to the occasion, to the sounds that express it--this is poetry. The musical in sound is the sustained and continuous; the musical in thought is the sustained and continuous also. There is a near connection between music and deep-rooted passion.

Mad people sing. As often as articulation passes naturally into intonation, there poetry begins. Where one idea gives a tone and colour to others, where one feeling melts others into it, there can be no reason why the same principle should not be extended to the sounds by which the voice utters these emotions of the soul, and blends syllables and lines into each other. It is to supply the inherent defect of harmony in the customary mechanism of language, to make the sound an echo to the sense, when the sense becomes a sort of echo to itself--to mingle the tide of verse, "the golden cadences of poetry", with the tide of feeling, flowing and murmuring as it flows--in short, to take the language of the imagination from off the ground, and enable it to spread its wings where it may indulge its own impulses:

Sailing with supreme dominion
Through the azure deep of air--

without being stopped, or fretted, or diverted with the abruptnesses and petty obstacles, and discordant flats and sharps of prose, that poetry was invented. It is to common language what springs are to a carriage, or wings to feet. In ordinary speech we arrive at a certain harmony by the modulations of the voice: in poetry the same thing is done systematically by a regular collocation of syllables. It has been well observed, that every one who declaims warmly, or grows intent upon a subject, rises into a sort of blank verse or measured prose. The merchant, as described in Chaucer, went on his way "sounding always the increase of his winning". Every prose writer has more or less of rhythmical adaptation, except poets who, when deprived of the regular mechanism of verse, seem to have no principle of modulation left in their writings.

An excuse might be made for rhyme in the same manner. It is but fair that the ear should linger on the sounds that delight it, or avail itself of the same brilliant coincidence and unexpected recurrence of syllables, that have been displayed in the invention and collocation of images. It is allowed that rhyme assists the memory; and a man of wit and shrewdness has been heard to say, that the only four good lines of poetry are the well-known ones which tell the number of days in the months of the year:

Thirty days hath September, &c.

But if the jingle of names assists the memory, may it not also quicken the fancy? and there are other things worth having at our fingers' ends, besides the contents of the almanac. Pope's versification is tiresome from its excessive sweetness and uniformity. Shakespeare's blank verse is the perfection of dramatic dialogue.

All is not poetry that passes for such: nor does verse make the whole difference between poetry and prose. The Iliad does not cease to be poetry in a literal translation; and Addison's Campaign has been very properly denominated a Gazette in rhyme. Common prose differs from poetry, as treating for the most part either of such trite, familiar, and irksome matters of fact, as convey no extraordinary impulse to the imagination, or else of such difficult and laborious processes of the understanding, as do not admit of the wayward or violent movements either of the imagination or the passions.

I will mention three works which come as near to poetry as possible without absolutely being so; namely, the Pilgrim's Progress, Robinson Crusoe, and the Tales of Boccaccio. Chaucer and Dryden have translated some of the last into English rhyme, but the essence and the power of poetry was there before. That which lifts the spirit above the earth, which draws the soul out of itself with indescribable longings, is poetry in kind, and generally fit to become so in name, by being "married to immortal verse". If it is of the essence of poetry to strike and fix the imagination, whether we will or no, to make the eye of childhood glisten with the starting tear, to be never thought of afterwards with indifference, John Bunyan and Daniel Defoe may be permitted to pass for poets in their way.

The mixture of fancy and reality in the Pilgrim's Progress was never equalled in any allegory. His pilgrims walk above the earth, and yet are on it. What zeal, what beauty, what truth of fiction! What deep feeling in the description of Christian's swimming across the water at last, and in the picture of the Shining Ones within the gates, with wings at their backs and garlands on their heads, who are to wipe all tears from his eyes! The writer's genius, though not "dipped in dews of Castalie", was baptized with the Holy Spirit and with fire. The prints in this book are no small part of it. If the confinement of Philoctetes in the island of Lemnos was a subject for the most beautiful of all the Greek tragedies, what shall we say to Robinson Crusoe in his? Take the speech of the Greek hero on leaving his cave, beautiful as it is, and compare it with the reflections of the English adventurer in his solitary place of confinement. The thoughts of home, and of all from which he is for ever cut off, swell and press against his bosom, as the heaving ocean rolls its ceaseless tide against the rocky shore, and the very beatings of his heart become audible in the eternal silence that surrounds him. Thus he says:

> As I walked about, either in my hunting, or for viewing the country, the anguish of my soul at my condition would break out upon me on a sudden, and my very heart would die within me to think of the woods, the mountains, and deserts I was in; and how I was a prisoner, locked up with the eternal bars and bolts of the ocean, in an uninhabited wilderness, without redemption. In the midst of the greatest composures of my mind, this would break out upon me like a storm, and make me wring my hands, and weep like a child. Sometimes it would take me in the middle of my work, and I would immediately sit down and sigh, and look upon the ground for an hour or two together, and this was still worse to me, for if I could burst into tears or vent myself in words, it would go off, and the grief having exhausted itself would abate.

The story of his adventures would not make a poem like the Odyssey, it is true; but the relater had the true genius of a poet. It has been made a question whether Richardson's romances are poetry; and the answer perhaps is, that they are not poetry, because they are not romance. The interest-is worked up to an inconceivable height; but it is by an infinite number of little things, by incessant labour and calls upon the attention, by a repetition of blows that have no rebound in them. The sympathy excited is not a voluntary contribution, but a tax. Nothing is unforced and spontaneous. There is a want of elasticity and motion. The story does not "give an echo to the seat where love is throned".

The heart does not answer of itself like a chord in music. The fancy does not run on before the writer with breathless expectation, but is dragged along with an infinite number of pins and wheels, like those with which the Liliputians dragged Gulliver pinioned to the royal palace. Sir Charles Grandison is a coxcomb. What sort of a figure would he cut, translated into an epic poem, by the side of Achilles? Clarissa, the divine Clarissa, is too interesting by half. She is interesting in her ruffles, in her gloves, her samplers, her aunts and uncles--she is interesting in all that is uninteresting. Such things, however intensely they may be brought home to us, are not conductors to the imagination. There is infinite truth and feeling in Richardson; but it is extracted from a caput mortuum of circumstances: it does not evaporate of itself. His poetical genius is like Ariel confined in a pine-tree, and requires an artificial process to let it out. Shakespeare says:

Our poesy is as a gum, which oozes
From whence 'tis nourished... our gentle flame
Provokes itself, and, like the current, flies
Each bound it chafes.

I shall conclude this general account with some remarks on four of the principal works of poetry in the world, at different periods of history--Homer, the Bible, Dante, and, let me add, Ossian. In Homer, the principle of action or life is predominant: in the Bible, the principle of faith and the idea of Providence; Dante is a personification of blind will; and in Ossian we see the decay of life and the lag end of the world. Homer's poetry is the heroic: it is full of life and action: it is bright as the day, strong as a river. In the vigour of his intellect, he grapples with all the objects of nature, and enters into all the relations of social life. He saw many countries, and the manners of many men; and he has brought them all together in his poem.

He describes his heroes going to battle with a prodigality of life, arising from an exuberance of animal spirits: we see them before us, their number and their order of battle, poured out upon the plain "all plumed like ostriches, like eagles newly bathed, wanton as goats, wild as young bulls, youthful as May, and gorgeous as the sun at midsummer", covered with glittering armour, with dust and blood; while the gods quaff their nectar in golden cups, or mingle in the fray; and the old men assembled on the walls of Troy rise up with reverence as Helen passes by them. The multitude of things in Homer is wonderful; their splendour, their truth, their force and variety. His poetry is, like his religion, the poetry of number and form: he describes the bodies as well as the souls of men.

The poetry of the Bible is that of imagination and of faith: it is abstract and disembodied: it is not the poetry of form, but of power; not of multitude, but of immensity. It does not divide into many, but aggrandizes into one. Its ideas of nature are like its ideas of God. It is not the poetry of social life, but of solitude: each man seems alone in the world, with the original forms of nature, the rocks, the earth, and the sky. It is not the poetry of action or heroic enterprise, but of faith in a supreme Providence, and resignation to the power that governs the universe.

As the idea of God was removed farther from humanity and a scattered polytheism, it became more profound and intense, as it became more universal, for the Infinite is present to everything: "If we fly into the uttermost parts of the earth, it is there also; if we turn to the east or the west, we cannot escape from it". Man is thus aggrandized in the image of his Maker. The history of the patriarchs is of this kind; they are founders of a chosen race of people, the inheritors of the earth; they exist in the generations which are to come after them. Their poetry, like their religious creed, is vast, unformed, obscure, and infinite; a vision is upon it; an invisible hand is suspended over it.

The spirit of the Christian religion consists in the glory hereafter to be revealed; but in the Hebrew dispensation Providence took an immediate share in the affairs of this life.

Jacob's dream arose out of this intimate communion between heaven and earth: it was this that let down, in the sight of the youthful patriarch, a golden ladder from the sky to the earth, with angels ascending and descending upon it, and shed a light upon the lonely place, which can never pass away.

The story of Ruth, again, is as if all the depth of natural affection in the human race was involved in her breast. There are descriptions in the book of Job more prodigal of imagery, more intense in passion, than anything in Homer; as that of the state of his prosperity, and of the vision that came upon him by night.

The metaphors in the Old Testament are more boldly figurative. Things were collected more into masses, and gave a greater momentum to the imagination.

Dante was the father of modern poetry, and he may therefore claim a place in this connection. His poem is the first great step from Gothic darkness and barbarism; and the struggle of thought in it, to burst the thraldom in which the human mind had been so long held, is felt in every page. He stood bewildered, not appalled, on that dark shore which separates the ancient and the modern world; and saw the glories of antiquity dawning through the abyss of time, while revelation opened its passage to the other world.

He was lost in wonder at what had been done before him, and he dared to emulate it. Dante seems to have been indebted to the Bible for the gloomy tone of his mind, as well as for the prophetic fury which exalts and kindles his poetry; but he is utterly unlike Homer. His genius is not a sparkling flame, but the sullen heat of a furnace.

He is power, passion, self-will personified. In all that relates to the descriptive or fanciful part of poetry, he bears no comparison to many who had gone before, or who have come after him; but there is a gloomy abstraction in his conceptions, which lies like a dead weight upon the mind--a benumbing stupor, a breathless awe, from the intensity of the impression--a terrible obscurity, like that which oppresses us in dreams--an identity of interest, which moulds every object to its own purposes, and clothes all things with the passions and imaginations of the human soul--that make amends for all other deficiencies.

The immediate objects he presents to the mind are not much in themselves; they want grandeur, beauty, and order; but they become everything by the force of the character he impresses upon them.

His mind lends its own power to the objects which it contemplates, instead of borrowing it from them. He takes advantage even of the nakedness and dreary vacuity of his subject. His imagination peoples the shades of death, and broods over the silent air.

He is the severest of all writers, the most hard and impenetrable, the most opposite to the flowery and glittering; the writer who relies most on his own power, and the sense of it in others, and who leaves most room to the imagination of his readers. Dante's only endeavour is to interest; and he interests by exciting our sympathy with the emotion by which he is himself possessed. He does not place before us the objects by which that emotion has been created; but he seizes on the attention, by showing us the effect they produce on his feelings; and his poetry accordingly gives the same thrilling and overwhelming sensation which is caught by gazing on the face of a person who has seen some object of horror.

The improbability of the events, the abruptness and monotony in the Inferno, are excessive: but the interest never flags, from the continued earnestness of the author's mind. Dante's great power is in combining internal feelings with external objects.

Thus the gate of hell, on which that withering inscription is written, seems to be endowed with speech and consciousness, and to utter its dread warning, not without a sense of mortal woes. This author habitually unites the absolutely local and individual with the greatest wildness and mysticism.

In the midst of the obscure and shadowy regions of the lower world, a tomb suddenly rises up with the inscription, "I am the tomb of Pope Anastasius the Sixth": and half the personages whom he has crowded into the Inferno are his own acquaintance.

All this, perhaps, tends to heighten the effect by the bold intermixture of realities, and by an appeal, as it were, to the individual knowledge and experience of the reader. He affords few subjects for picture. There is, indeed, one gigantic one, that of Count Ugolino, of which Michael Angelo made a basrelief, and which Sir Joshua Reynolds ought not to have painted.

Another writer whom I shall mention last, and whom I cannot persuade myself to think a mere modern in the groundwork, is Ossian. He is a feeling and a name that can never be destroyed in the minds of his readers. As Homer is the first vigour and lustihead, Ossian is the decay and old age of poetry.

He lives only in the recollection and regret of the past. There is one impression which he conveys more entirely than all other poets; namely, the sense of privation, the loss of all things, of friends, of good name, of country; he is even without God in the world. He converses only with the spirits of the departed; with the motionless and silent clouds. The cold moonlight sheds its faint lustre on his head; the fox peeps out of the ruined tower; the thistle waves its beard to the wandering gale; and the strings of his harp seem, as the hand of age, as the tale of other times, passes over them, to sigh and rustle like the dry reeds in the winter's wind!

The feeling of cheerless desolation, of the loss of the pith and sap of existence, of the annihilation of the substance, and the clinging to the shadow of all things, as in a mock-embrace, is here perfect.

In this way, the lamentation of Selma for the loss of Salgar is the finest of all. If it were indeed possible to show that this writer was nothing, it would only be another instance of mutability, another blank made, another void left in the heart, another confirmation of that feeling which makes him so often complain, "Roll on, ye dark brown years, ye bring no joy on your wing to Ossian!"

7

THE ARTIFICIAL COMEDY OF THE LAST CENTURY

CHARLES LAMB

The essay on the Artificial Comedy of the Last Century is one of the Essays of Elia, published in the London Magazine between 1820 and 1822. The paradox started by Lamb was taken up by Leigh Hunt in his edition of the Comic Dramatists of the Restoration, and was attacked by Macaulay in his well-known review of Hunt's work. It is characteristic of Lamb to have bound up his defence of these writers with an account of Kemble and other actors of the day. His peculiar strength lay in his power of throwing himself into the very mood and temper of the writers he admired, and no critic has more completely possessed the secret of living over again the life of a literary masterpiece.

His genius was, in fact, akin to the genius of an actor, an actor who, not for the moment but permanently, becomes the part that he seeks to represent. And he was never so much at home as when he was illustrating his own reading of a drama from the tones and gestures of the stage. It may be doubted whether, under stress of this impulse, he was not led to force the analogy between Sheridan and the dramatists of the Restoration. The analogy doubtless exists, but in his wish to bring home to his readers the inner meaning of plays, then no longer acted, he was perhaps tempted to press a resemblance to works, familiar to every play-goer, further than it could fairly be made to go.

The mistake, if mistake it were, is pardonable. And it serves to illustrate the essential nature of Lamb's genius as a critic, and of the new element that he brought into criticism. This was the invincible belief that poetry is not merely an art for the few, but something that finds an echo in the common instincts of all men, something that, coming from the heart, naturally clothes itself in fitting words and gives individual colour to each tone, gesture, and expression. These, therefore, we must study if we would penetrate to the open secret of the artist, if we would seize the vital spirit of his utterance and make it our own. Lamb's sense of poetic form, his instinct for subtle shades of difference, was far keener than Hazlitt's. And for that very reason he may be said to have seen yet more clearly than Hazlitt saw, how inseparable is the tie that binds poetry to life. It is not only in its deeper undertones, Lamb seems to remind us, but in its finest shades of voice and phrasing, that poetry is the echo of some mood or temper of the soul. This is the vein that he opened, and which, with wider scope and a touch still more delicate, has since been explored by Mr. Pater.

The two shorter pieces speak for themselves. They are taken from the Specimens of English Dramatic Poets (1808).

The artificial comedy, or comedy of manners, is quite extinct on our stage. Congreve and Farquhar show their heads once in seven years only, to be exploded and put down instantly. The times cannot bear this. Is it for a few wild speeches, an occasional licence of dialogue? I think not altogether. The business of their dramatic characters will not stand the moral test. We screw everything up to that. Idle gallantry in a fiction, a dream, the passing pageant of an evening, startles us in the same way as the alarming indications of profligacy in a son or ward in real life should startle a parent or guardian. We have no such middle emotions as dramatic interests left. We see a stage libertine playing his loose pranks of two hours' duration, and of no after consequence, with the severe eyes which inspect real vices with their bearings upon two worlds. We are spectators to a plot or intrigue (not reducible in life to the point of strict morality), and take it all for truth. We substitute a real for a dramatic person, and judge him accordingly. We try him in our courts, from which there is no appeal to the dramatis persona, his peers.

We have been spoiled with--not sentimental comedy--but a tyrant far more pernicious to our pleasures which has succeeded to it, the exclusive and all-devouring drama of common life; where the moral point is everything; where, instead of the fictitious half-believed personages of the stage (the phantoms of old comedy), we recognize ourselves, our brothers, aunts, kinsfolk, allies, patrons, enemies,--the same as in life,--with an interest in what is going on so hearty and substantial, that we cannot afford our moral judgment, in its deepest and most vital results, to compromise or slumber for a moment.

What is there transacting, by no modification is made to affect us in any other manner than the same events or characters would do in our relationships of life. We carry our fireside concerns to the theatre with us. We do not go thither like our ancestors, to escape from the pressure of reality, so much as to confirm our experience of it; to make assurance double, and take a bond of fate. We must live our toilsome lives twice over, as it was the mournful privilege of Ulysses to descend twice to the shades. All that neutral ground of character, which stood between vice and virtue; or which in fact was indifferent to neither, where neither properly was called in question; that happy breathing-place from the burthen of a perpetual moral questioning--the sanctuary and quiet Alsatia of hunted casuistry--is broken up and disfranchised, as injurious to the interests of society.

The privileges of the place are taken away by law. We dare not dally with images, or names, of wrong. We bark like foolish dogs at shadows. We dread infection from the scenic representation of disorder, and fear a painted pustule. In our anxiety that our morality should not take cold, we wrap it up in a great blanket surtout of precaution against the breeze and sunshine.

I confess for myself that (with no great delinquencies to answer for) I am glad for a season to take an airing beyond the diocese of the strict conscience,--not to live always in the precincts of the law- courts,--but now and then, for a dream-while or so, to imagine a world with no meddling restrictions--to get into recesses, whither the hunter cannot follow me-

Secret shades
Of woody Ida's inmost grove,
While yet there was no fear of Jove.

I come back to my cage and my restraint the fresher and more healthy for it. I wear my shackles more contentedly for having respired the breath of an imaginary freedom. I do not know how it is with others, but I feel the better always for the perusal of one of Congreve's-- nay, why should I not add even of Wycherley's--comedies. I am the gayer at least for it; and I could never connect those sports of a witty fancy in any shape with any result to be drawn from them to imitation in real life. They are a world of themselves almost as much as fairy-land.

Take one of their characters, male or female (with few exceptions they are alike), and place it in a modern play, and my virtuous indignation shall rise against the profligate wretch as warmly as the Catos of the pit could desire; because in a modern play I am to judge of the right and the wrong. The standard of police is the measure of political justice. The atmosphere will blight it; it cannot live here. It has got into a moral world, where it has no business, from which it must needs fall headlong; as dizzy, and incapable of making a stand, as a Sweden-borgian bad spirit that has wandered unawares into the sphere of one of his Good Men, or Angels. But in its own world do we feel the creature is so very bad?--The Fainalls and the Mirabels, the Dorimants and the Lady - Touchwoods, in their own sphere, do not offend my moral sense; in fact, they do not appeal to it at all.

They seem engaged in their proper element. They break through no laws or conscientious restraints. They know of none. They have got out of Christendom into the land--what shall I call it?-of cuckoldry--the Utopia of gallantry, where pleasure is duty, and the manners perfect freedom. It is altogether a speculative scene of things, which has no reference whatever to the world that is. No good person can be justly offended as a spectator, because no good person suffers on the stage. Judged morally, every character in these plays--the few exceptions only are mistakes--is alike essentially vain and worthless. The great art of Congreve is specially shown in this, that he has entirely excluded from his scenes--some little generosities in the part of Angelica In Love for Love perhaps excepted--not only anything like a faultless character, but any pretensions to goodness or good feelings whatsoever.

Whether he did this designedly, or instinctively, the effect is as happy as the design (if design) was bold. I used to wonder at the strange power which his Way of the World in particular possesses of interesting you all along in the pursuits of characters, for whom you absolutely care nothing--for you neither hate nor love his personages--and I think it is owing to this very indifference for any, that you endure the whole. He has spread a privation of moral light, I will call it, rather than by the ugly name of palpable darkness, over his creations; and his shadows flit before you without distinction or preference. Had he introduced a good character, a single gush of moral feeling, a revulsion of the judgment to actual life and actual duties, the impertinent Goshen would have only lighted to the discovery of deformities, which now are none, because we think them none.

Translated into real life, the characters of his, and his friend Wycherley's dramas, are profligates and strumpets,--the business of their brief existence, the undivided pursuit of lawless gallantry. No other spring of action, or possible motive of conduct, is recognized; principles which, universally acted upon, must reduce this frame of things to a chaos. But we do them wrong in so translating them. No such effects are produced, in their world. When we are among them, we are amongst a chaotic people. We are not to judge them by our usages. No reverend institutions are insulted by their proceedings--for they have none among them. No peace of families is violated--for no family ties exist among them. No purity of the marriage bed is stained--for none is supposed to have a being. No deep affections are disquieted, no holy wedlock bands are snapped asunder--for affection's depth and wedded faith are not of the growth of that soil. There is neither right nor wrong,--gratitude or its opposite,--claim or duty,--paternity or sonship. Of what consequence is it to Virtue, or how is she at all concerned about it, whether Sir Simon or Dapperwit steal away Miss Martha; or who is the father of Lord Froth's or Sir Paul Pliant's children?

The whole is a passing pageant, where we should sit as unconcerned at the issues, for life or death, as at the battle of the frogs and mice. But, like Don Quixcte, we take part against the puppets, and quite as impertinently. We dare not contemplate an Atlantis, a scheme out of which our coxcombical moral sense is for a little transitory ease excluded. We have not the courage to imagine a state of things for which there is neither reward nor punishment. We cling to the painful necessities of shame and blame. We would indict our very dreams.

Amidst the mortifying circumstances attendant upon growing old, it is something to have seen the School for Scandal in its glory. This comedy grew out of Congreve and Wycherley, but gathered some allays of the sentimental comedy which followed theirs. It is impossible that it should be now acted, though it continues, at long intervals, to be announced in the bills. Its hero, when Palmer played it at least, was Joseph Surface. When I remember the gay boldness, the graceful solemn plausibility, the measured step, the insinuating voice--to express it in a word--the downright acted villany of the part, so different from the pressure of conscious actual wickedness,--the hypocritical assumption of hypocrisy,--which made Jack so deservedly a favourite in that character, I must needs conclude the present generation of playgoers more virtuous than myself, or more dense.

I freely confess that he divided the palm with me with his better brother; that, in fact, I liked him quite as well. Not but there are passages,--like that, for instance, where Joseph is made to refuse a pittance to a poor relation,--incongruities which Sheridan was forced upon by the attempt to join the artificial with the sentimental comedy, either of which must destroy the other--but over these obstructions Jack's manner floated him so lightly, that a refusal from him no more shocked you, than the easy compliance of Charles gave you in reality any pleasure; you got over the paltry question as quickly as you could, to get back into the regions of pure comedy, where no cold moral reigns.

The highly artificial manner of Palmer in this character counteracted every disagreeable impression which you might have received from the contrast, supposing them real, between the two brothers. You did not believe in Joseph with the same faith with which you believed in Charles. The latter was a pleasant reality, the former a no less pleasant poetical foil to it.

The comedy, I have said, is incongruous; a mixture of Congreve with sentimental incompatibilities; the gaiety upon the whole is buoyant; but it required the consummate art of Palmer to reconcile the discordant elements.

A player with Jack's talents, if we had one now, would not dare to do the part in the same manner. He would instinctively avoid every turn which might tend to unrealize, and so to make the character fascinating.

He must takē his cue from his spectators, who would expect a bad man and a good man as rigidly opposed to each other as the deathbeds of those geniuses are contrasted in the prints, which I am sorry to say have disappeared from the windows of my old friend Carrington Bowles, of St. Paul's Churchyard memory--(an exhibition as venerable as the adjacent cathedral, and almost coeval) of the bad and good man at the hour of death; where the ghastly apprehensions of the former,--and truly the grim phantom with his reality of a toasting-fork is not to be despised,--so finely contrast with the meek complacent kissing of the rod,--taking it in like honey and butter,--with which the latter submits to the scythe of the gentle bleeder, Time, who wields his lancet with the apprehensive finger of a popular young ladies' surgeon.

What flesh, like loving grass, would not covet to meet half-way the stroke of such a delicate mower?

John Palmer was twice an actor in this exquisite part. He was playing to you all the while that he was playing upon Sir Peter and his lady. You had the first intimation of a sentiment before it was on his lips.

His altered voice was meant to you, and you were to suppose that his fictitious co-flutterers on the stage perceived nothing at all of it. What was it to you if that half reality, the husband, was overreached by the puppetry--or the thin thing (Lady Teazle's reputation) was persuaded it was dying of a plethory?

The fortunes of Othello and Desdemona were not concerned in it. Poor Jack has passed from the stage in good time, that he did not live to this our age of seriousness. The pleasant old Teazle King, too, is gone in good time.

His manner would scarce have passed current in our day. We must love or hate--acquit or condemn--censure or pity--exert our detestable coxcombry of moral judgment upon everything. Joseph Surface, to go down now, must be a downright revolting villain--no compromise--his first appearance must shock and give horror--his specious plausibilities, which the pleasurable faculties of our fathers welcomed with such hearty greetings, knowing that no harm (dramatic harm even) could come, or was meant to come, of them, must inspire a cold and killing aversion.

Charles (the real canting person of the scene--for the hypocrisy of Joseph has its ulterior legitimate ends, but his brother's professions of a good heart centre in down right self-satisfaction) must be loved and Joseph hated.

To balance one disagreeable reality with another, Sir Peter Teazle must be no longer the comic idea of a fretful old bachelor bridegroom, whose teasings (while King acted it) were evidently as much played off at you, as they were meant to concern anybody on the stage,--he must be a real person, capable in law of sustaining an injury--a person towards whom duties are to be acknowledged--the genuine crim. con. antagonist of the villainous seducer Joseph.

To realize him more, his sufferings under his unfortunate match must have the downright pungency of life--must (or should) make you not mirthful but uncomfortable, just as the same predicament would move you in a neighbour or old friend.

The delicious scenes which give the play its name and zest, must affect you in the same serious manner as if you heard the reputation of a dear female friend attacked in your real presence. Crabtree and Sir Benjamin--those poor snakes that live but in the sunshine of your mirth--must be ripened by this hot-bed process of realization into asps or amphisbaenas; and Mrs. Candour--O! frightful!--become a hooded serpent.

Oh! who that remembers Parsons and Dodd--the wasp and butterfly of the School for Scandal --in those two characters; and charming natural Miss Pope, the perfect gentle woman as distinguished from the fine lady of comedy, in the latter part--would forego the true scenic delight--the escape from life--the oblivion of consequences--the holiday barring out of the pedant Reflection--those Saturnalia of two or three brief hours, well won from the world--to sit instead at one of our modern plays--to have his coward conscience (that forsooth must not be left for a moment) stimulated with perpetual appeals--dulled rather, and blunted, as a faculty without repose must be--and his moral vanity pampered with images of notional justice, notional beneficence, lives saved without the spectator's risk, and fortunes given away that cost the author nothing?

No piece was, perhaps, ever so completely cast in all its parts as this manager's comedy. Miss Farren had succeeded to Mrs. Abington in Lady Teazle; and Smith, the original Charles, had retired when I first saw it.

The rest of the characters, with very slight exceptions, remained. I remember it was then the fashion to cry down John Kemble, who took the part of Charles after Smith; but, I thought, very unjustly.

Smith, I fancy, was more airy, and took the eye with a certain gaiety of person. He brought with him no sombre recollections of tragedy. He had not to expiate the fault of having pleased beforehand in lofty declamation. He had no sins of Hamlet or of Richard to atone for. His failure in these parts was a passport to success in one of so opposite a tendency. But, as far as I could judge, the weighty sense of Kemble made up for more personal incapacity than he had to answer for.

His harshest tones in this part came steeped and dulcified in good-humour. He made his defects a grace. His exact declamatory manner, as he managed it, only served to convey the points of his dialogue with more precision. It seemed to head the shafts to carry them deeper. Not one of his sparkling sentences was lost. I remember minutely how he delivered each in succession, and cannot by any effort imagine how any of them could be altered for the better.

No man could deliver brilliant dialogue-the dialogue of Congreve or of Wycherley-because none understood it-half so well as John Kemble. His Valentine, in Love for Love, was, to my recollection, faultless. He flagged sometimes in the intervals of tragic passion. He would slumber over the level parts of an heroic character.

His Macbeth has been known to nod. But he always seemed to me to be particularly alive to pointed and witty dialogue. The relaxing levities of tragedy have not been touched by any since him--the playful court-bred spirit in which he condescended to the players in Hamlet--the sportive relief which he threw into the darker shades of Richard--disappeared with him.

He had his sluggish moods, his torpors--but they were the halting-stones and resting-place of his tragedy--politic savings, and fetches of the breath--husbandry of the lungs, where nature pointed him to be an economist--rather, I think, than errors of the judgment. They were, at worst, less painful than the eternal, tormenting, unappeasable vigilance,--the "lidless dragon eyes", of present fashionable tragedy.

WEBSTER'S DUCHESS OF MALFI

All the several parts of the dreadful apparatus with which the Duchess's death is ushered in, are not more remote from the conceptions of ordinary vengeance, than the strange character of suffering which they seem to bring upon their victims is beyond the imagination of ordinary poets.

As they are not like inflictions of this life, so her language seems not of this world. She has lived among horrors till she is become "native and endowed unto that element". She speaks the dialect of despair, her tongue has a snatch of Tartarus and the souls in bale.--What are "Luke's iron crown", the brazen bull of Perillus, Procrustes' bed, to the waxen images which counterfeit death, to the wild masque of madmen, the tomb-maker, the bellman, the living person's dirge, the mortification by degrees!

To move a horror skilfully, to touch a soul to the quick, to lay upon fear as much as it can bear, to wean and weary a life till it is ready to drop, and then step in with mortal instruments to take its last forfeit--this only a Webster can do. Writers of an inferior genius may "upon horror's head horrors accumulate", but they cannot do this. They mistake quantity for quality, they "terrify babes with painted devils", but they know not how a soul is capable of being moved; their terrors want dignity, their affrightments are without decorum.

ON FORD'S BROKEN HEART

I do not know where to find in any play a catastrophe so grand, so solemn, and so surprising as this. This is indeed, according to Milton, to "describe high passions and high actions". The fortitude of the Spartan boy who let a beast gnaw out his bowels till he died without expressing a groan, is a faint bodily image of this dilaceration of the spirit and exenteration of the inmost mind, which Calantha with a holy violence against her nature keeps closely covered, till the last duties of a wife and a queen are fulfilled. Stories of martyrdom are but of chains and the stake; a little bodily suffering; these torments

On the purest spirits prey

As on entrails, joints, and limbs,

With answerable pains, but more intense.

What a noble thing is the soul in its strengths and in its weaknesses! who would be less weak than Calantha? who can be so strong? the expression of this transcendent scene almost bears me in imagination to Calvary and the Cross; and I seem to perceive some analogy between the scenical sufferings which I am here contemplating, and the real agonies of that final completion to which I dare no more than hint a reference.

Ford was of the first order of poets. He sought for sublimity, not by parcels in metaphors or visible images, but directly where she has her full residence in the heart of man; in the actions and sufferings of the greatest minds.

There is a grandeur of the soul above mountains, seas, and the elements. Even in the poor perverted reason of Giovanni and Annabella (in the play which precedes this) we discern traces of that fiery particle, which in the irregular starting out of the road of beaten action, discovers something of a right line even in obliquity and shows hints of an improvable greatness in the lowest descents and degradations of our nature.

8

A Defence of Poetry

PERCY BYSSHE SHELLEY

The Defence of Poetry was written in the early months of 1821, the year before Shelley's death. Its immediate occasion was an essay on The Four Ages of Poetry by T L Peacock. But all allusions to Peacock's work were cut out by John Hunt when he prepared it--in vain, as things proved--for publication in The Liberal, and it remains, as Peacock said, "a defence without an attack". For all essential purposes, the Defence can only be said to have gained by shaking off its local and temporary reference. It expresses Shelley's deepest thoughts about poetry, and marks, as clearly as any writing of the last hundred years, the width of the gulf that separates the ideals of recent poetry from those of the century preceding the French Revolution. It may be compared with Sidney's Apologie on the one hand, and with Wordsworth's Preface to the Lyrical Ballads, or the more abstract parts of Carlyle's critical writings upon the other.

The fundamental conceptions of Shelley are the same as those of the Elizabethan critic and of his own great contemporaries. But he differs from Sidney and Wordsworth, and perhaps from Carlyle also, in laying more stress upon the outward form, and particularly the musical element, of poetry, and from Sidney in laying less stress upon its directly moral associations. He thus attains to a wider and truer view of his subject, and, while insisting as strongly as Wordsworth insists upon the kinship between the matter of poetry and that of truth or science, he also recognizes, as Wordsworth commonly did not, that there is a harmony between the imaginative conception of that matter and its outward expression, and that beautiful thought must necessarily clothe itself in beauty of language and of sound. There is not in our literature any clearer presentment of the inseparable connection between the matter and form of poetry, nor of the ideal element which, under different shapes, is the life and soul of both.

According to one mode of regarding those two classes of me 'al action, which are called reason and imagination, the former may be considered as mind contemplating the relations borne by one thought to another, however produced; and the latter, as mind acting upon those thoughts so as to colour them with its own light, and composing from them, as from elements, other thoughts, each containing within itself the principle of its own integrity.

The one is the Greek transliterated: to poiein, or the principle of synthesis, and has for its objects those forms which are common to universal nature and existence itself; the other is the Greek transliterated: to logizein, or principle of analysis, and its action regards the relations of things simply as relations; considering thoughts, not in their integral unity, but as the algebraical representations which conduct to certain general results. Reason is the enumeration of qualities already known; imagination is the perception of the value of those quantities, both separately and as a whole. Reason respects the differences, and imagination the similitudes of things. Reason is to imagination as the instrument to the agent, as the body to the spirit, as the shadow to the substance.

Poetry, in a general sense, may be defined to be "the expression of the imagination": and poetry is connate with the origin of man. Man is an instrument over which a series of external and internal impressions are driven, like the alternations of an ever-changing wind over an Aolian lyre, which move it by their motion to ever-changing melody. But there is a principle within the human being, and perhaps within all sentient beings, which acts otherwise than in the lyre, and produces not melody alone, but harmony, by an internal adjustment of the sounds or motions thus excited to the impressions which excite them. It is as if the lyre could accommodate its chords to the motions of that which strikes them, in a determined proportion of sound; even as the musician can accommodate his voice to the sound of the lyre.

A child at play by itself will express its delight by its voice and motions; and every inflexion of tone and every gesture will bear exact relation to a corresponding antitype in the pleasurable impressions which awakened it; it will be the reflected image of that impression; and as the lyre trembles and sounds after the wind has died away, so the child seeks, by prolonging in its voice and motions the duration of the effect, to prolong also a consciousness of the cause. In relation to the objects which delight a child, these expressions are what poetry is to higher objects. The savage (for the savage is to ages what the child is to years) expresses the emotions produced in him by surrounding objects in a similar manner; and language and gesture, together with plastic or pictorial imitation, become the image of the combined effect of those objects, and of his apprehension of them.

Man in society, with all his passions and his pleasures, next becomes the object of the passions and pleasures of man; an additional class of emotions produces an augmented treasure of expressions; and language, gesture, and the imitative arts become at once the representation and the medium, the pencil and the picture, the chisel and the statue, the chord and the harmony. The social sympathies, or those laws from which, as from its elements, society results, begin to develop themselves from the moment that two human beings coexist; the future is contained within the present, as the plant within the seed: and equality, diversity, unity, contrast, mutual dependence, become the principles alone capable of affording the motives according to which the will of a social being is determined to action, inasmuch as he is social; and constitute pleasure in sensation, virtue in sentiment, beauty in art, truth in reasoning, and love in the intercourse of kind. Hence men, even in the infancy of society, observe a certain order in their words and actions, distinct from that of the objects and the impressions represented by them, all expression being subject to the laws of that from which it proceeds. But let us dismiss those more general considerations which might involve an inquiry into the principles of society itself, and restrict our view to the manner in which the imagination is expressed upon its forms.

In the youth of the world, men dance and sing and imitate natural objects, observing in these actions, as in all others, a certain rhythm or order. And, although all men observe a similar, they observe not the same order, in the motions of the dance, in the melody of the song, in the combinations of language, in the series of their imitations of natural objects. For there is a certain order or rhythm belonging to each of these classes of mimetic representation, from which the hearer and the spectator receive an intenser and purer pleasure than from any other: the sense of an approximation to this order has been called taste by modern writers. Every man in the infancy of art observes an order which approximates more or less closely to that from which this highest delight results; but the diversity is not sufficiently marked, as that its gradations should be sensible, except in those instances where the predominance of this faculty of approximation to the beautiful (for so we may be permitted to name the relation between this highest pleasure and its cause) is very great.

Those in whom it exists in excess are poets, in the most universal sense of the word; and the pleasure resulting from the manner in which they express the influence of society or nature upon their own minds, communicates itself to others, and gathers a sort of reduplication from that community. Their language is vitally metaphorical; that is, it marks the before unapprehended relations of things and perpetuates their apprehension, until the words which represent them, become, through time, signs for portions or classes of thoughts instead of pictures of integral thoughts; and then, if no new poets should arise to create afresh the associations which have been thus disorganized, language will be dead to all the nobler purposes of human intercourse.

These similitudes or relations are finely said by Lord Bacon to be "the same footsteps of nature impressed upon the various subjects of the world" De Augment. Scient., cap. I, lib. iii.--and he considers the faculty which perceives them as the storehouse of axioms common to all knowledge. In the infancy of society every author is necessarily a poet, because language itself is poetry; and to be a poet is to apprehend the true and the beautiful; in a word, the good which exists in the relation subsisting, first between existence and perception, and secondly between perception and expression. Every original language near to its source is in itself the chaos of a cyclic poem: the copiousness of lexicography and the distinctions of grammar are the works of a later age, and are merely the catalogue and the form of the creations of poetry.

But poets, or those who imagine and express this indestructible order, are not only the authors of language and of music, of the dance, and architecture, and statuary, and painting: they are the institutors of laws, and the founders of civil society, and the inventors of the arts of life, and the teachers, who draw into a certain propinquity with the beautiful and the true, that partial apprehension of the agencies of the invisible world which is called religion. Hence all original religions are allegorical, or susceptible of allegory, and, like Janus, have a double face of false and true. Poets, according to the circumstances of the age and nation in which they appeared, were called, in the earlier epochs of the world, legislators, or prophets: a poet essentially comprises and unites both these characters.

For he not only beholds intensely the present as it is, and discovers those laws according to which present things ought to be ordered, but he beholds the future in the present, and his thoughts are the germs of the flower and the fruit of latest time. Not that I assert poets to be prophets in the gross sense of the word, or that they can foretell the form as surely as they foreknow the spirit of events: such is the pretence of superstition, which would make poetry an attribute of prophecy rather than prophecy an attribute of poetry. A poet participates in the eternal, the infinite, and the one; as far as relates to his conceptions, time and place and number are not. The grammatical forms which express the moods of time, and the difference of persons, and the distinction of place, are convertible with respect to the highest poetry without injuring it as poetry; and the choruses of Aschylus, and the book of Job, and Dante's Paradise, would afford, more than any other writings, examples of this fact, if the limits of this essay did not forbid citation. The creations of sculpture, painting, and music are illustrations still more decisive.

Language, colour, form, and religious and civil habits of action are all the instruments and materials of poetry; they may be called poetry by that figure of speech which considers the effect as a synonym of the cause. But poetry in a more restricted sense expresses those arrangements of language, and especially metrical language, which are created by that imperial faculty, whose throne is curtained within the invisible nature of man. And this springs from the nature itself of language, which is a more direct representation of the actions and passions of our internal being, and is susceptible of more various and delicate combinations than colour, form, or motion, and is more plastic and obedient to the control of that faculty of which it is the creation. For language is arbitrarily produced by the imagination, and has relation to thoughts alone; but all other materials, instruments, and conditions of art have relations among each other, which limit and interpose between conception and expression.

The former is as a mirror which reflects, the latter as a cloud which enfeebles, the light of which both are mediums of communication. Hence the fame of sculptors, painters, and musicians, although the intrinsic powers of the great masters of these arts may yield in no degree to that of those who have employed language as the hieroglyphic of their thoughts, has never equalled that of poets in the restricted sense of the term; as two performers of equal skill will produce unequal effects from a guitar and a harp. The fame of legislators and founders of religions, so long as their institutions last, alone seems to exceed that of poets in the restricted sense; but it can scarcely be a question whether, if we deduct the celebrity which their flattery of the gross opinions of the vulgar usually conciliates, together with that which belonged to them in their higher character of poets, any excess will remain.

We have thus circumscribed the word poetry within the limits of that art which is the most familiar and the most perfect expression of the faculty itself. It is necessary, however, to make the circle still narrower, and to determine the distinction between measured and unmeasured language; for the popular division into prose and verse is inadmissible in accurate philosophy.

Sounds as well as thoughts have relation both between each other and towards that which they represent, and a perception of the order of those relations has always been found connected with a perception of the order of the relations of thoughts. Hence the language of poets has ever affected a certain uniform and harmonious recurrence of sound, without which it were not poetry, and which is scarcely less indispensable to the communication of its influence than the words themselves, without reference to that peculiar order. Hence the vanity of translation; it were as wise to cast a violet into a crucible that you might discover the formal principle of its colour and odour, as seek to transfuse from one language into another the creations of a poet. The plant must spring again from its seed, or it will bear no flower--and this is the burthen of the curse of Babel.

An observation of the regular mode of the recurrence of harmony in the language of poetical minds, together with its relation to music, produced metre, or a certain system of traditional forms of harmony and language. Yet it is by no means essential that a poet should accommodate his language to this traditional form, so that the harmony, which is its spirit, be observed.

The practice is indeed convenient and popular, and to be preferred, especially in such composition as includes much action: but every great poet must inevitably innovate upon the example of his predecessors in the exact structure of his peculiar versification. The distinction between poets and prose writers is a vulgar error.

The distinction between philosophers and poets has been anticipated. Plato was essentially a poet--the truth and splendour of his imagery, and the melody of his language, are the most intense that it is possible to conceive. He rejected the measure of the epic, dramatic, and lyrical forms, because he sought to kindle a harmony in thoughts divested of shape and action, and he forbore to invent any regular plan of rhythm which would include, under determinate forms, the varied pauses of his style.

Cicero sought to imitate the cadence of his periods, but with little success. Lord Bacon was a poet. See the Filum Labyrinthi, and the Essay on Death particularly. His language has a sweet and majestic rhythm, which satisfies the sense, no less than the almost superhuman wisdom of his philosophy satisfies the intellect; it is a strain which distends, and then bursts the circumference of the reader's mind, and pours itself forth together with it into the universal element with which it has perpetual sympathy.

All the authors of revolutions in opinion are not only necessarily poets as they are inventors, nor even as their words unveil the permanent analogy of things by images which participate in the life of truth; but as their periods are harmonious and rhythmical, and contain in themselves the elements of verse; being the echo of the eternal music. Nor are those supreme poets, who have employed traditional forms of rhythm on account of the form and action of their subjects, less capable of perceiving and teaching the truth of things, than those who have omitted that form. Shakespeare, Dante, and Milton (to confine ourselves to modern writers) are philosophers of the very loftiest power.

A poem is the very image of life expressed in its eternal truth. There is this difference between a story and a poem, that a story is a catalogue of detached facts, which have no other connection than time, place, circumstance, cause and effect; the other is the creation of actions according to the unchangeable forms of human nature, as existing in the mind of the Creator, which is itself the image of all other minds. The one is partial, and applies only to a definite period of time, and a certain combination of events which can never again recur; the other is universal, and contains within itself the germ of a relation to whatever motives or actions have place in the possible varieties of human nature. Time, which destroys the beauty and the use of the story of particular facts, stripped of the poetry which should invest them, augments that of poetry, and for ever develops new and wonderful applications of the eternal truth which it contains. Hence epitomes have been called the moths of just history; they eat out the poetry of it. A story of particular facts is as a mirror which obscures and distorts that which should be beautiful: poetry is a mirror which makes beautiful that which is distorted.

The parts of a composition may be poetical, without the composition as a whole being a poem. A single sentence may be considered as a whole, though it may be found in the midst of a series of unassimilated portions; a single word even may be a spark of inextinguishable thought. And thus all the great historians, Herodotus, Plutarch, Livy, were poets; and although the plan of these writers, especially that of Livy, restrained them from developing this faculty in its highest degree, they made copious and ample amends for their subjection by filling all the interstices of their subjects with living images.

Having determined what is poetry, and who are poets, let us proceed to estimate its effects upon society.

Poetry is ever accompanied with pleasure: all spirits on which it falls open themselves to receive the wisdom which is mingled with its delight. In the infancy of the world, neither poets themselves nor their auditors are fully aware of the excellence of poetry: for it acts in a divine and unapprehended manner, beyond and above consciousness; and it is reserved for future generations to contemplate and measure the mighty cause and effect in all the strength and splendour of their union. Even in modern times, no living poet ever arrived at the fulness of his fame; the jury which sits in judgment upon a poet, belonging as he does to all time, must be composed of his peers: it must be impanelled by Time from the selectest of the wise of many generations.

A poet is a nightingale, who sits in darkness and sings to cheer its own solitude with sweet sounds; his auditors are as men entranced by the melody of an unseen musician, who feel that they are moved and softened, yet know not whence or why. The poems of Homer and his contemporaries were the delight of infant Greece; they were the elements of that social system which is the column upon which all succeeding civilization has reposed. Homer embodied the ideal perfection of his age in human character; nor can we doubt that those who read his verses were awakened to an ambition of becoming like to Achilles, Hector, and Ulysses: the truth and beauty of friendship, patriotism, and persevering devotion to an object, were unveiled to the depths in these immortal creations: the sentiments of the auditors must have been refined and enlarged by a sympathy with such great and lovely impersonations, until from admiring they imitated, and from imitation they identified themselves with the objects of their admiration.

Nor let it be objected that these characters are remote from moral perfection, and that they can by no means be considered as edifying patterns for general imitation. Every epoch, under names more or less specious, has deified its peculiar errors; Revenge is the naked idol of the worship of a semi-barbarous age; and Self-deceit is the veiled image of unknown evil, before which luxury and satiety lie prostrate. But a poet considers the vices of his contemporaries as the temporary dress in which his creations must be arrayed, and which cover without concealing the eternal proportions of their beauty. An epic or dramatic personage is understood to wear them around his soul, as he may the ancient armour or the modern uniform around his body; whilst it is easy to conceive a dress more graceful than either.

The beauty of the internal nature cannot be so far concealed by its accidental vesture but that the spirit of its form shall communicate itself to the very disguise, and indicate the shape it hides from the manner in which it is worn. A majestic form and graceful motions will express themselves through the most barbarous and tasteless costume. Few poets of the highest class have chosen to exhibit the beauty of their conceptions in its naked truth and splendour; and it is doubtful whether the alloy of costume, habit, &c., be not necessary to temper this planetary music for mortal ears.

The whole objection, however, of the immorality of poetry rests upon a misconception of the manner in which poetry acts to produce the moral improvement of man. Ethical science arranges the elements which poetry has created, and propounds schemes and proposes examples of civil and domestic life: nor is it for want of admirable doctrines that men hate, and despise, and censure, and deceive, and subjugate one another. But poetry acts in another and diviner manner. It awakens and enlarges the mind itself by rendering it the receptacle of a thousand unapprehended combinations of thought. Poetry lifts the veil from the hidden beauty of the world, and makes familiar objects be as if they were not familiar; it reproduces all that it represents, and the impersonations clothed in its Elysian light stand thenceforward in the minds of those who have once contemplated them as memorials of that gentle and exalted content which extends itself over all thoughts and actions with which it coexists.

The great secret of morals is love; or a going out of our nature, and an identification of ourselves with the beautiful which exists in thought, action, or person, not our own. A man, to be greatly good, must imagine intensely and comprehensively; he must put himself in the place of another and of many others; the pains and pleasures of his species must become his own. The great instrument of moral good is the imagination; and poetry administers to the effect by acting upon the cause. Poetry enlarges the circumference of the imagination by replenishing it with thoughts of ever new delight, which have the power of attracting and assimilating to their own nature all other thoughts, and which form new intervals and interstices whose void for ever craves fresh food. Poetry strengthens the faculty which is the organ of the moral nature of man, in the same manner as exercise strengthens a limb.

A poet therefore would do ill to embody his own conceptions of right and wrong, which are usually those of his place and time, in his poetical creations, which participate in neither. By this assumption of the inferior office of interpreting the effect, in which perhaps after all he might acquit himself but imperfectly, he would resign a glory in a participation in the cause. There was little danger that Homer, or any of the eternal poets, should have so far misunderstood themselves as to have abdicated this throne of their widest dominion. Those in whom the poetical faculty, though great, is less intense, as Euripides, Lucan, Tasso, Spenser, have frequently affected a moral aim, and the effect of their poetry is diminished in exact proportion to the degree in which they compel us to advert to this purpose.

Homer and the cyclic poets were followed at a certain interval by the dramatic and lyrical poets of Athens, who flourished contemporaneously with all that is most perfect in the kindred expressions of the poetical faculty; architecture, painting, music, the dance, sculpture, philosophy, and we may add, the forms of civil life. For although the scheme of Athenian society was deformed by many imperfections which the poetry existing in chivalry and Christianity has erased from the habits and institutions of modern Europe; yet never at any other period has so much energy, beauty, and virtue been developed; never was blind strength and stubborn form so disciplined and rendered subject to the will of man, or that will less repugnant to the dictates of the beautiful and the true, as during the century which preceded the death of Socrates.

Of no other epoch in the history of our species have we records and fragments stamped so visibly with the image of the divinity in man. But it is poetry alone, in form, in action, or in language, which has rendered this epoch memorable above all others, and the storehouse of examples to everlasting time. For written poetry existed at that epoch simultaneously with the other arts, and it is an idle inquiry to demand which gave and which received the light, which all, as from a common focus, have scattered over the darkest periods of succeeding time. We know no more of cause and effect than a constant conjunction of events: poetry is ever found to coexist with whatever other arts contribute to the happiness and perfection of man. I appeal to what has already been established to distinguish between the cause and the effect.

It was at the period here adverted to that the drama had its birth; and however a succeeding writer may have equalled or surpassed those few great specimens of the Athenian drama which have been preserved to us, it is indisputable that the art itself never was understood or practised according to the true philosophy of it, as at Athens. For the Athenians employed language, action, music, painting, the dance, and religious institutions to produce a common effect in the representation of the highest idealisms of passion and of power; each division in the art was made perfect in its kind by artists of the most consummate skill, and was disciplined into a beautiful proportion and unity one towards the other.

On the modern stage a few only of the elements capable of expressing the image of the poet's conception are employed at once. We have tragedy without music and dancing; and music and dancing without the highest impersonations of which they are the fit accompaniment, and both without religion and solemnity. Religious institution has indeed been usually banished from the stage. Our system of divesting the actor's face of a mask, on which the many expressions appropriate to his dramatic character might be moulded into one permanent and unchanging expression, is favourable only to a partial and inharmonious effect; it is fit for nothing but a monologue, where all the attention may be directed to some great master of ideal mimicry. The modern practice of blending comedy with tragedy, though liable to great abuse in point of practice, is undoubtedly an extension of the dramatic circle; but the comedy should be, as in King Lear, universal, ideal, and sublime. It is perhaps the intervention of this principle which determines the balance in favour of King Lear against the OEdipus Tyrannus or the Agamemnon, or, if you will, the trilogies with which they are connected; unless the intense power of the choral poetry, especially that of the latter, should be considered as restoring the equilibrium.

King Lear, if it can sustain this comparison, may be judged to be the most perfect specimen of the dramatic art existing in the world; in spite of the narrow conditions to which the poet was subjected by the ignorance of the philosophy of the drama which has prevailed in modern Europe. Calderon, in his religious Autos, has attempted to fulfill some of the high conditions of dramatic representation neglected by Shakespeare; such as the establishing a relation between the drama and religion, and the accommodating them to music and dancing; but he omits the observation of conditions still more important, and more is lost than gained by the substitution of the rigidly-defined and ever-repeated idealisms of a distorted superstition for the living impersonations of the truth of human passion.

But I digress.--The connection of scenic exhibitions with the improvement or corruption of the manners of men has been universally recognized; in other words, the presence or absence of poetry in its most perfect and universal form has been found to be connected with good and evil in conduct or habit. The corruption which has been imputed to the drama as an effect, begins when the poetry employed in its constitution ends: I appeal to the history of manners whether the periods of the growth of the one and the decline of the other have not corresponded with an exactness equal to any example of moral cause and effect.

The drama at Athens, or wheresoever else it may have approached to its perfection, ever coexisted with the moral and intellectual greatness of the age. The tragedies of the Athenian poets are as mirrors in which the spectator beholds himself, under a thin disguise of circumstance, stript of all but that ideal perfection and energy which every one feels to be the internal type of all that he loves, admires, and would become. The imagination is enlarged by a sympathy with pains and passions so mighty that they distend in their conception the capacity of that by which they are conceived; the good affections are strengthened by pity, indignation, terror, and sorrow; and an exalted calm is prolonged from the satiety of this high exercise of them into the tumult of familiar life: even crime is disarmed of half its horror and all its contagion by being represented as the fatal consequence of the unfathomable agencies of nature; error is thus divested of its willfulness; men can no longer cherish it as the creation of their choice.

In a drama of the highest order there is little food for censure or hatred; it teaches rather self-knowledge and self-respect. Neither the eye nor the mind can see itself, unless reflected upon that which it resembles. The drama, so long as it continues to express poetry, is as a prismatic and many-sided mirror, which collects the brightest rays of human nature and divides and reproduces them from the simplicity of these elementary forms, and touches them with majesty and beauty, and multiplies all that it reflects, and endows it with the power of propagating its like wherever it may fall.

But in periods of the decay of social life, the drama sympathizes with that decay. Tragedy becomes a cold imitation of the form of the great masterpieces of antiquity, divested of all harmonious accompaniment of the kindred arts; and often the very form misunderstood, or a weak attempt to teach certain doctrines, which the writer considers as moral truths; and which are usually no more than specious flatteries of some gross vice or weakness with which the author, in common with his auditors, are infected. Hence what has been called the classical and domestic drama. Addison's Cato is a specimen of the one; and would it were not superfluous to cite examples of the other! To such purposes poetry cannot be made subservient. Poetry is a sword of lightning, ever unsheathed, which consumes the scabbard that would contain it.

And thus we observe that all dramatic writings of this nature are unimaginative in a singular degree; they affect sentiment and passion, which, divested of imagination, are other names for caprice and appetite. The period in our own history of the grossest degradation of the drama is the reign of Charles II., when all forms in which poetry had been accustomed to be expressed became hymns to the triumph of kingly power over liberty and virtue. Milton stood alone illuminating an age unworthy of him. At such periods the calculating principle pervades all the forms of dramatic exhibition, and poetry ceases to be expressed upon them. Comedy loses its ideal universality: wit succeeds to humour; we laugh from self-complacency and triumph, instead of pleasure; malignity, sarcasm, and contempt succeed to sympathetic merriment; we hardly laugh, but we smile.

Obscenity, which is ever blasphemy against the divine beauty in life, becomes, from the very veil which it assumes, more active if less disgusting: it is a monster for which the corruption of society for ever brings forth new food, which it devours in secret.

The drama being that form under which a greater number of modes of expression of poetry are susceptible of being combined than any other, the connection of poetry and social good is more observable in the drama than in whatever other form. And it is indisputable that the highest perfection of human society has ever corresponded with the highest dramatic excellence; and that the corruption or the extinction of the drama in a nation where it has once flourished, is a mark of a corruption of manners, and an extinction of the energies which sustain the soul of social life. But, as Machiavelli says of political institutions, that life may be preserved and renewed, if men should arise capable of bringing back the drama to its principles. And this is true with respect to poetry in its most extended sense: all language, institution and form, require not only to be produced, but to be sustained: the office and character of a poet participates in the divine nature as regards providence, no less than as regards creation.

Civil war, the spoils of Asia, and the fatal predominance, first of the Macedonian, and then of the Roman arms, were so many symbols of the extinction or suspension of the creative faculty in Greece. The bucolic writers, who found patronage under the lettered tyrants of Sicily and Egypt, were the latest representatives of its most glorious reign. Their poetry is intensely melodious; like the odour of the tuberose, it overcomes and sickens the spirit with excess of sweetness; whilst the poetry of the preceding age was as a meadow-gale of June, which mingles the fragrance of all the flowers of the field, and adds a quickening and harmonizing spirit of its own which endows the sense with a power of sustaining its extreme delight.

The bucolic and erotic delicacy in written poetry is correlative with that softness in statuary, music, and the kindred arts, and even in manners and institutions, which distinguished the epoch to which I now refer. Nor is it the poetical faculty itself, or any misapplication of it, to which this want of harmony is to be imputed. An equal sensibility to the influence of the senses and the affections is to be found in the writings of Homer and Sophocles: the former, especially, has clothed sensual and pathetic images with irresistible attractions. Their superiority over these succeeding writers consists in the presence of those thoughts which belong to the inner faculties of our nature, not in the absence of those which are connected with the external: their incomparable perfection consists in a harmony of the union of all. It is not what the erotic poets have, but what they have not, in which their imperfection consists. It is not inasmuch as they were poets, but inasmuch as they were not poets, that they can be considered with any plausibility as connected with the corruption of their age.

Had that corruption availed so as to extinguish in them the sensibility to pleasure, passion, and natural scenery, which is imputed to them as an imperfection, the last triumph of evil would have been achieved. For the end of social corruption is to destroy all sensibility to pleasure; and, therefore, it is corruption. It begins at the imagination and the intellect as at the core, and distributes itself thence as a paralysing venom, through the affections into the very appetites, until all become a torpid mass in which hardly sense survives. At the approach of such a period, poetry ever addresses itself to those faculties which are the last to be destroyed, and its voice is heard, like the footsteps of Astraa, departing from the world. Poetry ever communicates all the pleasure which men are capable of receiving: it is ever still the light of life; the source of whatever of beautiful or generous or true can have place in an evil time.

It will readily be confessed that those among the luxurious citizens of Syracuse and Alexandria, who were delighted with the poems of Theocritus, were less cold, cruel, and sensual than the remnant of their tribe. But corruption must utterly have destroyed the fabric of human society before poetry can ever cease. The sacred links of that chain have never been entirely disjointed, which descending through the minds of many men is attached to those great minds, whence as from a magnet the invisible effluence is sent forth, which at once connects, animates, and sustains the life of all. It is the faculty which contains within itself the seeds at once of its own and of social renovation.

And let us not circumscribe the effects of the bucolic and erotic poetry within the limits of the sensibility of those to whom it was addressed. They may have perceived the beauty of those immortal compositions, simply as fragments and isolated portions: those who are more finely organized, or, born in a happier age, may recognize them as episodes to that great poem, which all poets, like the co-operating thoughts of one great mind, have built up since the beginning of the world.

The same revolutions within a narrower sphere had place in ancient Rome; but the actions and forms of its social life never seem to have been perfectly saturated with the poetical element. The Romans appear to have considered the Greeks as the selectest treasuries of the selectest forms of manners and of nature, and to have abstained from creating in measured language, sculpture, music, or architecture anything which might bear a particular relation to their own condition, whilst it should bear a general one to the universal constitution of the world. But we judge from partial evidence, and we judge perhaps partially. Ennius, Varro, Pacuvius, and Accius, all great poets, have been lost. Lucretius is in the highest, and Virgil in a very high sense, a creator.

The chosen delicacy of expressions of the latter are as a mist of light which conceal from us the intense and exceeding truth of his conceptions of nature. Livy is instinct with poetry. Yet Horace, Catullus, Ovid, and generally the other great writers of the Virgilian age, saw man and nature in the mirror of Greece. The institutions also, and the religion of Rome, were less poetical than those of Greece, as the shadow is less vivid than the substance. Hence poetry in Rome seemed to follow, rather than accompany, the perfection of political and domestic society. The true poetry of Rome lived in its institutions; for whatever of beautiful, true, and majestic they contained, could have sprung only from the faculty which creates the order in which they consist.

The life of Camillus, the death of Regulus; the expectation of the senators, in their godlike state, of the victorious Gauls; the refusal of the republic to make peace with Hannibal after the battle of Cannae, were not the consequences of a refined calculation of the probable personal advantage to result from such a rhythm and order in the shows of life, to those who were at once the poets and the actors of these immortal dramas. The imagination, beholding the beauty of this order, created it out of itself according to its own idea; the consequence was empire, and the reward ever-living fame. These things are not the less poetry, quia carent vate sacro. They are the episodes of that cyclic poem written by Time upon the memories of men. The Past, like an inspired rhapsodist, fills the theatre of everlasting generations with their harmony.

At length the ancient system of religion and manners had fulfilled the circle of its revolutions. And the world would have fallen into utter anarchy and darkness, but that there were found poets among the authors of the Christian and chivalric systems of manners and religion, who created forms of opinion and action never before conceived; which, copied into the imaginations of men, became as generals to the bewildered armies of their thoughts.

It is foreign to the present purpose to touch upon the evil produced by these systems: except that we protest, on the ground of the principles already established, that no portion of it can be attributed to the poetry they contain.

It is probable that the poetry of Moses, Job, David, Solomon, and Isaiah had produced a great effect upon the mind of Jesus and his disciples. The scattered fragments preserved to us by the biographers of this extraordinary person are all instinct with the most vivid poetry.

But his doctrines seem to have been quickly distorted. At a certain period after the prevalence of a system of opinions founded upon those promulgated by him, the three forms into which Plato had distributed the faculties of mind underwent a sort of apotheosis, and became the object of the worship of the civilized world. Here it is to be confessed that "Light seems to thicken", and

"The crow makes wing to the rooky wood,

Good things of day begin to droop and drowse,

And night's black agents to their preys do rouse".

But mark how beautiful an order has sprung from the dust and blood of this fierce chaos! how the world, as from a resurrection, balancing itself on the golden wings of knowledge and of hope, has reassumed its yet unwearied flight into the heaven of time. Listen to the music, unheard by outward ears, which is as a ceaseless and invisible wind, nourishing its everlasting course with strength and swiftness.

The poetry in the doctrines of Jesus Christ, and the mythology and institutions of the Celtic The confusion between Celtic and Teutonic is constant in the writers of the eighteenth century and the early part of this. conquerors of the Roman empire, outlived the darkness and the convulsions connected with their growth and victory, and blended themselves in a new fabric of manners and opinion. It is an error to impute the ignorance of the dark ages to the Christian doctrines or the predominance of the Celtic nations. Whatever of evil their agencies may have contained sprang from the extinction of the poetical principle, connected with the progress of despotism and superstition.

Men, from causes too intricate to be here discussed, had become insensible and selfish: their own will had become feeble, and yet they were its slaves, and thence the slaves of the will of others: lust, fear, avarice, cruelty, and fraud characterized a race amongst whom no one was to be found capable of creating in form, language, or institution. The moral anomalies of such a state of society are not justly to be charged upon any class of events immediately connected with them, and those events are most entitled to our approbation which could dissolve it most expeditiously. It is unfortunate for those who cannot distinguish words from thoughts, that many of these anomalies have been incorporated into our popular religion.

It was not until the eleventh century that the effects of the poetry of the Christian and chivalric systems began to manifest themselves. The principle of equality had been discovered and applied by Plato in his Republic, as the theoretical rule of the mode in which the materials of pleasure and of power produced by the common skill and labour of human beings ought to be distributed among them. The limitations of this rule were asserted by him to be determined only by the sensibility of each, or the utility to result to all. Plato, following the doctrines of Timaeus and Pythagoras, taught also a moral and intellectual system of doctrine, comprehending at once the past, the present, and the future condition of man. Jesus Christ divulged the sacred and eternal truths contained in these views to mankind, and Christianity, in its abstract purity, became the exoteric expression of the esoteric doctrines of the poetry and wisdom of antiquity.

The incorporation of the Celtic nations with the exhausted population of the south, impressed upon it the figure of the poetry existing in their mythology and institutions. The result was a sum of the action and reaction of all the causes included in it; for it may be assumed as a maxim that no nation or religion can supersede any other without incorporating into itself a portion of that which it supersedes. The abolition of personal and domestic slavery, and the emancipation of women from a great part of the degrading restraints of antiquity, were among the consequences of these events.

The abolition of personal slavery is the basis of the highest political hope that it can enter into the mind of man to conceive. The freedom of women produced the poetry of sexual love. Love became a religion, the idols of whose worship were ever present. It was as if the statues of Apollo and the Muses had been endowed with life and motion, and had walked forth among their worshippers; so that earth became peopled by the inhabitants of a diviner world. The familiar appearance and proceedings of life became wonderful and heavenly, and a paradise was created as out of the wrecks of Eden. And as this creation itself is poetry, so its creators were poets; and language was the instrument of their art: Galeotto fu il libro, e chi lo scrisse.

The Provencal Trouveurs, or inventors, preceded Petrarch, whose verses are as spells, which unseal the inmost enchanted fountains of the delight which is in the grief of love. It is impossible to feel them without becoming a portion of that beauty which we contemplate: it were superfluous to explain how the gentleness and the elevation of mind connected with these sacred emotions can render men more amiable, more generous and wise, and lift them out of the dull vapours of the little world of self. Dante understood the secret things of love even more than Petrarch. His Vita Nuova is an inexhaustible fountain of purity of sentiment and language: it is the idealized history of that period, and those intervals of his life which were dedicated to love.

His apotheosis of Beatrice in Paradise, and the gradations of his own love and her loveliness, by which as by steps he feigns himself to have ascended to the throne of the Supreme Cause, is the most glorious imagination of modern poetry. The acutest critics have justly reversed the judgment of the vulgar, and the order of the great acts of the Divine Drama, in the measure of the admiration which they accord to the Hell, Purgatory, and Paradise.

The latter is a perpetual hymn of everlasting love. Love, which found a worthy poet in Plato alone of all the ancients, has been celebrated by a chorus of the greatest writers of the renovated world; and the music has penetrated the caverns of society, and its echoes still drown the dissonance of arms and superstition. At successive intervals, Ariosto, Tasso, Shakespeare, Spenser, Calderon, Rousseau, and the great writers of our own age, have celebrated the dominion of love, planting, as it were, trophies in the human mind of that sublimest victory over sensuality and force. The true relation borne to each other by the sexes into which human kind is distributed has become less misunderstood; and if the error which confounded diversity with inequality of the powers of the two sexes has been partially recognized in the opinions and institutions of modern Europe, we owe this great benefit to the worship of which chivalry was the law, and poets the prophets.

The poetry of Dante may be considered as the bridge thrown over the stream of time, which unites the modern and ancient world. The distorted notions of invisible things which Dante and his rival Milton have idealized are merely the mask and the mantle in which these great poets walk through eternity enveloped and disguised: It is a difficult question to determine how far they were conscious of the distinction which must have subsisted in their minds between their own creeds and that of the people. Dante at least appears to wish to mark the full extent of it by placing Rhipaus, whom Virgil calls justissimus unus, in Paradise, Paradiso, xx. 68. and observing a most heretical caprice in his distribution of rewards and punishments.

And Milton's poem contains within itself a philosophical refutation of that system, of which, by a strange and natural antithesis, it has been a chief popular support. Nothing can exceed the energy and magnificence of the character of Satan as expressed in Paradise Lost. It is a mistake to suppose that he could ever have been intended for the popular personification of evil. Implacable hate, patient cunning, and a sleepless refinement of device to inflict the extremest anguish on an enemy, these things are evil; and, although venial in a slave, are not to be forgiven in a tyrant; although redeemed by much that ennobles his defeat in one subdued, are marked by all that dishonours his conquest in the victor. Milton's Devil as a moral being is as far superior to his God as one who perseveres in some purpose which he has conceived to be excellent in spite of adversity and torture, is to one who in the cold security of undoubted triumph inflicts the most horrible revenge upon his enemy, not from any mistaken notion of inducing him to repent of a perseverance in enmity, but with the alleged design of exasperating him to deserve new torments.

Milton has so far violated the popular creed (if this shall be judged to be a violation) as to have alleged no superiority of moral virtue to his God over his Devil. And this bold neglect of a direct moral purpose is the most decisive proof of the supremacy of Milton's genius. He mingled, as it were, the elements of human nature as colours upon a single pallet, and arranged them in the composition of his great picture according to the laws of epic truth; that is, according to the laws of that principle by which a series of actions of the external universe and of intelligent and ethical beings is calculated to excite the sympathy of succeeding generations of mankind. The Divina Commedia and Paradise Lost have conferred upon modern mythology a systematic form; and when change and time shall have added one more superstition to the mass of those which have arisen and decayed upon the earth, commentators will be learnedly employed in elucidating the religion of ancestral Europe, only not utterly forgotten because it will have been stamped with the eternity of genius.

Homer was the first and Dante the second epic poet: that is, the second poet, the series of whose creations bore a defined and intelligible relation to the knowledge and sentiment and religion of the age in which he lived, and of the ages which followed it, developing itself in correspondence with their development. For Lucretius had limed the wings of his swift spirit in the dregs of the sensible world; and Virgil, with a modesty that ill became his genius, had affected the fame of an imitator, even whilst he created anew all that he copied; and none among the flock of mock-birds, though their notes were sweet, Apollonius Rhodius, Quintus Calaber, Nonnus, Lucan, Statius, or Claudian, have sought even to fulfil a single condition of epic truth. Milton was the third epic poet. For if the title of epic in its highest sense be refused to the Aneid still less can it be conceded to the Orlando Furioso, the Gerusalemme Liberata, the Lusiad, or the Fairy Queen.

Dante and Milton were both deeply penetrated with the ancient religion of the civilized world; and its spirit exists in their poetry probably in the same proportion as its forms survived in the unreformed worship of modern Europe. The one preceded and the other followed the Reformation at almost equal intervals. Dante was the first religious reformer, and Luther surpassed him rather in the rudeness and acrimony than in the boldness of his censures of papal usurpation. Dante was the first awakener of entranced Europe; he created a language, in itself music and persuasion, out of a chaos of inharmonious barbarisms. He was the congregator of those great spirits who presided over the resurrection of learning; the Lucifer of that starry flock which in the thirteenth century shone forth from republican Italy, as from a heaven, into the darkness of the benighted world.

His very words are instinct with spirit; each is as a spark, a burning atom of inextinguishable thought; and many yet lie covered in the ashes of their birth, and pregnant with the lightning which has yet found no conductor. All high poetry is infinite; it is as the first acorn, which contained all oaks potentially. Veil after veil may be undrawn, and the inmost naked beauty of the meaning never exposed. A great poem is a fountain for ever overflowing with the waters of wisdom and delight; and after one person and one age has exhausted all its divine effluence which their peculiar relations enable them to share, another and yet another succeeds, and new relations are ever developed, the source of an unforeseen and an unconceived delight.

The age immediately succeeding to that of Dante, Petrarch, and Boccaccio was characterized by a revival of painting, sculpture, and architecture. Chaucer caught the sacred inspiration, and the superstructure of English literature is based upon the materials of Italian invention.

But let us not be betrayed from a defence into a critical history of poetry and its influence on society. Be it enough to have pointed out the effects of poets, in the large and true sense of the word, upon their own and all succeeding times.

But poets have been challenged to resign the civic crown to reasoners and mechanists on another plea. It is admitted that the exercise of the imagination is most delightful, but it is alleged that that of reason is more useful. Let us examine, as the grounds of this distinction, what is here meant by utility. Pleasure or good, in a general sense, is that which the consciousness of a sensitive and intelligent being seeks, and in which, when found, it acquiesces. There are two kinds of pleasure, one durable, universal, and permanent; the other transitory and particular. Utility may either express the means of producing the former or the latter. In the former sense, whatever strengthens and purifies the affections, enlarges the imagination, and adds spirit to sense, is useful. But a narrower meaning may be assigned to the word utility, confining it to express that which banishes the importunity of the wants of our animal nature, the surrounding men with security of life, the dispersing the grosser delusions of superstition, and the conciliating such a degree of mutual forbearance among men as may consist with the motives of personal advantage.

Undoubtedly the promoters of utility, in this limited sense, have their appointed office in society. They follow the footsteps of poets, and copy the sketches of their creations into the book of common life. They make space, and give time. Their exertions are of the highest value, so long as they confine their administration of the concerns of the inferior powers of our nature within the limits due to the superior ones. But whilst the sceptic destroys gross superstitions, let him spare to deface, as some of the French writers have defaced, the eternal truths charactered upon the imaginations of men. Whilst the mechanist abridges, and the political economist combines labour, let them beware that their speculations, for want of correspondence with those first principles which belong to the imagination, do not tend, as they have in modern England, to exasperate at once the extremes of luxury and want. They have exemplified the saying, "To him that hath, more shall be given; and from him that hath not, the little that he hath shall be taken away". The rich have become richer, and the poor have become poorer; and the vessel of the state is driven between the Scylla and Charybdis of anarchy and despotism. Such are the effects which must ever flow from an unmitigated exercise of the calculating faculty.

It is difficult to define pleasure in its highest sense; the definition involving a number of apparent paradoxes. For, from an inexplicable defect of harmony in the constitution of human nature, the pain of the inferior is frequently connected with the pleasures of the superior portions of our being. Sorrow, terror, anguish, despair itself, are often the chosen expressions of an approximation to the highest good. Our sympathy in tragic fiction depends on this principle; tragedy delights by affording a shadow of the pleasure which exists in pain. This is the source also of the melancholy which is inseparable from the sweetest melody. The pleasure that is in sorrow is sweeter than the pleasure of pleasure itself. And hence the saying, "It is better to go to the house of mourning than to the house of mirth". Not that this highest species of pleasure is necessarily linked with pain. The delight of love and friendship, the ecstasy of the admiration of nature, the joy of the perception, and still more of the creation of poetry, is often wholly unalloyed.

The production and assurance of pleasure in this highest sense is true utility. Those who produce and preserve this pleasure are poets or poetical philosophers.

The exertions of Locke, Hume, Gibbon, Voltaire, Rousseau Although Rousseau has been thus classed, he was essentially a poet. The others, even Voltaire, were mere reasoners., and their disciples, in favour of oppressed and deluded humanity, are entitled to the gratitude of mankind. Yet it is easy to calculate the degree of moral and intellectual improvement which the world would have exhibited had they never lived. A little more nonsense would have been talked for a century or two; and perhaps a few more men, women, and children burnt as heretics. We might not at this moment have been congratulating each other on the abolition of the Inquisition in Spain. But it exceeds all imagination to conceive what would have been the moral condition of the world if neither Dante, Petrarch, Boccaccio, Chaucer, Shakespeare, Calderon, Lord Bacon, nor Milton had ever existed; if Raphael and

Michael Angelo had never been born; if the Hebrew poetry had never been translated; if a revival of the study of Greek literature had never taken place; if no monuments of ancient sculpture had been handed down to us; and if the poetry of the religion of the ancient world had been extinguished together with its belief. The human mind could never, except by the intervention of these excitements, have been awakened to the invention of the grosser sciences, and that application of analytical reasoning to the aberrations of society, which it is now attempted to exalt over the direct expression of the inventive and creative faculty itself.

We have more moral, political, and historical wisdom than we know how to reduce into practice; we have more scientific and economical knowledge than can be accommodated to the just distribution of the produce which it multiplies. The poetry in these systems of thought is concealed by the accumulation of facts and calculating processes. There is no want of knowledge respecting what is wisest and best in morals, government, and political economy, or, at least, what is wiser and better than what men now practise and endure. But we let " I dare not wait upon I would, like the poor cat in the adage". We want the creative faculty to imagine that which we know; we want the generous impulse to act that which we imagine; we want the poetry of life: our calculations have outrun conception; we have eaten more than we can digest.

The cultivation of those sciences which have enlarged the limits of the empire of man over the external world, has, for want of the poetical faculty, proportionally circumscribed those of the internal world; and man, having enslaved the elements, remains himself a slave. To what but a cultivation of the mechanical arts in a degree disproportioned to the presence of the creative faculty, which is the basis of all knowledge, is to be attributed the abuse of all invention for abridging and combining labour, to the exasperation of the inequality of mankind? From what other cause has it arisen that the discoveries which should have lightened have added a weight to the curse imposed on Adam? Poetry, and the principle of Self, of which money is the visible incarnation, are the God and Mammon of the world.

The functions of the poetical faculty are twofold: by one it creates new materials of knowledge, and power, and pleasure; by the other it engenders in the mind a desire to reproduce and arrange them according to a certain rhythm and order which may be called the beautiful and the good. The cultivation of poetry is never more to be desired than at periods when, from an excess of the selfish and calculating principle, the accumulation of the materials of external life exceeds the quantity of the power of assimilating them to the internal laws of human nature. The body has then become too unwieldy for that which animates it.

Poetry is indeed something divine. It is at once the centre and circumference of knowledge; it is that which comprehends all science, and that to which all science must be referred. It is at the same time the root and blossom of all other systems of thought; it is that from which all spring, and that which adorns all; and that which, if blighted, denies the fruit and the seed, and withholds from the barren world the nourishment and the succession of the scions of the tree of life. It is the perfect and consummate surface and bloom of all things; it is as the odour and the colour of the rose to the texture of the elements which compose it, as the form and splendour of unfaded beauty to the secrets of anatomy and corruption.

What were virtue, love, patriotism, friendship--what were the scenery of this beautiful universe which we inhabit; what were our consolations on this side of the grave--and what were our aspirations beyond it, if poetry did not ascend to bring light and fire from those eternal regions where the owl-winged faculty of calculation dare not ever soar? Poetry is not like reasoning, a power to be exerted according to the determination of the will. A man cannot say, "I will compose poetry". The greatest poet even cannot say it; for the mind in creation is as a fading coal, which some invisible influence, like an inconstant wind, awakens to transitory brightness; this power arises from within, like the colour of a flower which fades and changes as it is developed, and the conscious portions of our natures are unprophetic either of its approach or its departure. Could this influence be durable in its original purity and force, it is impossible to predict the greatness of the results; but when composition begins, inspiration is already on the decline, and the most glorious poetry that has ever been communicated to the world is probably a feeble shadow of the original conceptions of the poet.

I appeal to the greatest poets of the present day whether it is not an error to assert that the finest passages of poetry are produced by labour and study. The toil and the delay recommended by critics can be justly interpreted to mean no more than a careful observation of the inspired moments, and an artificial connection of the spaces between their suggestions by the intermixture of conventional expressions; a necessity only imposed by the limitedness of the poetical faculty itself: for Milton conceived the Paradise Lost as a whole before he executed it in portions. We have his own authority also for the muse having "dictated" to him the "unpremeditated song".

And let this be an answer to those who would allege the fifty-six various readings of the first line of the Orlando Furioso. Compositions so produced are to poetry what mosaic is to painting. This instinct and intuition of the poetical faculty is still more observable in the plastic and pictorial arts; a great statue or picture grows under the power of the artist as a child in the mother's womb; and the very mind which directs the hands in formation is incapable of accounting to itself for the origin, the gradations, or the media of the process.

Poetry is the record of the best and happiest moments of the happiest and best minds. We are aware of evanescent visitations of thought and feeling sometimes associated with place or person, sometimes regarding our own mind alone, and always arising unforeseen and departing unbidden, but elevating and delightful beyond all expression: so that even in the desire and the regret they leave, there cannot but be pleasure, participating as it does in the nature of its object.

It is, as it were, the interpenetration of a diviner nature through our own; but its footsteps are like those of a wind over the sea, which the coming calm erases, and whose traces remain only as on the wrinkled sands which paves it. These and corresponding conditions of being are experienced principally by those of the most delicate sensibility and the most enlarged imagination; and the state of mind produced by them is at war with every base desire.

The enthusiasm of virtue, love, patriotism, and friendship is essentially linked with such emotions; and whilst they last, self appears as what it is, an atom to a universe.

Poets are not only subject to these experiences as spirits of the most refined organization, but they can colour all that they combine with the evanescent hues of this ethereal world; a word, a trait in the representation of a scene or a passion will touch the enchanted chord, and reanimate, in those who have ever experienced these emotions, the sleeping, the cold, the buried image of the past.

Poetry thus makes immortal all that is best and most beautiful in the world; it arrests the vanishing apparitions which haunt the interlunations of life, and veiling them, or in language or in form, sends them forth among mankind, bearing sweet news of kindred joy to those with whom their sisters abide--abide, because there is no portal of expression from the caverns of the spirit which they inhabit into the universe of things. Poetry redeems from decay the visitations of the divinity in man.

Poetry turns all things to loveliness; it exalts the beauty of that which is most beautiful, and it adds beauty to that which is most deformed; it marries exultation and horror, grief and pleasure, eternity and change; it subdues to union under its-light yoke all irreconcilable things.

It transmutes all that it touches, and every form moving within the radiance of its presence is changed by wondrous sympathy to an incarnation of the spirit which it breathes: its secret alchemy turns to potable gold the poisonous waters which flow from death through life; it strips the veil of familiarity from the world, and lays bare the naked and sleeping beauty, which is the spirit of its forms.

All things exist as they are perceived: at least in relation to the percipient. "The mind is its own place, and of itself can make a heaven of hell, a hell of heaven." But poetry defeats the curse which binds us to be subjected to the accident of surrounding impressions.

And whether it spreads its own figured curtain, or withdraws life's dark veil from before the scene of things, it equally creates for us a being within our being. It makes us the inhabitants of a world to which the familiar world is a chaos. It reproduces the common universe of which we are portions and percipients, and it purges from our inward sight the film of familiarity which obscures from us the wonder of our being.

It compels us to feel that which we perceive, and to imagine that which we know. It creates anew the universe, after it has been annihilated in our minds by the recurrence of impressions blunted by reiteration. It justifies the bold and true words of Tasso --Non merita nome di creatore, se non Iddio ed il Poeta.

A poet, as he is the author to others of the highest wisdom, pleasure, virtue, and glory, so he ought personally to be the happiest, the best, the wisest, and the most illustrious of men. As to his glory, let time be challenged to declare whether the fame of any other institutor of human life be comparable to that of a poet.

That he is the wisest, the happiest, and the best, inasmuch as he is a poet, is equally incontrovertible: the greatest poets have been men of the most spotless virtue, of the most consummate prudence, and, if we would look into the interior of their lives, the most fortunate of men: and the exceptions, as they regard those who possessed the poetic faculty in a high yet inferior degree, will be found on consideration to confine rather than destroy the rule.

Let us for a moment stoop to the arbitration of popular breath, and usurping and uniting in our own persons the incompatible characters of accuser, witness, judge, and executioner, let us decide, without trial, testimony, or form, that certain motives of those who are "there sitting where we dare not soar", are reprehensible.

Let us assume that Homer was a drunkard, that Virgil was a flatterer, that Horace was a coward, that Tasso was a madman, that Lord Bacon was a peculator, that Raphael was a libertine, that Spenser was a poet-laureate. It is inconsistent with this division of our subject to cite living poets, but posterity has done ample justice to the great names now referred to.

Their errors have been weighed and found to have been dust in the balance; if their sins "were as scarlet, they are now white as snow"; they have been washed in the blood of the mediator and redeemer, Time. Observe in what a ludicrous chaos the imputations of real or fictitious crime have been confused in the contemporary calumnies against poetry and poets; consider how little is, as it appears--or appears, as it is; look to your own motives, and judge not, lest ye be judged.

Poetry, as has been said, differs in this respect from logic, that it is not subject to the control of the active powers of the mind, and that its birth and recurrence have no necessary connection with the consciousness or will. It is presumptuous to determine that these are the necessary conditions of all mental causation, when mental effects are experienced unsusceptible of being referred to them. The frequent recurrence of the poetical power, it is obvious to suppose, may produce in the mind a habit of order and harmony correlative with its own nature and with its effects upon other minds.

But in the intervals of inspiration, and they may be frequent without being durable, a poet becomes a man, and is abandoned to the sudden reflux of the influences under which others habitually live.

But as he is more delicately organized than other men, and sensible to pain and pleasure, both his own and that of others, in a degree unknown to them, he will avoid the one and pursue the other with an ardour proportioned to this difference. And he renders himself obnoxious to calumny when he neglects to observe the circumstances under which these objects of universal pursuit and flight have disguised themselves in one another's garments.

But there is nothing necessarily evil in this error, and thus cruelty, envy, revenge, avarice, and the passions purely evil have never formed any portion of the popular imputations on the lives of poets.

I have thought it most favourable to the cause of truth to set down these remarks according to the order in which they were suggested to my mind by a consideration of the subject itself, instead of observing the formality of a polemical reply; but if the view which they contain be just, they will be found to involve a refutation of the arguers against poetry, so far at least as regards the first division of the subject.

I can readily conjecture what should have moved the gall of some learned and intelligent writers who quarrel with certain versifiers; I confess myself, like them, unwilling to be stunned by the Theseids of the hoarse Codri of the day. Bavius and Maevius undoubtedly are, as they ever were, insufferable persons. But it belongs to a philosophical critic to distinguish rather than confound.

The first part of these remarks has related to poetry in its elements and principles; and it has been shown, as well as the narrow limits assigned them would permit, that what is called poetry, in a restricted sense, has a common source with all other forms of order and of beauty, according to which the materials of human life are susceptible of being arranged, and which is poetry in an universal sense.

The second part It was never written. will have for its object an application of these principles to the present state of the cultivation of poetry, and a defence of the attempt to idealize the modern forms of manners and opinions, and compel them into a subordination to the imaginative and creative faculty.

For the literature of England, an energetic development of which has ever preceded or accompanied a great and free development of the national will, has arisen, as it were, from a new birth. In spite of the low- thoughted envy which would undervalue contemporary merit, our own will be a memorable age in intellectual achievements, and we live among such philosophers and poets as surpass beyond comparison any who have appeared since the last national struggle for civil and religious liberty.

The most unfailing herald, companion, and follower of the awakening of a great people to work a beneficial change in opinion or institution is poetry. At such periods there is an accumulation of the power of communicating and receiving intense and impassioned conceptions respecting men and nature. The persons in whom this power resides may often, as far as regards many portions of their nature, have little apparent correspondence with that spirit of good of which they are the ministers. But even whilst they deny and abjure, they are yet compelled to serve, the power which is seated on the throne of their own soul.

It is impossible to read the compositions of the most celebrated writers of the present day without being startled with the electric life which burns within their words.

They measure the circumference and sound the depths of human nature with a comprehensive and all-penetrating spirit, and they are themselves perhaps the most sincerely astonished at its manifestations; for it is less their spirit than the spirit of the age.

Poets are the hierophants of an unapprehended inspiration; the mirrors of the gigantic shadows which futurity casts upon the present; the words which express what they understand not; the trumpets which sing to battle, and feel not what they inspire; the influence which is moved not, but moves. Poets are the unacknowledged legislators of the world.

9

The Goethe

THOMAS CARLYLE

The brief account here given of the work of Goethe was originally published as part of the introduction to the volume of translations called German Romance which was published in 1827. It is now commonly printed as an appendix to the first volume of Carlyle's Miscellanies. Carlyle was probably never at his best when he gave himself to the study of a particular author. His genius rather lay in the more general aspects of his work, and in the force with which he gave an entirely new turn to the currents of English criticism. Of his studies upon particular authors, the essay on Burns is perhaps the most complete and the most penetrating. But it is too long for the purposes of this selection. Nor is it amiss that he should here be represented by a work which may remind us that, among his services to English letters, to have opened the stores of German poetry and thought was by no means the least memorable.

Of a nature so rare and complex as Goethe's it is difficult to form a true comprehension; difficult even to express what comprehension one has formed. In Goethe's mind, the first aspect that strikes us is its calmness, then its beauty; a deeper inspection reveals to us its vastness and unmeasured strength. This man rules, and is not ruled. The stern and fiery energies of a most passionate soul lie silent in the centre of his being; a trembling sensibility has been inured to stand, without flinching or murmur, the sharpest trials. Nothing outward, nothing inward, shall agitate or control him. The brightest and most capricious fancy, the most piercing and inquisitive intellect, the wildest and deepest imagination; the highest thrills of joy, the bitterest pangs of sorrow: all these are his, he is not theirs.

While he moves every heart from its steadfastness, his own is firm and still: the words that search into the inmost recesses of our nature, he pronounces with a tone of coldness and equanimity; in the deepest pathos he weeps not, or his tears are like water trickling from a rock of adamant. He is king of himself and of his world; nor does he rule it like a vulgar great man, like a Napoleon or Charles Twelfth, by the mere brute exertion of his will, grounded on no principle, or on a false one: his faculties and feelings are not fettered or prostrated under the iron sway of Passion, but led and guided in kindly union under the mild sway of Reason; as the fierce primeval elements of Nature were stilled at the coming of Light, and bound together, under its soft vesture, into a glorious and beneficent Creation.

This is the true Rest of man; no stunted unbelieving callousness, no reckless surrender to blind Force, no opiate delusion; but the harmonious adjustment of Necessity and Accident, of what is changeable and what is unchangeable in our destiny; the calm supremacy of the spirit over its circumstances; the dim aim of every human soul, the full attainment of only a chosen few. It comes not unsought to any; but the wise are wise because they think no price too high for it. Goethe's inward home has been reared by slow and laborious efforts; but it stands on no hollow or deceitful basis: for his peace is not from blindness, but from clear vision; not from uncertain hope of alteration, but from sure insight into what cannot alter.

His world seems once to have been desolate and baleful as that of the darkest sceptic: but he has covered it anew with beauty and solemnity, derived from deeper sources, over which Doubt can have no sway. He has inquired fearlessly, and fearlessly searched out and denied the False; but he has not forgotten, what is equally essential and infinitely harder, to search out and admit the True. His heart is still full of warmth, though his head is clear and cold; the world for him is still full of grandeur, though he clothes it with no false colours; his fellow-creatures are still objects of reverence and love, though their basenesses are plainer to no eye than to his.

To reconcile these contradictions is the task of all good men, each for himself, in his own way and manner; a task which, in our age, is encompassed with difficulties peculiar to the time; and which Goethe seems to have accomplished with a success that few can rival. A mind so in unity with itself, even though it were a poor and small one, would arrest our attention, and win some kind regard from us; but when this mind ranks among the strongest and most complicated of the species, it becomes a sight full of interest, a study full of deep instruction.

Such a mind as Goethe's is the fruit not only of a royal endowment by nature, but also of a culture proportionate to her bounty. In Goethe's original form of spirit we discern the highest gifts of manhood, without any deficiency of the lower: he has an eye and a heart equally for the sublime, the common, and the ridiculous; the elements at once of a poet, a thinker, and a wit. Of his culture we have often spoken already; and it deserves again to be held up to praise and imitation. This, as he himself unostentatiously confesses, has been the soul of all his conduct, the great enterprise of his life; and few that understand him will be apt to deny that he has prospered.

As a writer, his resources have been accumulated from nearly all the provinces of human intellect and activity; and he has trained himself to use these complicated instruments with a light expertness which we might have admired in the professor of a solitary department. Freedom, and grace, and smiling earnestness are the characteristics of his works: the matter of them flows along in chaste abundance, in the softest combination; and their style is referred to by native critics as the highest specimen of the German tongue. On this latter point the vote of a stranger may well be deemed unavailing; but the charms of Goethe's style lie deeper than the mere words; for language, in the hands of a master, is the express image of thought, or rather it is the body of which thought is the soul; the former rises into being together with the latter, and the graces of the one are shadowed forth in the movements of the other.

Goethe's language, even to a foreigner, is full of character and secondary meanings; polished, yet vernacular and cordial, it sounds like the dialect of wise, ancient, and true-hearted men: in poetry, brief, sharp, simple, and expressive; in prose, perhaps still more pleasing; for it is at once concise and full, rich, clear, unpretending and melodious; and the sense, not presented in alternating flashes, piece after piece revealed and withdrawn, rises before us as in continuous dawning, and stands at last simultaneously complete, and bathed in the mellowest and ruddiest sunshine. It brings to mind what the prose of Hooker, Bacon, Milton, Browne, would have been, had they written under the good, without the bad influences, of that French precision, which has polished and attenuated, trimmed and impoverished, all modern languages; made our meaning clear, and too often shallow as well as clear.

But Goethe's culture as a writer is perhaps less remarkable than his culture as a man. He has learned not in head only, but also in heart: not from Art and Literature, but also by action and passion, in the rugged school of Experience. If asked what was the grand characteristic of his writings, we should not say knowledge, but wisdom. A mind that has seen, and suffered, and done, speaks to us of what it has tried and conquered. A gay delineation will give us notice of dark and toilsome experiences, of business done in the great deep of the spirit; a maxim, trivial to the careless eye, will rise with light and solution over long perplexed periods of our own history.

It is thus that heart speaks to heart, that the life of one man becomes a possession to all. Here is a mind of the most subtle and tumultuous elements; but it is governed in peaceful diligence, and its impetuous and ethereal faculties work softly together for good and noble ends. Goethe may be called a Philosopher; for he loves and has practised as a man the wisdom which, as a poet, he inculcates. Composure and cheerful seriousness seem to breathe over all his character. There is no whining over human woes: it is understood that we must simply all strive to alleviate or remove them. There is no noisy battling for opinions; but a persevering effort to make Truth lovely, and recommend her, by a thousand avenues, to the hearts of all men. Of his personal manners we can easily believe the universal report, as often given in the way of censure as of praise, that he is a man of consummate breeding and the stateliest presence: for an air of polished tolerance, of courtly, we might almost say majestic repose, and serene humanity, is visible throughout his works. In no line of them does he speak with asperity of any man; scarcely ever even of a thing.

He knows the good, and loves it; he knows the bad and hateful, and rejects it; but in neither case with violence: his love is calm and active; his rejection is implied, rather than pronounced; meek and gentle, though we see that it is thorough, and never to be revoked. The noblest and the basest he not only seems to comprehend, but to personate and body forth in their most secret lineaments: hence actions and opinions appear to him as they are, with all the circumstances which extenuate or endear them to the hearts where they originated and are entertained. This also is the spirit of our Shakespeare, and perhaps of every great dramatic poet. Shakespeare is no sectarian; to all he deals with equity and mercy; because he knows all, and his heart is wide enough for all. In his mind the world is a whole; he figures it as Providence governs it; and to him it is not strange that the sun should be caused to shine on the evil and the good. and the rain to fall on the just and the unjust.

Goethe has been called the German Voltaire; but it is a name which does him wrong, and describes him ill. Except in the corresponding variety of their pursuits and knowledge, in which, perhaps, it does Voltaire wrong, the two cannot be compared.

Goethe is all, or the best of all, that Voltaire was, and he is much that Voltaire did not dream of. To say nothing of his dignified and truthful character as a man, he belongs, as a thinker and a writer, to a far higher class than this enfant gate du monde qu'il gata.

He is not a questioner and a despiser, but a teacher and a reverencer; not a destroyer, but a builder-up; not a wit only, but a wise man. Of him Montesquieu could not have said, with even epigrammatic truth: Il a plus que personne l'esprit que tout le monde a. Voltaire was the cleverest of all past and present men; but a great man is something more, and this he surely was not.

As poets, the two live not in the same hemisphere, not in the same world. Of Voltaire's poetry, it were blindness to deny the polished intellectual vigour, the logical symmetry, the flashes that from time to time give it the colour, if not the warmth, of fire: but it is in a far other sense than this that Goethe is a poet; in a sense of which the French literature has never afforded any example. We may venture to say of him, that his province is high and peculiar; higher than any poet but himself, for several generations, has so far succeeded in, perhaps even has steadfastly attempted. In reading Goethe's poetry, it perpetually strikes us that we are reading the poetry of our own day and generation. No demands are made on our credulity; the light, the science, the scepticism of the age, are not hid from us.

He does not deal in antiquated mythologies, or ring changes on traditionary poetic forms; there are no supernal, no infernal influences, for Faust is an apparent rather than a real exception: but there is the barren prose of the nineteenth century, the vulgar life which we are all leading; and it starts into strange beauty in his hands; and we pause in delighted wonder to behold the flower of Poesy blooming in that parched and rugged soil.

This is the end of his Mignons and Harpers of his Tassos and Meisters. Poetry, as he views it, exists not in time or place, but in the spirit of man; and Art, with Nature, is now to perform for the poet, what Nature alone performed of old.

The divinities and demons, the witches, spectres, and fairies, are vanished from the world, never again to be recalled: but the Imagination which created these still lives, and will forever live in man's soul; and can again pour its wizard light over the Universe, and summon forth enchantments as lovely or impressive, and which its sister faculties will not contradict.

To say that Goethe has accomplished all this, would be to say that his genius is greater than was ever given to any man: for if it was a high and glorious mind, or rather series of minds, that peopled the first ages with their peculiar forms of poetry, it must be a series of minds much higher and more glorious that shall so people the present.

The angels and demons that can lay prostrate our hearts in the nineteenth century must be of another and more cunning fashion than those that subdued us in the ninth. To have attempted, to have begun this enterprise, may be accounted the greatest praise.

That Goethe ever meditated it, in the form here set forth, we have no direct evidence: but indeed such is the end and aim of high poetry at all times and seasons; for the fiction of the poet is not falsehood, but the purest truth; and if he would lead captive our whole being, not rest satisfied with a part of it, he must address us on interests that are not that were ours; and in a dialect which finds a response, and not a contradiction, within our bosoms.

How Goethe has fulfilled these conditions in addressing us, an inspection of his works, but no description, can inform us. Let me advise the reader to study them, and see. If he come to the task with an opinion that poetry is an amusement, a passive recreation; that its highest object is to supply a languid mind with fantastic shows and indolent emotions, his measure of enjoyment is likely to be scanty, and his criticisms will be loud, angry, and manifold.

But if he know and believe that poetry is the essence of all science, and requires the purest of all studies; if he recollect that the new may not always be the false; that the excellence which can be seen in a moment is not usually a very deep one; above all, if his own heart be full of feelings and experiences, for which he finds no name and no solution, but which lie in pain imprisoned and unuttered in his breast, till the Word be spoken, the spell that is to unbind them, and bring them forth to liberty and light; then, if I mistake not, he will find that in this Goethe there is a new world set before his eyes; a world of Earnestness and Sport, of solemn cliff and gay plain; some such temple--far inferior, as it may well be, in magnificence and beauty, but a temple of the same architecture--some such temple for the Spirit of our age, as the Shakespeares and Spensers have raised for the Spirit of theirs.

This seems a bold assertion: but it is not made without deliberation, and such conviction as it has stood within my means to obtain. If it invite discussion, and forward the discovery of the truth in this matter, its best purpose will be answered. Goethe's genius is a study for other minds than have yet seriously engaged with it among us.

By and by, apparently ere long, he will be tried and judged righteously; he himself, and no cloud instead of him;

for he comes to us in such a questionable shape, that silence and neglect will not always serve our purpose. England, the chosen home of justice in all its senses, where the humblest merit has been acknowledged, and the highest fault not unduly punished, will do no injustice to this extraordinary man.

And if, when her impartial sentence has been pronounced and sanctioned, it shall appear that Goethe's earliest admirers have wandered too far into the language of panegyric, I hope it may be reckoned no unpardonable sin. It is spirit-stirring rather than spirit-sharpening, to consider that there is one of the Prophets here with us in our own day: that a man who is to be numbered with the Sages and Sacri Vates the Shakespeares, the Tassos, the Cervanteses of the world, is looking on the things which we look on, has dealt with the very thoughts which we have to deal with, is reigning in serene dominion over the perplexities and contradictions in which we are still painfully entangled.

That Goethe's mind is full of inconsistencies and shortcomings, can be a secret to no one who has heard of the Fall of Adam. Nor would it be difficult, in this place, to muster a long catalogue of darknesses defacing our perception of this brightness: but it might be still less profitable than it is difficult; for in Goethe's writings, as in those of all true masters, an apparent blemish is apt, after maturer study, to pass into a beauty.

His works cannot be judged in fractions, for each of them is conceived and written as a whole; the humble and common may be no less essential there than the high and splendid: it is only Chinese pictures that have no shade.

There is a maxim, far better known than practised, that to detect faults is a much lower occupation than to recognize merits. We may add also, that though far easier in the execution, it is not a whit more certain in the result. What is the detecting of a fault, but the feeling of an incongruity, of a contradiction, which may exist in ourselves as well as in the object? Who shall say in which? None but he who sees this object as it is, and himself as he is. We have all heard of the critic fly; but none of us doubts the compass of his own vision.

It is thus that a high work of art, still more that a high and original mind, may at all times calculate on much sorriest criticism. In looking at an extraordinary man, it were good for an ordinary man to be sure of seeing him, before attempting to oversee him. Having ascertained that Goethe is an object deserving study, it will be time to censure his faults when we have clearly estimated his merits; and if we are wise judges, not till then.

10

SANDRO BOTTICELLI

WALTER PATER

Of the critics who have written during the last sixty years, Mr. Pater is probably the most remarkable. His work is always weighted with thought, and his thought is always fused with imagination. He unites, in a singular degree of intensity, the two crucial qualities of the critic, on the one hand a sense of form and colour and artistic utterance, on the other hand a speculative instinct which pierces behind these to the various types of idea and mood and character that underlie them. He is equally alive to subtle resemblances and to subtle differences, and art is to him not merely an intellectual enjoyment, but something which is to be taken into the spirit of a man and to become part of his life. Of the history of literature, and the problems that rise out of it, he takes but small account.

But for the other function assigned by Carlyle to criticism, for criticism as a "creative art, aiming to reproduce under a different shape the existing product of the artist, and painting to the intellect what already lay painted to the heart and the imagination"--for this no man has done more than Mr. Pater. With wider knowledge and a clearer consciousness of the deeper issues involved, he may be said to have taken up the work of Lamb and to have carried it forward in a spirit which those who best love Lamb will be the most ready to admire.

Of Mr. Pater's literary criticisms, those on Wordsworth and Coleridge are perhaps the most striking. But he was probably still more at home in interpreting the work of the great painters. And of his "appreciations" of painters none is more characteristic than his study of Botticelli. It was written in 1870, and published in The Renaissance in 1873.

In Leonardo's treatise on painting only one contemporary is mentioned by name--Sandro Botticelli. This pre-eminence may be due to chance only, but to some it will appear a result of deliberate judgment; for people have begun to find out the charm of Botticelli's work, and his name, little known in the last century, is quietly becoming important. In the middle of the fifteenth century he had already anticipated much of that meditative subtlety, which is sometimes supposed peculiar to the great imaginative workmen of its close.

Leaving the simple religion which had occupied the followers of Giotto for a century, and the simple naturalism which had grown out of it, a thing of birds and flowers only, he sought inspiration in what to him were works of the modern world, the writings of Dante and Boccaccio, and in new readings of his own of classical stories: or, if he painted religious incidents, painted them with an undercurrent of original sentiment, which touches you as the real matter of the picture through the veil of its ostensible subject. What is the peculiar sensation, what is the peculiar quality of pleasure, which his work has the property of exciting in us, and which we cannot get elsewhere? For this, especially when he has to speak of a comparatively unknown artist, is always the chief question which a critic has to answer.

In an age when the lives of artists were full of adventure, his life is almost colourless. Criticism, indeed, has cleared away much of the gossip which Vasari accumulated, has touched the legend of Lippo and Lucrezia, and rehabilitated the character of Andrea del Castagno. But in Botticelli's case there is no legend to dissipate. He did not even go by his true name: Sandro is a nickname, and his true name is

Filipepi, Botticelli being only the name of the goldsmith who first taught him art. Only two things happened to him--two things which he shared with other artists: he was invited to Rome to paint in the Sistine Chapel, and he fell in later life under the influence of Savonarola, passing apparently almost out of men's sight in a sort of religious melancholy, which lasted till his death in 1515, according to the received date. Vasari says that he plunged into the study of Dante, and even wrote a comment on the Divine Comedy. But it seems strange that he should have lived on inactive so long; and one almost wishes that some document might come to light, which, fixing the date of his death earlier, might relieve one, in thinking of him, of his dejected old age.

He is before all things a poetical painter, blending the charm of story and sentiment, the medium of the art of poetry, with the charm of line and colour, the medium of abstract painting. So he becomes the illustrator of Dante. In a few rare examples of the edition of 1481, the blank spaces left at the beginning of every canto, for the hand of the illuminator, have been filled, as far as the nineteenth canto of the Inferno with impressions of engraved plates, seemingly by way of experiment, for in the copy in the Bodleian Library, one of the three impressions it contains has been printed upside down, and much awry, in the midst of the luxurious printed page.

Giotto, and the followers of Giotto, with their almost childish religious aim, had not learned to put that weight of meaning into outward things--light, colour, everyday gesture, which the poetry of the Divine Comedy involves, and before the fifteenth century Dante could hardly have found an illustrator. Botticelli's illustrations are crowded with incident, blending, with a naive carelessness of pictorial propriety, three phases of the same scene into one plate. The grotesques, so often a stumbling-block to painters, who forget that the words of a poet, which only feebly present an image to the mind, must be lowered in key when translated into visible form, make one regret that he has not rather chosen for illustration the more subdued imagery of the Purgatorio.

Yet in the scene of those who "go down quick into hell", there is an inventive force about the fire taking hold on the upturned soles of the feet, which proves that the design is no mere translation of Dante's words, but a true painter's vision; while the scene of the Centaurs wins one at once, for, forgetful of the actual circumstances of their appearance, Botticelli has gone off with delight on the thought of the Centaurs themselves, bright, small creatures of the woodland, with arch baby faces and mignon forms, drawing their tiny bows.

Botticelli lived in a generation of naturalists, and he might have been a mere naturalist among them. There are traces enough in his work of that alert sense of outward things, which, in the pictures of that period, fills the lawns with delicate living creatures, and the hillsides with pools of water, and the pools of water with flowering reeds. But this was not enough for him; he is a visionary painter, and in his visionariness he resembles Dante. Giotto, the tried companion of Dante, Masaccio, Ghirlandajo even, do but transcribe, with more or less refining, the outward image; they are dramatic, not visionary painters; they are almost impassive spectators of the action before them. But the genius of which Botticelli is the type usurps the data before it as the exponent of ideas, moods, visions of its own; in this interest it plays fast and loose with those data, rejecting some and isolating others, and always combining them anew. To him, as to Dante, the scene, the colour, the outward image or gesture, comes with all its incisive and importunate reality; but awakes in him, moreover, by some subtle law of his own structure, a mood which it awakes in no one else, of which it is the double or repetition, and which it clothes, that all may share it, with visible circumstance.

But he is far enough from accepting the conventional orthodoxy of Dante which, referring all human action to the simple formula of purgatory, heaven, and hell, leaves an insoluble element of prose in the depths of Dante's poetry. One picture of his, with the portrait of the donor, Matteo Palmieri, below, had the credit or discredit of attracting some shadow of ecclesiastical censure. This Matteo Palmieri (two dim figures move under that name in contemporary history) was the reputed author of a poem, still unedited, La Citta Divina which represented the human race as an incarnation of those angels who, in the revolt of Lucifer, were neither for Jehovah nor for His enemies, a fantasy of that earlier Alexandrian philosophy about which the Florentine intellect in that century was so curious. Botticelli's picture may have been only one of those familiar compositions in which religious reverie has recorded its impressions of the various forms of beatified existence-- Glorias as they were called, like that in which Giotto painted the portrait of Dante; but somehow it was suspected of embodying in a picture the wayward dream of Palmieri, and the chapel where it hung was closed. Artists so entire as Botticelli are usually careless about philosophical theories, even when the philosopher is a Florentine of the fifteenth century, and his work a poem in terza rima. But Botticelli, who wrote a commentary on Dante, and became the disciple of Savonarola, may well have let such theories come and go across him. True or false, the story interprets much of the peculiar sentiment with which he infuses his profane and sacred persons, comely, and in a certain sense like angels, but with a sense of displacement or loss about them--the wistfulness of exiles, conscious of a passion and energy greater than any known issue of them explains, which runs through all his varied work with a sentiment of ineffable melancholy.

So just what Dante scorns as unworthy alike of heaven and hell, Botticelli accepts: that middle world in which men take no side in great conflicts, and decide no great causes, and make great refusals. He thus sets for himself the limits within which art, undisturbed by any moral ambition, does its most sincere and surest work. His interest is neither in the untempered goodness of Angelico's saints, nor the untempered evil of Orcagna's Inferno ; but with men and women, in their mixed and uncertain condition, always attractive, clothed sometimes by passion with a character of loveliness and energy, but saddened perpetually by the shadow upon them of the great things from which they shrink.

His morality is all sympathy; and it is this sympathy, conveying into his work somewhat more than is usual of the true complexion of humanity, which makes him, visionary as he is, so forcible a realist.

It is this which gives to his Madonnas their unique expression and charm. He has worked out in them a distinct and peculiar type, definite enough in his own mind, for he has painted it over and over again, sometimes one might think almost mechanically, as a pastime during that dark period when his thoughts were so heavy upon him.

Hardly any collection of note is without one of these circular pictures, into which the attendant angels depress their heads so naively. Perhaps you have sometimes wondered why those peevish-looking Madonnas, conformed to no acknowledged or obvious type of beauty, attract you more and more, and often come back to you when the Sistine Madonna and the Virgins of Fra Angelico are forgotten.

At first, contrasting them with those, you may have thought that there was something in them mean or abject even, for the abstract lines of the face have little nobleness, and the colour is wan.

For with Botticelli she too, though she holds in her hands the "Desire of all nations", is one of those who are neither for Jehovah nor for His enemies; and her choice is on her face. The white light on it is cast up hard and cheerless from below, as when snow lies upon the ground, and the children look up with surprise at the strange whiteness of the ceiling. Her trouble is in the very caress of the mysterious child, whose gaze is always far from her, and who has already that sweet look of devotion which men have never been able altogether to love, and which still makes the born saint an object almost of suspicion to his earthly brethren.

Once, indeed, he guides her hand to transcribe in a book the words of her exaltation, the Ave and the Magnificat and the Gaude Maria and the young angels, glad to rouse her for a moment from her dejection, are eager to hold the inkhorn and to support the book.

But the pen almost drops from her hand, and the high cold words have no meaning for her, and her true children are those others, among whom, in her rude home, the intolerable honour came to her, with that look of wistful inquiry on their irregular faces which you see in startled animals--gipsy children, such as those who, in Apennine villages, still hold out their long brown arms to beg of you, but on Sundays become enfants du choeur with their thick black hair nicely combed, and fair white linen on their sunburnt throats.

What is strangest is that he carries this sentiment into classical subjects, its most complete expression being a picture in the Uffizii of Venus rising from the sea, in which the grotesque emblems of the middle age, and a landscape full of its peculiar feeling, and even its strange draperies, powdered all over in the Gothic manner with a quaint conceit of daisies, frame a figure that reminds you of the faultless nude studies of Ingres.

At first, perhaps, you are attracted only by a quaintness of design, which seems to recall all at once whatever you have read of Florence in the fifteenth century; afterwards you may think that this quaintness must be incongruous with the subject, and the colour is cadaverous or at least cold. And yet, the more you come to understand what imaginative colouring really is, that all colour is no mere delightful quality of natural things, but a spirit upon them by which they become expressive to the spirit, the better you will like this peculiar quality of colour; and you will find that quaint design of Botticelli's a more direct inlet into the Greek temper than the works of the Greeks themselves even of the finest period.

Of the Greeks as they really were, of their difference from ourselves, of the aspects of their outward life, we know far more than Botticelli, or his most learned contemporaries; but for us long familiarity has taken off the edge of the lesson, and we are hardly conscious of what we owe to the Hellenic spirit.

But in pictures like this of Botticelli's you have a record of the first impression made by it on minds turned back towards it, in almost painful aspiration, from a world in which it had been ignored so long; and in the passion, the energy, the industry of realization, with which Botticelli carries out his intention, is the exact measure of the legitimate influence over the human mind of the imaginative system of which this is perhaps the central subject.

The light is indeed cold--mere sunless dawn; but a later painter would have cloyed you with sunshine; and you can see the better for that quietness in the morning air each long promontory, as it slopes down to the water's edge. Men go forth to their labours until the evening; but she is awake before them, and you might think that the sorrow in her face was at the thought of the whole long day of love yet to come.

An emblematical figure of the wind blows hard across the gray water, moving forward the dainty-lipped shell on which she sails, the sea "showing his teeth", as it moves, in thin lines of foam, and sucking in, one by one, the falling roses, each severe in outline, plucked off short at the stalk, but embrowned a little, as Botticelli's flowers always are. Botticelli meant all this imagery to be altogether pleasurable, and it was partly an incompleteness of resources, inseparable from the art of that time, that subdued and chilled it. But his predilection for minor tones counts also; and what is unmistakable is the sadness with which he has conceived the goddess of pleasure, as the depository of a great power over the lives of men.

I have said that the peculiar character of Botticelli is the result of a blending in him of a sympathy for humanity in its uncertain condition, its attractiveness, its investiture at rarer moments in a character of loveliness and energy, with his consciousness of the shadow upon it of the great things from which it shrinks, and that this conveys into his work somewhat more than painting usually attains of the true complexion of humanity.

He paints the story of the goddess of pleasure in other episodes besides that of her birth from the sea, but never without some shadow of death in the gray flesh and wan flowers. He paints Madonnas, but they shrink from the pressure of the divine child, and plead in unmistakable undertones for a warmer, lower humanity.

The same figure--tradition connects it with Simonetta, the mistress of Giuliano de' Medici-appears again as Judith, returning home across the hill country, when the great deed is over, and the moment of revulsion come, when the olive branch in her hand is becoming a burthen; as Justice sitting on a throne, but with a fixed look of self-hatred which makes the sword in her hand seem that of a suicide; and again as Veritas in the allegorical picture of Calumnia where one may note in passing the suggestiveness of an accident which identifies the image of Truth with the person of Venus. We might trace the same sentiment through his engravings; but his share in them is doubtful, and the object of this brief study has been attained if I have defined aright the temper in which he worked.

But, after all, it may be asked, is a painter like Botticelli--a secondary painter--a proper subject for general criticism? There are a few great painters, like Michelangelo or Leonardo, whose work has become a force in general culture, partly for this very reason that they have absorbed into themselves all such workmen as Sandro Botticelli; and, over and above mere technical or antiquarian criticism, general criticism may be very well employed in that sort of interpretation which adjusts the position of these men to general culture, whereas smaller men can be the proper subjects only of technical or antiquarian treatment.

But, besides those great men, there is a certain number of artists who have a distinct faculty of their own by which they convey to us a peculiar quality of pleasure which we cannot get elsewhere; and these, too, have their place in general culture, and must be interpreted to it by those who have felt their charm strongly, and are often the object of a special diligence and a consideration wholly affectionate, just because there is not about them the stress of a great name and authority.

Of this select number Botticelli is one. He has the freshness, the uncertain and diffident promise, which belong to the earlier Renaissance itself, and make it perhaps the most interesting period in the history of the mind. In studying his work one begins to understand to how great a place in human culture the art of Italy had been called.

Bibliography

Allen, Ernst: *The English Novel: a Short Critical History*, London: Phoenix House, 1954.

Arthur Miller: *As a Critic of Drama*, New Delhi, Anmol, 2004.

Authors, Texts, Issues: *Essays on Indian Literature*, Delhi, Pencraft International, 2003.

Ball, M. J. : *Phonetics: The Science of Speech*, London, Arnold, 1999.

Bennett, J. A. W.: *Middle English Literature*, Oxford, Clarendon Press, 1986.

Beyond Borders: *An Anthology of SAARC Poetry*, Noida, Rainbow, 2002.

Bhattacharyya, Nath: *Indian Religious Historiography*, New Delhi, Munshiram Manoharlal Publishers, 1996.

Brown, J. M.: *Ireland in Fiction; a Guide to Irish Novels, Tales, Romances, and Folk-lore*, London: Maunsel, 1919.

Cahalan, M.: *The Irish Novel: a Critical History*, Boston, Twayne Publishers, 1988.

Cavanagh, John: *British Theatre: a Bibliography, 1901 to 1985*, Hampshire, Motley, 1989.

Classe, A.: *The Rhythm of English Prose*, Oxford, Blackwell, 1939.

Couper-Kuhlen, E.: *An Introduction to English Prosody*, London, Edward Arnold, 1986.

Courthope, John: *A History of English Poetry*, London, MacMillan and Co., 1903.

Crystal, D.: *Prosodic Systems and Intonation in English*, Cambridge, Cambridge University Press, 1969.

Davis, Brian L. : *Uniforms and Insignia of the Luftwaffe*, London, Arms and Armor, 1999.

Davis, Gwenn: *Drama by Women to 1900: a Bibliography of American and British Writers*, London, Mansell, 1992.

Dobree, Bonamy: *English Literature in the Early Eighteenth Century, 1700-1740*, Oxford, Clarendon Press, 1959.

Edmund Spenser: *A Critical Study*, New Delhi, Anmol Pub., 2005.

Ferrence, G.: *Deadly Fashion: the Rise and Fall of Cigarette Smoking in North America*, New York, Garland, 1989.

Francis, Russell: *The Scottish Novel: from Smollett to Spark*, Cambridge, Harvard University Press, 1978.

Halliday, M. A. K.: *Intonation and Grammar in British English*, The Hague, Mouton, 1967.

Harivansh R.B.: *In the Afternoon of Time: An Autobiography*, New Delhi, Penguin, 2001.

Hogan, Robert Goode: *The Modern Irish Drama: a Documentary History*, NJ: Humanities Press, 1975.

Jack, Ian Robert James: *English Literature, 1815-1832*, Oxford, Clarendon Press, 1963.

James, Ernest: *Principles of Textual Criticism*, San Marino, Huntington Library, 1972.

James, Runcieman: *English Literature of the Late Seventeenth Century*, New York, Oxford University Press, 1969.

Jhumpa Lahiri: *The Master Storyteller: A Critical Response to Interpreter of Maladies*, New Delhi, KPH, 2002.

John Milton: *A Critical Study*, New Delhi, Anmol, 2005.

Laver, J.: *Principles of Phonetics*, Cambridge, Cambridge University Press, 1994.

Logan, P.: *The Later Jacobean and Caroline Dramatists*, Lincoln, University of Nebraska Press, 1978.

Matricardi, Paolo: *Complete Book of World War II Combat Aircraft*, NY, Military Press, 1988

Naipaul, V.S. : *A House for Mr. Biswas: With an Introduction by Ian Buruma*, New Delhi, Penguin, 1992.

Nath, Narendra: *Indian Religious Historiography*, New Delhi, Munshiram Manoharlal Publishers, 1996.

Neil Bissoondath: *Indo-Caribbean-Canadian Diaspora*, New Delhi, Rawat, 2005.

Perkins, David: *A History of Modern Poetry*, Cambridge, Belknap Press of Harvard University Press, 1976.

Philip Roth: *A Novelist in Crisis*, New Delhi, Classical Publishing, 2001.

Rahilly, J.: *Phonetics: The Science of Speech*, London, Arnold, 1999.

Raja Rao: *The Fictionist*, Delhi, B.R. Publishing, 2003.

Rogers, H.: *The Sounds of Language: An Introduction to Phonetics*, Harlow, Longman, 2000.

Royle, Trevor: *The Macmillan Companion to Scottish Literature*, London, MacMillan Reference Books, 1983.

Seidlhofer, B.: *Pronunciation, Oxford*, Oxford University Press, 1994.

Stevenson, Lionel: *Victorian Fiction: a Guide to Research*, Cambridge, Harvard University Press, 1966.

Terence, P.: *The Later Jacobean and Caroline Dramatists*, Lincoln, University of Nebraska Press, 1978.

Underhill, A.: *Sound Foundations*, London, Heineman, 1994.

Vikram Seth: *Multiple Locations, Multiple Affiliation*, New Delhi, Rawat, 2001.

Wearing, J. P.: *The London Stage, 1890-1899: a Calendar of Plays and Players*, NJ, Scarecrow Press, 1976.

Wickham, Glynne William Gladstone: *Early English Stages, 1300 to 1660*, London, Routledge and Paul; 1959.

William Blake: *A Critical Study*, New Delhi, Anmol, 2005.

William, John: *A History of English Poetry*, London, MacMillan and Co., 1903.

Yeats, W.B. : *Poetry and Plays*, New Delhi, Atlantic, 2002.

Index

A

Administration, 260.
Approach, 2, 26, 45, 251, 264.
Aristotle, 4, 5, 9, 39, 84, 93, 97, 98, 113, 116, 123, 128, 152.
Artificial Comedy, 220, 221.
Atmosphere, 8, 75, 223.

B

Bible, 49, 62, 214, 215, 216.

C

Charles Lamb, 220.
Chirurgery, 170.
Christian, 8, 144, 146, 216, 253, 254.
Church, 52, 82, 144, 154, 175.
Civilization, 207, 242.
Climax, 202.
Combination, 159, 182, 187, 241, 274.
Comedy, 13, 18, 25, 101, 102, 122, 204, 220, 221, 222, 225, 226, 229, 246, 249, 283.
Communication, 183, 239.
Community, 1, 114, 237.
Company, 2, 18, 31, 43, 118, 148.
Comparisons, 16, 31, 34, 37, 159.
Conception, 11, 13, 26, 38, 60, 61, 62, 64, 65, 69, 75, 159, 204, 234, 239, 246, 247, 262.
Court, 50, 77, 132, 135, 158, 172, 230.
Culture, 9, 273, 274, 290.
Customs, 149, 177.

D

Daniel Defoe, 212.
Development, 75, 195, 258, 269.
Devotion, 3, 170, 243, 287.
Dimensions, 200.
Diversity, 75, 236, 256.
Drama, 6, 7, 13, 18, 19, 20, 21, 23, 24, 25, 26, 27, 28, 29, 30, 31, 37, 43, 46, 54, 188, 193, 220, 222, 246, 247, 248, 249, 256.
Dramatic Power, 22.

E

Education, 124.
Elizabeth, 2, 14, 15, 22, 34, 53, 131.
Emotion, 159, 186, 189, 210, 217.

English Drama, 20.
English Literature, 2, 4, 18, 36, 37, 39, 53, 57, 157, 259.
Essays, 8, 16, 18, 37, 46, 47, 58, 66, 220.

F

Freedom, 3, 17, 33, 67, 71, 223, 224, 255, 273.

G

Generations, 216, 242, 252, 258, 276.
Governor, 81.

H

Humanity, 47, 72, 173, 209, 215, 261, 275, 286, 289.

I

Idealism, 49.
Independence, 29, 55.
Influence, 2, 3, 11, 12, 21, 36, 37, 38, 51, 58, 63, 66, 71, 199, 236, 239, 250, 259, 264, 270, 283, 288.
Information, 48.
Institution, 246, 249, 254, 269.
Intellect, 56, 74, 158, 204, 215, 240, 251, 272, 273, 281, 285.

J

John Bunyan, 212.
John Dryden, 130.
Judge, 1, 19, 42, 50, 59, 60, 133, 141, 150, 151, 156, 222, 223, 225, 229, 252, 267.
Judgement, 8.
Justice, 12, 47, 64, 90, 98, 104, 146, 153, 200, 205, 223, 229, 267, 279, 289.

K

Kinship, 22, 234.

L

Lectures, 5, 58, 66, 71, 178, 195.
Letters, 7, 8, 44, 45, 50, 109, 169, 271.
Library, 112, 283.
Literature, 1, 2, 4, 14, 16, 18, 20, 33, 34, 36, 37, 39, 46, 47, 51, 53, 57, 58, 59, 63, 64, 66, 68, 69, 70, 71, 75, 157, 234, 259, 262, 269, 274, 276, 281.
Lyric, 4, 6, 20, 21, 23, 86, 103, 110, 157.
Lyrics, 119.

M

Management, 193.
Matthew Arnold, 63.
Metaphysical Poets, 20, 21, 157, 158, 159.
Mission, 65, 76.
Modern Literature, 34.
Movements, 200, 209, 212, 274.
Mysticism, 218.

N

Novels, 132, 146, 151, 183.

O

Occupation, 279.

P

Paradox, 60, 220.
Percy Bysshe Shelley, 233.
Plato, 4, 5, 7, 9, 10, 79, 89, 98, 104, 108, 113, 114, 115, 116, 147, 185, 198, 240, 253, 254, 256.
Poetic Diction, 26, 178.
Poetic Genius, 65, 178, 185, 186, 187, 188, 191.
Powers, 42, 62, 91, 161, 178, 239, 256, 260, 267.
Press, 148, 213, 220.
Propagation, 172.
Prose, 1, 11, 25, 26, 27, 35, 86, 100, 107, 120, 125, 132, 133, 134, 151, 178, 182, 185, 196, 202, 203, 207, 209, 210, 211, 212, 239, 240, 274, 277, 285.

R

Reformation, 133, 258.
Relations, 215, 234, 237, 239, 259.
Renaissance, 63, 282, 290.
Restoration, 3, 4, 7, 15, 16, 17, 18, 20, 22, 25, 32, 33, 34, 36, 37, 39, 42, 50, 155, 220.
Revolution, 4, 39, 50, 58, 69, 75, 76, 233.
Romance, 1, 122, 127, 213, 271.

S

Samuel Johnson, 157.
Samuel Taylor Coleridge, 178.
Sandro Botticelli, 281, 282, 290.
Scholarship, 48.
Sir Thomas More, 92.
Speakers, 93, 117.
Struggles, 189.

T

Theology, 115.
Thomas Carlyle, 271.
Trade, 187, 203.
Traditions, 72.

V

Violence, 92, 103, 159, 181, 231, 275.
Visions, 206, 284.

W

Walter Pater, 281.
William Hazlitt, 195.
Writers, 4, 16, 17, 18, 32, 33, 35, 37, 38, 40, 41, 42, 44, 45, 48, 49, 50, 52, 58, 59, 62, 63, 70, 78, 80, 89, 107, 109, 122, 126, 132, 141, 158, 160, 176, 177, 217, 220, 231, 236, 240, 241, 242, 250, 252, 254, 256, 260, 268, 270.